John Keble, Edward Bouverie Pusey

Village Sermons on the Baptismal Service

John Keble, Edward Bouverie Pusey

Village Sermons on the Baptismal Service

ISBN/EAN: 9783744742535

Printed in Europe, USA, Canada, Australia, Japan

Cover: Foto ©Lupo / pixelio.de

More available books at **www.hansebooks.com**

VILLAGE SERMONS

ON

THE BAPTISMAL SERVICE.

VILLAGE SERMONS

ON

THE BAPTISMAL SERVICE.

BY

THE REV. JOHN KEBLE,
AUTHOR OF "THE CHRISTIAN YEAR."

𝔗𝔥𝔦𝔯𝔡 𝔗𝔥𝔬𝔲𝔰𝔞𝔫𝔡.

SOLD BY JAMES PARKER & CO., OXFORD,
AND 377, STRAND, LONDON;
AND RIVINGTONS,
LONDON, OXFORD, AND CAMBRIDGE.
1869.

NOTICE.

The following Sermons were given to me for publication by my revered friend John Keble now many years ago. It was at a time when, sermons of our common friends Newman and Manning having been withdrawn from circulation, the want was felt, of some to replace them. I did not *then* publish these sermons, on a ground which in the eyes of some will give them now a special charm; their simplicity. I wanted sermons for the intellectual classes, and these were written for the poor. I feared too that, since they were written under circumstances, which required the writer to withhold so much of his thought, their publication would rather be disappointing. I asked him, from time to time, for sermons, like those of his, which were preached at the Consecration of St. Saviour's, Leeds. He told me last; "They said to me, that I was preaching over the people's heads, and so I changed my style."

The characteristic then of these sermons is their affectionate simplicity. Here and there, there occur hints of an accurate theology, or gleams of poetic thought, or what would have been eloquence, had it been developed. But so, through human mismanagement, it was arranged, that the writer of "the Christian Year" should, for the chief part of his life, preach to a peasant flock, of average mental capacity. He had been chosen as one of the "select Preachers" before the University when not yet 30, and again seven years later in 1828. In 1833, at the appointment of the Vice-Chancellor, Dr Rowley, he preached an Assize sermon at Oxford, which formed an era in the Oxford movement.

One more Sermon, "On Church and State," he preached at the appointment of the same Vice-Chancellor, on the anniversary of the accession of King William IV in 1835. On the following year, 1836, at the visitation of Dr Dealtry, Chancellor of Winchester, he preached a remarkable Sermon, "Primitive Tradition recognised in Holy Scripture." Thenceforth, as far as I know, no one gave any opportunity for that voice (whose every word, in our early years, rivetted the thoughts of us all) to be heard by any intellectual audience, until, when he had reached the threescore years and ten, the late Vice-Chancellor, Dr Lightfoot, asked him to undertake the office of select Preacher. The invitation drew out an answer of his characteristic modesty; that "his voice was no longer strong enough to be heard, and that he himself was not of the calibre for such a congregation." With these rare exceptions, his high intellectual gifts were (as far as man gave him the opportunities) confined to teaching his Hampshire village-children and his peasant flock.

And so ended the history of his preaching, according to that wide law of God's Providence, Who, while He accepts what would be done, as if it were done, and forms, the more, active souls through the inaction to which they are assigned, allows or orders that so many of His gifts should in human sight be wasted. It is not in the English Church alone, that gifts are wasted and those whose talents might be treasures to the Church are misplaced. What the Mind of Him, Who formed their minds in so rare a mould, was in this apparent waste, will be known in that Day alone, when He "maketh up His jewels," and the light, which men hid here, shall shine the more brightly in the Eternal Day.

E. B. P.

Christ Church,
       Trinity Sunday. 1868.

CONTENTS.

SERMON I.

JUNE 17, 1849.

ACTS xix. 5.

"They were baptized in the Name of the Lord Jesus."   Page 1

SERMON II.

FEAST OF St. JOHN BAPTIST. 1849.

St. LUKE iii. 16.

"I indeed baptize with water, but One mightier than I cometh, the latchet of Whose shoes I am not worthy to unloose, He shall baptize you with the Holy Ghost and with fire." 10

SERMON III.

JULY 1, 1849.

EPH. iv. 5.

"One Lord, one Faith, one Baptism." . . . 19

SERMON IV.

JULY 8, 1849.

Ps. li. 6.

"*Behold, I was shapen in wickedness, and in sin hath my mother conceived me.*" 29

SERMON V.

JULY 15, 1849.

Ezekiel xxxvi. 25.

"*Then will I sprinkle clean water upon you, and you shall be clean.*" 36

SERMON VI.

JULY 22, 1849.

St. John vi. 44.

"*No man can come unto Me, except the Father which hath sent Me draw him.*" 46

SERMON VII.

JULY 29, 1849.

1 St. Peter iii. 20, 21.

"*The long-suffering of God waited in the days of Noah, while the ark was a preparing, wherein few, that is, eight souls, were saved by water: the like figure whereunto, even Baptism, doth now save us.*" 56

SERMON VIII.

SEPTEMBER 2, 1849.

1 Cor. x. 1, 2.

✝ "*All our fathers were under the cloud, and all passed through the sea: and were all baptized unto Moses in the cloud and in the sea.*" 65

SERMON IX.

SEPTEMBER 9, 1849.

St. Matt. iii. 15.

"*Thus it becometh us to fulfil all righteousness.*" . 76

SERMON X.

SEPTEMBER 18, 1849.

1 Cor. vi. 11.

"*But ye are washed, but ye are sanctified, in the Name of the Lord Jesus, and by the Spirit of our God.*" 86

SERMON XI.

SEPTEMBER 23, 1849.

St. Matt. vii. 11.

"*If ye then, being evil, know how to give good gifts unto your children, how much more shall your Father which is in heaven give good things to them that ask Him.*" 96

SERMON XII.

SEPTEMBER 30, 1849.

St. Mark x. 14.

"*Suffer the little children to come unto Me, and forbid them not; for of such is the kingdom of God.*" 106

SERMON XIII.

OCTOBER 7, 1849.

Deut. xxxiii. 27.

"*The Eternal God is thy refuge, and underneath are the Everlasting Arms.*" 116

CONTENTS.

SERMON XIV.

OCTOBER 14, 1849.

PSALM cxix. 32.

"*I will run the way of Thy Commandments, when Thou hast set my heart at liberty.*" . . . 126

SERMON XV.

OCTOBER 21, 1849.

PSALM l. 5.

"*Gather My saints together unto Me, those that have made a covenant with Me by sacrifice.*" . . 135

SERMON XVI.

OCTOBER 28, 1849.

2 COR. vi. 14.

"*What Communion hath light with darkness?*" . 144

SERMON XVII.

NOVEMBER 4, 1849.

ACTS viii. 36, 37.

"*The eunuch said, See here is water; what does hinder me to be baptized? and Philip said, If thou believest with all thine heart, thou mayest.*" . . 154

SERMON XVIII.

NOVEMBER 11, 1849.

ST. LUKE xiv. 23.

"*Compel them to come in.*" 163

SERMON XIX.

NOVEMBER 18, 1849.

JEREMIAH vii. 23.

"*This thing commanded I them, saying, Obey My Voice, and I will be your God and ye shall be My people.*" 173

SERMON XX.

JANUARY 20, 1850.

COLOSSIANS ii. 12.

"*Buried with Him in Baptism, wherein also ye are risen with Him.*" 181

SERMON XXI.

JUNE 2, 1850.

COLOSSIANS i. 23.

"*If ye continue in the Faith, grounded and settled, and be not moved away from the hope of the Gospel which ye have heard.*" 189

SERMON XXII.

JUNE 9, 1850.

ST. JOHN xix. 34, 35.

"*One of the soldiers with a spear pierced His side, and forthwith came there out Blood and Water; and he that saw it bare record, and his record is true, and he knoweth that he saith true, that ye might believe.*" 197

SERMON XXIII.

JUNE 16, 1850.

ST. MATT. xxviii. 19.

"*Go ye therefore, and teach all nations, baptizing them in the Name of the Father and of the Son and of the Holy Ghost.*" 207

SERMON XXIV.

JUNE 23, 1850.

ZECHARIAH xiii. 1.

"*In that day there shall be a fountain opened to the house of David and to the inhabitants of Jerusalem for sin and for uncleanness.*" 217

SERMON XXV.

JULY 7, 1850.

REV. iii. 12.

"*I will write upon him My new Name.*" . . . 227

SERMON XXVI.

JULY 14, 1850.

PROVERBS xviii. 10.

"*The Name of the Lord is a strong tower; the righteous runneth into it, and is safe.*" . . . 237

SERMON XXVII.

JULY 21, 1850.

ROMANS vi. 4.

"*We are buried with Him by Baptism into death; that like as Christ was raised up from the dead by the glory of the Father, even so we also should walk in newness of life.*" 246

SERMON XXVIII.

AUGUST 11, 1850.

ST. MATT. x. 38.

"*He that taketh not his Cross and followeth after Me, is not worthy of Me.*" 254

SERMON XXIX.

AUGUST 18, 1850.

MARK viii. 38.

"*Whosoever therefore shall be ashamed of Me and of My words in this adulterous and sinful generation, of him also shall the Son of Man be ashamed, when He cometh in the glory of His Father with the holy Angels.*" 264

SERMON XXX.

AUGUST 25, 1850.

ST. JOHN xv. 3, 4.

"*Now ye are clean through the word which I have spoken unto you. Abide in Me, and I in you.*" . 272

SERMON XXXI.

SEPTEMBER 1, 1850.

1 THESS. v. 23, 24.

"*The very God of peace sanctify you wholly; and I pray God your whole spirit and soul and body be preserved blameless unto the Coming of our Lord Jesus Christ. Faithful is He that calleth you, Who also will do it.*" 282

SERMON XXXII.

SEPTEMBER 8, 1850.

1 Sam. i. 22.

"*I will bring him, that he may appear before the Lord, and there abide for ever.*" 292

SERMON XXXIII.

SEPTEMBER 15, 1850.

Psalm lxxxiv. 7.

"*They will go from strength to strength, and unto the God of gods appeareth every one of them in Sion.*" 301

SERMON I.

Acts xix. 5.

"They were baptized in the Name of the Lord Jesus."

You know that there are in our Prayer Book, besides the regular morning and evening services, appointed for the use of the whole Church every day throughout the year:—I say you know that besides these there are certain services, sometimes called occasional, because they are only needed on certain special occasions. Such as the Offices for Holy Baptism and Holy Communion, for the Visitation of the Sick, the Burial of the Dead, and others. For as the Church by her morning and evening prayer does as it were sanctify and offer to God through Christ all our ordinary course of life, so she is careful, like a good and perfect Mother, to sanctify and offer up also, on our behalf, all the chief events and changes of every Christian man's life, his birth, his growth and nourishment, his coming to man's estate, his marriage, his sickness, his death. Our birth she sanctifies by giving us Holy Baptism; our growth and nourishment by Holy Communion; our coming of age, by Confirmation; our marriage, by the office of Holy Matrimony; our sickness, by the Visitation office; our death by the office of Burial. Thus from beginning to end, our gracious Mother the Church waits upon us all; and these, the occasional Services in the Prayer Book, are the means whereby she waits upon us.

Not a sore, not a sickness in our life, but she is there to heal it: not a hope, not a blessing, but she is there to make it doubly blessed. Oh! happy and comfortable indeed are they, who go on in this faith from their cradles to their graves: accounting it their greatest privilege, that Christ died to receive them, newly-born, in His Arms: their chief help, that whatever happens to them for joy or for sorrow, He still holds their hands; and their best and only hope, that, whenever they die, He will be at hand, enabling them to offer their death as well as their life in sacrifice to Him. I am sure, my beloved Brethren, it must do us much good, if we can get into a way of thinking deeply and steadily on these things: remembering all our life long, that, whatever happens to us, the Church our Mother is at hand to turn it into a great blessing. Therefore I intend, please God, to go on from time to time in a course of regularly explaining some of the occasional Services of the Church; and of course I begin with Baptism, because Baptism is the beginning, the first thing whereby each one of us has to do with the Church of God.

Now we all know in a general way, out of the Catechism, what Holy Baptism is.

We know in the first place, that it is a Sacrament ordained by Christ in His Church: that is to say, that it has in it something inward and something outward; the water which we see, and the grace of God which we do not see: both appointed by Jesus Christ Himself, Who did also appoint the words which should go along with the water in order to give the grace, viz. that the Person baptizing should say, "In the Name of the Father and of the Son and of the Holy Ghost."

All this we know well, whether we have thought much of it or no. We have been used to see children so baptized: we know that we were so baptized ourselves, and we should account it a very wrong and inexcusable thing, if we knew of any person omitting to have his children so baptized. Because Baptism is the regular way out of the world into the Church, out of Satan's kingdom into the Kingdom of God; and any one wilfully neglecting it, wilfully leaves himself, or those belonging to him, in the world and out of the Church, in the power of Satan and not in the family of God. And therefore as Baptism is a blessing, whereof the world hath not the like, so neglect of Baptism, and unthankfulness for it, is one of the most grievous sins which a Christian can be guilty of. All this, as I said, we all of us know in a way. Let us now see what special care Holy Church has taken in our Prayer Book to put us in mind of all this, and warn us against making light of it.

First, if you will look in the Rubric i. e. in the directions of the Church, set before the Baptismal Service, you will see that we the Clergy are to admonish you, that Baptism should not be administered but upon Sundays and Holydays, when the most number of people come together. For being so great an act, it ought to be transacted in the most solemn manner possible. When a king or queen is crowned, you know, the day is set beforehand, and all the chief people in the country are gathered together. All the nobles and great men of the land are made witnesses of what is done. So when persons are married, it is not a thing to be done in secret, but publicly in the face of the Church. They are to come into the Church with their friends and neighbours, after notice publicly given.

Now Baptism is in some respects a coronation and a marriage. The child of the very meanest beggar, though he be brought to the Font in rags, and have no home to be carried to afterwards, yet is he then and there most truly crowned a great king. For it is written, "He hath made us kings and priests unto God and His Father." Every Christian is a king, for he is a member of Christ the Great King; and therefore every Baptism is a Coronation, more solemn and glorious in the sight of God than the crowning of the greatest Emperor on earth: and as the princes and nobles of the land make haste to be present when a king is crowned, so the Holy Angels and the Saints reigning in Heaven are no doubt present unseen by us, whenever a little child is Christened. Again, every Baptism is a marriage, because in it by a wonderful working the Holy and Almighty Spirit of God unites the baptized person to the mystical Body of our Lord, making *him* a member of Christ, who was before but a child and limb of Adam, in all his natural uncleanness. Christ Himself teaches us to say that Baptism makes such an one "bone of His Bone and flesh of His Flesh." Therefore it is a marriage and more than a marriage, being indeed that of which earthly marriage is but a figure: and being a marriage it is best to be public as a marriage solemnly contracted and proclaimed before proper witnesses, and blessed by the Lord in the hearing of men and Angels.

For such reasons as these, it is convenient that Baptisms should generally be celebrated, not at home but in Church; and not on ordinary days but on Sundays and those Holy days when the most people come together. From that time forward there can be no doubt of the person or child so received being a Christian,—and all the congregation, being made witnesses of it, are bound thenceforward to treat him as a Christian: to pray for him, and shew all brotherly love towards him. So that neither he himself nor any one else may any more doubt of his being a Christian, than of his being a man born naturally into the world. And every one present at his Baptism will be a witness against him hereafter, that, if he go wrong, it is not because he never received God's grace, but because through wilful sin he received it in vain.

Our Church mentions also another reason why Baptism should be as public as possible: viz. that every man there present should be reminded of his own Baptism. I am sure we must all feel how great need we have of being so reminded. Although Baptism is the greatest of blessings and makes the greatest difference to us all, yet we are apt to pass days and weeks with very little thought of it, because it was provided for us without our knowledge or trouble, and because we see that almost all whom we know of are baptized. And yet the Angels, who are all around us invisibly, know that God in giving us Baptism gave us the greatest of all favours, a favour which He has bestowed on very few of the children of Adam: for the most part, by very far, never even heard of the Name of Christ. We ought therefore to make very much of the opportunities which God gives us of being present at Baptism and joining in the prayers and thanksgivings there. When there is a pause, as the manner is, after the second Lesson, and you see the Minister go towards the Font, and the nurses with the children waiting to meet him there, and hear him ask of each one of them, "hath this child been already baptized or no?" then think with yourself, "so it was with me one day: I was carried to the Font in like manner. I was met there by God's Minister, and God by him adopted me before the Congregation to be His own child. Alas! how little have I thought of it since! how unthankful have I been for that unspeakable gift! nay, have I not gone near to cast it away for ever by wilful grievous sin?" Again, when you see the congregation all turning towards the Font, and watching and listening as they are apt to do at a Baptism, think with yourself, "Even so do guardian angels, as many of them as here present in God's House, though to us invisible: even so they in this moment are turning in their heavenly watchfulness the very same way; they are waiting in all reverence for the Holy Ghost to come down and set His seal upon this child, that they may begin to take the little one into their especial charge: and did they not, so many years ago, wait in like manner on the christening of me unworthy? did they not take me also into their charge? and I alas! how have I requited their care? May I not fear that at this very moment they may be regarding me with a kind of disappointment, and hoping that this child now to be baptized may prove far other than I have been?"

My brethren, if such thoughts as these ever come into your mind when you are present at a christening, do not, I beseech you, let them pass quickly away: try to carry them home with you, and to renew them very often. For instance, when you see young and innocent children, and take notice of their happy ways, say sometimes to yourself; "Ah, they have a right to be happy, for they have received the Unspeakable Gift and have not yet cast it away. Christ's wonderworking Touch renewed the original Image of God in their souls, and they have not yet effaced it by wilful grievous sin, nor done anything to stamp there the image of the evil one instead. Well, then, may they be happy and joyous: but as for me, I know that in proportion to my sins I ought to go on with humble fear and trembling: and then (blessed be His Name) my lamp, kindled in Holy Baptism, will not have quite burned out when the Bridegroom cometh: then Baptismal grace will revive and flourish in me, and death and judgment will find me still a member of Christ, a child of God, and an Inheritor of the Kingdom of Heaven."

These, my Brethren, and such as these are the thoughts to do us good when we are present at others' Baptism, to remember, as we join in prayer for them, that the very same prayers were once said in Church for us: as we listen to the answers, made by their

Sponsors, that the very same engagements were made for us also: as we hear the Priest say the solemn words, and see him pour the water upon them, that over us also the water was poured, and the Thrice Holy Name pronounced:—and what if it should prove all in vain? What if this little simple child, whose Baptism we have been now attending, should rise up with us in the Judgment, and condemn us for not repenting now at least, now that God by this means has brought it all before our mind?

By this, you may partly understand how much good it might do us all, if we permitted the Baptism of others to remind us of our own Baptism: and therefore how like a Mother's love it is, that our holy Church takes order for one being so reminded as often as possible: directing not only the place of Baptism, that it should be in the Church, but the time also, that it should be when most come together.

As for the grace given to the infants baptized, that is as well provided for, be the Baptism never so private: in a Church with only the Sponsors, or, as you know often happens in sickness or alarm, in a private room. The Spiritual grace, we trust, is the same; but the profit of the example to others is likely to be greater, the more are present. The Church for such purposes is, "Wheresoever two or three are gathered together in Christ's Name." The priest, the nurse, and the infant, are three gathered in Christ's Name and in obedience to His Will. Doubt ye not therefore, but earnestly believe that a child so offered receives the fulness of baptismal blessings: only, as I said, the more witnesses are by, to be reminded of their own Baptism, the better.

Thus have you heard concerning the Church's care in ordaining that Baptism should be as public as possible. Let us see to it, brethren, that her motherly tenderness be not thrown away upon us. Let us not be careless unthankful children of such a wise and loving Parent. So often as we see others baptized, and hear what is promised in their name, surely we are without excuse, if we ever let a day pass without thanking God for our own Baptism and examining ourselves how we have kept our vows.

SERMON II.

St. Luke iii. 16.

"*I indeed baptize you with water, but One mightier than I cometh, the latchet of whose shoes I am not worthy to unloose; He shall baptize you with the Holy Ghost and with fire.*"

WHEN you come into Church, the first thing you see is the Font, close to the principal entrance. We all know, why it is placed there; it is, because Baptism is the beginning, the way into the Kingdom of Heaven, and, without Baptism, there is no ordinary way to the other good things which our Lord gives us in His Church. We must pass by the Font, in order to take our place among God's people for Prayer, before hearing of Scriptures, for Confession and Absolution, for Confirmation and all other Holy ordinances, and especially for Holy Communion. And as the Font stands at the entrance of the Church, so Baptism, if you mark it, stands at the beginning of the Gospel. The very first thing related in the history of the New Testament is the promise given to Zacharias that St. John Baptist should be born. St. Mark's Gospel opens as follows; "The beginning of the Gospel of Jesus Christ the Son of God; as it is written in the prophets, Behold I send My messenger before Thy Face, which shall prepare Thy way before Thee; The Voice of one crying in the wilderness, prepare ye the way of the Lord, make His paths straight. John did baptize in the wilderness, and preach the Baptism of repentance for the remission of sins." St. John, as soon as ever he has declared the Godhead of Jesus Christ, and His wonderful Incarnation, goes on to tell us of John the Baptist, how He came to bear witness of that Light, baptizing with water. St. Matthew relates at large, how our Lord, when He would begin His ministry, came to be baptized by St. John in Jordan. Thus in every one of the Gospels you see that Baptism was the beginning. But what Baptism? Not that of Christ, but that of him who was only the forerunner of Christ. The Master Himself did not for a long time begin to baptize, but left it entirely to His servant. St. John's Baptism, to which the people from all parts thronged so largely, was not at all the same thing with the Baptism which we have received, and at which we are continually present in the holy Church. It was no Sacrament of Christ, as our's is. No special promise of heavenly grace was added to it; much less the great and heavenly Promise, "He that believeth and is baptized shall be saved." Hear how the Holy Baptist himself points out the difference of the two. "One mightier than I cometh, the latchet of Whose shoes I am not worthy to stoop down and unloose." *That* was one unspeakable difference, namely in the *persons* baptizing: no lesser difference than between God and man.

Another was the difference in the Baptism itself. "I indeed baptize you with water, but He shall baptize you with the Holy Ghost and with fire." St. John had no power but to apply the outward sign. The Holy Ghost he could not give; but when our Lord began to baptize on and after the Day of Pentecost, He baptized with the Holy Ghost—the same Holy Ghost Who on that day came down as fire, as fiery tongues lighting on the Apostles.

And when St. John spake of our Lord thus baptizing, he meant no other than the Baptism which now goes on in the Christian Church. Wonderful as it is to think of, yet by God's mercy we believe it to be most certainly true, that this prophecy of the Baptist is fulfilled even among ourselves, as often as a young child is brought to yonder Font to be baptized. The person then and there baptizing is not St. John nor any mortal man, but it is our Lord Jesus Christ Himself: the Priest or Deacon standing there in his surplice, and taking up the child in his arms, is in himself nothing at all to the Baptism; whether he be good or bad, the infant is just as truly christened: because the minister is simply and only a token of the Presence of Jesus Christ, Who by him takes the child into His loving Arms, pours the water upon him, and blesses him with the very greatest of His gifts and blessings, i. e. with the Holy Spirit then and there given him, to make him "a member of Christ, a child of God, and an inheritor of the Kingdom of Heaven." This, I say, this great and miraculous work is truly wrought among Christians, whensoever and wheresoever any one is rightly baptized: and though there seem to be as many baptizers as there are ministers to apply the water, yet all the while there is but one Baptizer, even Jesus Christ Himself, even as all are baptized with one and the same Spirit. All this goes on as truly and as wonderfully, whenever a child is christened here, as it did in Jerusalem on the day of Pentecost, the first day of Christian Baptism, when they who gladly received St. Peter's words were baptized, not with water only, but with the Holy Ghost also and with fire.

As a certain proof, how much greater and holier the Baptism of Christ was than the Baptism of John, we read again and again in the Acts of the Apostles how they who had received John's Baptism only, were obliged, on becoming Christians, to be again baptized with water. And again, whereas St. John Baptist simply baptized men with water unto repentance, our Lord in His Baptism, i. e. His Apostles and Priests in His Name, always baptized in the Name of the Father and the Son and the Holy Ghost: for so He Himself had ordained. This again is a great difference, a hidden wonder of Christian Baptism, that in it the Name of the most Holy Trinity is put upon men, which it was not in St. John's Baptism. Thus every way is our Baptism so much higher and more blessed than St. John's, that there is no comparing them one with another.

See then how high and holy and sacred even St. John's Baptism was, how much it required of the baptized person, and consider thereupon what manner of persons we ought to be, who have received so much greater gift from a Person so much more holy and glorious.

For indeed St. John was a very holy person filled with the Holy Ghost even from his mother's womb: such an one that our Lord said, "Among them that were born of women there had not arisen a greater Prophet." And our Saviour gives us to understand that St. John's appearing among the Jews left them entirely without excuse, if they continued in their impenitence. "John came unto you in the way of righteousness, but ye received him not." But if the Jews of that time were without excuse for not receiving John the Baptist; what shall we say for ourselves, in so far as we stand off and refuse to receive Jesus Christ? John, when he had baptized any, went away generally from them or they from him, and they saw no more of him: yet the mere remembrance of him ought to have been enough to keep them in order. But we Christians know and are sure, that He who baptized us is with us always. He is with us always, by day and by night, watching to see whether we are keeping the promise which we made to Him, whether we are making use of the gift and grace which He trusted us with. And then, what great things He hath done for us! The Israelites, when St. John first appeared, thought it a great thing that he had spent so much time in the desert, hardly clothed and sparely fed, in order that he might prepare himself to do them good: but what is that to our Baptizer, Who left the glories of heaven to do us good, and made Himself one of us, to live a whole life in the wilderness of this world, among evil men and evil spirits, and at last had Himself crucified for us?

Again, the Baptism of St. John was a very serious matter for the Jews of that time, because it required a solemn confession of sin : as we read, "Then went out unto him all the land of Judea, and they of Jerusalem, and were all baptized of him in the river of Jordan, confessing their sins." It is a fearful thing to come into the presence of the Living and True God, bringing with you the sad account, how grievously you from time to time had offended Him. But if it was a sharp and severe trial to confess with a view to that Baptism by water only, much more is that confession sharp and severe, which Christian Baptism requires of all grown-up persons who have received, or are to receive It: because if we keep back anything from that confession, we do not only profane a holy ceremony, as persons coming lightly to St. John's Baptism did; but we make void the grace, the pardoning grace of our God, and cause His merciful absolving Words to be of none effect ; and besides, people coming to St. John had only to acknowledge what they had done amiss in their natural unregenerate condition: but our sins are the sins of the regenerate; so much worse than their's, by how much the grace we have received is greater. We alas! are so used to transgress and to see others transgress, as a matter of course, that it is very hard for the most thoughtful of us all to think seriously enough of the hideousness of his own sins: but let us use ourselves, when we confess, to recollect for a little moment what passed in the moment of our Baptism. Who was there: what a solemn promise we made Him : what a heavenly lift He gave us, that we may have power to keep that promise :—what a thing then it was for us wilfully and knowingly to break that promise, and to affront Him to His Face: and that, not once or twice, but as often as we have consented to known sin : hundreds, may be, or thousands of times. Whose heart, alas ! would not die down within him, when he thinks of all this, were it not that by the same Baptism he obtained an interest in that Saviour Who is always more ready to forgive, than we to sin; and so we may hope, that by true confession even now, by *true* confession I say, and *sincere* amendment—all may be set right, even with such an one as he has been? But all will depend on our being *quite* in earnest: *very* serious indeed, very much concerned for our souls.

And this so much the more, as there is another difference, a very remarkable one, between our case and their's who came to St. John the Baptist. He spake to them of the axe laid at the root of the trees, ready to be used at any moment against any tree that bore not fruit. Every such tree, he said, would be "hewn down and cast into the fire." It may be doubtful perhaps, whether St. John in those words did not refer in part to the grievous troubles and judgments, which were just then about to come on the Jewish people: but there is no doubt whatever, that, when the same words are uttered to *us*—when the Scriptures speak to *us* of the fire of judgment, and that " our God is a consuming fire,"—something is meant far more terrible than the destruction of Jerusalem. There is no doubt what the unquenchable fire is, nor who are meant by the chaff which it will burn up, and by the trees that will be cast into it, after they have been hewn down for bearing no good fruit. We sometimes, I daresay, think what a sad thing it must have been to have lived in those times when

Jerusalem was finally destroyed; and perhaps some, who are mothers among you, may have felt horror before now, on hearing or reading of the frightful suffering which came upon mothers and infants in that siege, when the Prophet's saying came true, "The hands of the pitiful tender-hearted women have sodden their own children," and, as our Lord said, the barren were blest, and it was woe to them that had children to nurse. But if that history is shocking to you, think, I pray you, this with yourselves, what if the children of your own body, the little ones over whom you have watched day and night, who seem more dear to you than your own life—what if you should see them one day cast into the unquenchable fire, far worse than anything that happened at Jerusalem,—because they cared not enough for their Baptism, because, being tempted by the world, the flesh and the devil, they sinned away the grace which the Great Baptizer had given them? What if some of you mothers should have to witness this horrible end of your children? And what if you should then have to reproach yourselves, that, although you brought them to be christened, you took no real and earnest care to bring them up afterwards in the memory of their christening?

Many such thoughts are brought into a considerate person's mind by the yearly return of St. John Baptist's day: and more so, perhaps, as the world grows older and the axe is more evidently laid at the root of the trees. All seems tending to decay and confusion: except so far as there are any, who are willing like the Baptist to lead holy and mortified lives—to deny themselves for the sake of their Lord

B

and Saviour. As Jerusalem in her latter days, when she was on the edge of the final reprobation and ruin, had the Holy Baptist sent to her for a solemn warning, if haply she would repent in time for our Lord's first coming: so this old worn-out world of ours now perhaps, in her latter days, may be favoured more or less with holy and self-denying examples, "witnesses" as the Scripture says, "clothed in sackcloth"—to warn her of the Judge standing before the door, the Lord of the harvest approaching with His fan in His Hand. Repentance and self-denial prepared the way for the first Advent of our Saviour: and if we would be ready for His second Advent, we must repent and deny ourselves. That is the only way to save ourselves, and it is the likeliest way to do good to the souls of others. Do you not see that, on the whole, he who is most in earnest can do most in winning hearts to God? and how are people to prove themselves in earnest, but by repenting of their sins and by denying themselves for the love of Christ and the Church? Do this, and your Baptism will be a joy to you at the last Day. But if you will not repent, nor deny yourself, it were better for you never to have been baptized, never to have been brought to Christ at all.

SERMON III.

Ephesians iv. 5.

" One Lord, one Faith, one Baptism."

Do you not perceive, by the very sound of these words, what a great and holy thing Baptism must be : seeing that it is reckoned up with the greatest and holiest Name of all—the Name of our Lord Jesus Christ, and of God the Father of all—and with faith in those Names? as though it were not altogether sufficient for us to have all one Lord, one faith and one God, but we must also have one Baptism.

Plainly we are here given to understand two great truths concerning that holy Sacrament : first, that it is a very solemn thing—one of the most solemn and important that can possibly be : and secondly, that it can come but once ; a man can be baptized only once in his life.

Now regarding the solemnity of Baptism I have shewn you from the Rubric in the Prayer Book, at the beginning of the Baptismal Service, what care the Church takes, to make it as public as she can, that all persons may think much of it, in that it is appointed to be, if possible, only on great days. Now I will remind you of some more things of the same kind, which have already been pointed out in the Catechising.

It is convenient that Baptism be administered in the vulgar tongue: i. e. in the English language, not in the Latin which has sometimes been used in the Church: in order that all persons present may be more effectually reminded of their own Baptism. Now see, how certainly this makes every one of us answerable before God for a devout remembrance of his Baptism, as being indeed that good work, whereby he was made a member of Christ, a child of God, and an inheritor of the Kingdom of Heaven. If we lived in Spain or Italy, or France, and did not understand the words of the service when we heard it, then of course we could not out of that Service learn the doctrine of Holy Baptism: but as it is, if we will but attend, we can hardly help learning a great deal: how that we were all conceived and born in sin, that we cannot get out of this miserable condition and enter into the Kingdom of God without being born again of water and the Holy Ghost; that this new birth takes place at Baptism, seeing that before the child is christened we pray to God that he may be regenerate, and after he is christened, we thank God that he is regenerate; and that, being once baptized, his great care must be to keep the good thing then given him, daily dying to sin, and rising again unto righteousness. All this and more those who will, may learn for themselves, by merely attending to the service of our Church whenever a child is baptized. And are we not then without excuse, if we think little of our own Baptism? Will not those Christians one day rise up in judgment against us, who, although they cannot understand the words of the Baptismal service, do yet believe and remember what a great gift they then received, saying to themselves as St. Paul says for us all, "If we live in the Spirit, let us also walk in the Spirit?"

Observe what the Church next appoints: "There shall be for every male child to be baptized two Godfathers and one Godmother, and for every female one Godfather and two Godmothers." Now this again is a very solemn circumstance: for the Godfathers and Godmothers are in a manner deputies appointed by the Church to bring the child to Almighty God and beseech Him to receive him: and by coming forward as they do, they not only make themselves answerable for the child, in the manner which is explained at the end of this service, and that, publicly before all men, but they also are a kind of token of the great care which the Church takes to make our Baptism as solemn as possible. It is a great honor done to them, that the Church should permit them to bring her little ones in their arms, and lay them as it were at the feet of the great King, that He may take them up in His Arms: just as it would be a great honor if the queen should trust her young children to any one to be carried any where, and to receive any good thing.

Observe further, that notice is to be given, the parents are to inform the Pastor of the parish over night or in the morning before the service. Because Baptism is a great Sacrament and nothing should be done in it hastily and without preparation: and because the Pastor should have time to enquire about the persons intended to be sponsors, and, if need be, to talk with them or with the parents, since we see and know of our own selves, that, in so holy a service as Baptism, all who take part should at least be trying to be holy; and, as it is greatly to be commended and a very charitable work, when sincere and thoughtful persons, young or old, come forward to present Christ's little ones at His Font, so it is a great pity for any to come in a light and thoughtless way; much more if they be known neglecters of Church-services and Sacraments; or if unhappily they be notorious evil livers. All this is plain of itself; and so is the motherly care of the Church in taking that order which she doth, that the sponsors may be such as to honor the Sacrament and do a good part by the babe.

We may notice also, in what part of the service the Sacrament of Baptism is appointed to be administered. It is to come after the second lesson; and the second lesson, as you know, is always taken from the New Testament. And do you not see how suitable it is, that immediately after the written Word of Christ should come the blessing of His Sacramental Word? that such as He has been declared in our hearing by His Holy apostles and prophets, such He should come in our sight by the no less Holy Mysteries which He Himself ordained? even as, when St. Peter first preached to the Jews, they that gladly received his word were baptized: and when he preached again to the gentiles, the Holy Ghost fell upon all them that heard the word.

The Rubric goes on. The sponsors and people are

to be ready at the Font, and then the Priest is to come to them: the Font being, as we have before noticed, close to the principal entrance, because Baptism is the entrance into Christ's Spiritual Body: it is the beginning of our Christian life, even as we begin each new day by washing with water. When we turn towards it, as we commonly do at the commencement of the baptismal service, well were it, if in heart we always turned back towards our own Baptism, remembering what a good beginning we then made, and how grievous it will be, if our latter end be not answerable.

Take notice that this Font is to be *filled* with pure water. The Water must be pure, because it is to represent and convey the purest of all beings, the Holy Spirit of God; and it must fill the Font, because God's mercy is overflowing; and because, as the service afterwards shews, it were well if the infant, not being weak or sickly, might be plunged entirely in the water, instead of merely having it poured on him.

All things being thus prepared for the solemn outward baptizing of the child, the Priest begins the office by asking, Hath this child been already baptized or no?—If they answer no, he goes on at once: if yes, he asks some three or four more questions, in order to make sure of its having been rightly made partaker of the Sacrament: of which questions I shall speak presently: but in no case is either the same Priest or any other ever to think of baptizing that child again. Baptism can in no case be repeated: it were a kind of sacrilege, an utter abomination to the Lord. Did you not hear, how solemnly St. Paul told his Ephesian converts, "As there is but one Lord, and one Faith, so there is but one Baptism." Nor is the reason hard to see. Baptism is a kind of birth, a second birth after the first, a new birth into a new and spiritual life. Therefore it can come to us once only. For as Nicodemus argued with our Saviour, "How can a man be born when he is old? can he enter the second time into his mother's womb, and be born?" And our Lord answered by telling him, not that a man could be born twice in the same kind of birth, but that He was speaking of a different birth, of quite another kind from that which Nicodemus was thinking of. But in the same kind, man cannot be born twice: so far Nicodemus was quite right: and for this reason, that birth is always a beginning of life, and there cannot be two beginnings of the same life. Therefore as a man cannot literally enter the second time into his mother's womb, so neither can a man be born more than once of water and of the Spirit. As we read in the Epistle to the Hebrews, "It is impossible for those who were once enlightened and have tasted of the heavenly gift and were made partakers of the Holy Ghost, and have tasted the good word of God and the powers of the world to come, if they shall fall away, to renew them again unto repentance." They cannot be baptized a second time, if they have once quite lost and forfeited for ever the blessings of their first baptism. The Church therefore in the Nicene Creed acknowledges but "one Baptism for the Remission of sins." Those who fall away after Baptism and repent and amend and are saved at last, are saved, not by a new Baptism, but by the mercy of God awakening, as it were, within them the virtue of their first Baptism which had gone to sleep. You cannot be baptized a second time : if a person tried to be so, it would be either in ignorance, and then I suppose it would just come to nothing—or, if he did it by way of disparaging his former Baptism, surely it would be a great and grievous sin, a sin and dishonour done to a very special grace and Gift of the Holy Ghost.

Nevertheless there are cases, in which the Church is not content with asking whether the child hath been before baptized or no : i. e. if a child is brought to Church and they say it hath been already baptized, still the Priest is to ask three or four questions (unless he was himself the baptizer). He is to ask, By whom was the child baptized ? and, Who was present ?—that the Church may have regular testimony of its having been done. And then, for fear something of importance might be left out, the Priest is to ask two questions more, With what matter was this child baptized ? and, With what words was this child baptized ? Because in the outward part of Baptism, there are two things of consequence, the element or matter, which is the water, to bury the child in, or to be poured or sprinkled upon it : and the form of words, ordained by our Lord Himself, "In the Name of the Father, and the Son and the Holy Ghost." If either of these two were wanting, i. e. if the child were washed or dipped in water, but not in the Sacred Name: or, again, if the Name were said over it, but no water applied to it ; then it would not be baptized : and it is to make sure of its being baptized, that those two questions are asked. When they are sufficiently answered, then, says our Church, we are to make no doubt that the child is lawfully and sufficiently baptized, and ought by no means to be baptized again. He is not half but wholly baptized, if the water have been once applied in the saving Name. Thenceforth it is a Christian; not for a time, but for ever, unless by its own wilful sin it finally cast away that grace. It needs no more christening; only, for its good and for the Church's satisfaction, it must be presented publicly in Church and make its profession before God by its godfathers. But by no means, and in no sense, can it ever be baptized or christened again.

"Once baptized and always baptized," that is a point for us all to muse deeply over. All of us naturally think a good deal of any thing that is done once for all: it seems such a sad thing, should it be wrongly done: we feel beforehand how miserable it will be, should we have bye and bye the feeling that it was all wrong, all ill done, and at the same time that it never can be mended. Think of the great turning point of this our earthly life, such as, choice of business or employment, e. g. when a lad enlists to be a soldier, or is bound apprentice to any trade; and more especially if a person marries; for that of course is the great turning point in respect of this world's happiness or discomfort. *This* is the fearful, anxious thing, that, when we make a choice in such matters, we choose for good and all: it settles one way through life: if we are right, it is well; but if wrong, we must bear it: it can hardly or at all be mended. But what is all the good or evil of this one short space of time here, compared with what depends on the moment of our Baptism? what signifies success or failure in this or that profession, this or that line of life, compared with our keeping or not keeping the grace of regeneration? To baptize is a thing done in a very short time: the water is poured on the child in a moment: the words are said in a very few moments: but to that brief and fleeting moment the soul will look back through all eternity, in joy and thanksgiving, or in bitter shame and remorse. All the children of Adam will look back to the moment of their natural birth, as to that which introduced them to an eternity of joy or despair: but we, his regenerate children, shall have to look back on the moment of our Baptism also, as lifting us to a far higher Heaven, or sinking us into a lower and more miserable Hell.

My brethren, you know, better than I can tell you, how you cherish, how you treasure and value this short life of our's: with what unfeigned horror, for the most part, you shrink from deadly sickness, from fatal and alarming accidents, from everything which you think apt to shorten your life. You know how eagerly you welcome every plan which at all promises to secure you from death, or those whom you love, though it be but for a short time. Why will you not as truly, as earnestly, treasure and value the baptismal grace of Christ—the Holy Spirit given you at the Font, to abide in you, if not driven away, not a few years, not all your life, but in the whole of your being, in life, in death, in Eternity? If you had a jewel in your keeping, most precious in itself, and of such virtue that, as long as you wore it, it kept you from all serious sickness, should you not prize that jewel very much, and not let it lie about, to be caught up by those who would do you a mischief? Such a jewel, my Brethren, is Baptismal Grace. O watch it well, hold it very dear, never forget it, for it is exceeding precious: and, if once entirely lost, it can never be recovered.

Life, this earthly mortal life, is still very dear to us, even in our sickness and old age: people generally cling to it, even when but little of it remains. May not this too teach us something in respect of our Baptismal life in Christ Jesus? Too often and too sadly is that life within us impaired by grievous sin: and not seldom are we tempted to put by all thought of it: to give ourselves up in despair saying, "Let us eat and drink; for to-morrow we die." I beseech you, never for one moment hearken to any such thought. What if you are grievously fallen? By His great mercy your Baptismal life remains, you are not given over by the heavenly Physician; else why are you here, caring at all about your sins? As you value and take care of your life, even when you are on your sick bed, so and much more, for Christ's sake, I pray you to value and take care of your soul, diseased but not yet dead: take care of it, nurse it well, keep it from evil, cleanse and chasten it with penitence; feed it, if God permit, with Holy Communion. Such methods, taken in earnest, cannot fail in time to effect a complete cure: by virtue of that holiest seal which the Spirit of Christ set on you in Baptism—the Name of the Father, the Son, and the Holy Ghost. What if you are weak and fallen? In that Name Christ bids you arise: in that Name He once for all gave you power to obey His bidding: and if you do obey it, in that Name He will bless you for ever.

SERMON IV.

Psalm li. 6.

"Behold, I was shapen in wickedness and in sin hath my mother conceived me."

THE first foundation and groundwork of the doctrine of Baptism, and that on which all the rest of it depends, is the doctrine of original sin. What original sin is, you will find explained in one of the XXXIX Articles of our Church which are printed at the end of the Prayer Book. The ninth Article says, "original sin is the fault and corruption of every man naturally engendered of the offspring of Adam—whereby man is very far gone from original righteousness, and is of his own nature inclined to evil, so that the flesh lusteth always contrary to the Spirit." That is to say, that in every child born into this world, however wise and good his parents, and however earnestly they pray to God for him, there is still something very bad, from the very first moment of that child's being, affecting both his soul and body. For so David says in the text, "I was shapen in wickedness, and in sin hath my mother conceived me." David was shapen and conceived like other men: his father Jesse was a good man: and, if David was shapen and conceived in wickedness, so must have been all other men. So it was in David's time as it is now; so it has been in all times; so it will be to the end. Only one of the children of Adam, that we are told of, was conceived without sin; and that one was our Lord and Saviour, the Child of Adam by the mother's side: but He was not naturally conceived, but in some miraculous and unspeakable way, by the power of the Holy Ghost. All the rest, as soon as we were born and before, were the worse for this original sin, this taint within us, very bad, very displeasing to Almighty God, and quite sure, like a bad seed, to ripen into all sorts of mischief, if only it were left to itself.

To some this may seem a hard saying, when they look at a little child, whether it be their own or another's, and see how sweet and innocent it looks; as sweet and as innocent, to all outward appearance, before it is christened as after. It may sound strange in their ears, that the Priest should look at the simple babe, lying so quietly in its nurse's arms, and pronounce it to be in a wretched and sinful state. For so he undoubtedly does, my brethren, when, having been told that it is yet unbaptized, he begins to speak to the people and say, "Dearly beloved, forasmuch as all men are conceived and born in sin:" so going on to rehearse the doctrine of Baptism. Unthinking persons might wonder at this: but after all, why need it appear to them so much out of the way? They would at once own how true it was, if one were to take up a child out of its cradle and say, "this child does indeed look for the present most fair and healthful; yet depend upon it, this child, like all other children, must one day die; nay, and he will die very soon, if you do not provide him with the food and medicine which are necessary for him." You might think it odd, if a man took such pains to teach you what you knew very well before; but at least you would not doubt the truth of it; for you have long since known that we are all mortal, all subject to pain and sickness: and this babe among the rest. Look at the most miserable helpless person you know, him who is most entirely worn out with age and disease, and fancy him what you know he once was, an infant in his mother's or nurse's arms; can you be sure, that he too was not just as fine and promising and happy a little creature as any that you most admire now? You are aware that it is very possible; therefore you would readily allow that any child, of which you are now proud, may one day be as the most deformed and decayed of your acquaintance.

Now why have I said all this about sickness and the change which it and old age and the wear and tear of life make in children? In order that you might better know, how to think on what the Prayer Book teaches of original sin. For sin is in many respects like sickness; and original sin is like a natural taint, a bad constitution which the child inherits from its father and mother. Adam and Eve, by their unhappy disobedience, brought the complaint upon themselves, and God in His wise and just judgments, secret to us, permitted it to be conveyed on to all their posterity: just as many sicknesses, sometimes the result of sin, are known to run in the blood of such and such families. As I said then about bodily sickness and affliction, so now I say about sin, which is the sickness of the soul. If it seems hard to you to say of the babe at the Font, "this infant is in original sin, he is subject to the wrath of God," imagine to yourself the worst criminal that ever lived. Imagine Judas Iscariot, who betrayed our Lord, and for whom, our Lord said, good were it, if he had not been born: and consider that he was once as harmless as any other little babe, and very likely looked so; and it may be his mother little thought of his proving so wicked. Therefore their sweet childish innocence is no proof that there is not something very evil lying hid in their nature. Does not the Bible tell us so plainly? "They are all gone out of the way; they are altogether become abominable, there is none good, no not one." "All have sinned and come short of the glory of God." "The Heavens are not pure in His Sight: how much less man that is a worm!" And then see how we turn out, if God leave us to ourselves. See how children go on, if they are turned loose into the world without education, and just permitted to go their own way. They bear a full crop of sin and vice of all kinds, as surely as a neglected piece of ground bears no good fruit, but only thorns and thistles. Why should not the ground as well bear wheat and barley, grapes and apples? It is cursed: cursed for the sin of man: that is the only account that can be given of the matter. So these hearts and bodies of ours, having the heavy curse and mark of that first transgression upon them, are naturally inclined to evil, and, left to ourselves, every imagination of our thoughts would be only evil continually. It is a sad thing, but there is no disputing it. The best way is to leave off wondering, why or how such a burden should be laid upon us, and thankfully and gladly to accept the sure and certain remedy which God has provided—Jesus Christ crucified, taught in His Gospel, given in His Sacraments, present evermore in His Church.

And indeed you do all accept Him, and I am most thankful that you do, in one very chief matter, the matter of which we are speaking: you all make a point of bringing your young children to be christened in good time. I only wish you thought as much of this Sacrament of Food as you do of the Sacrament of birth. It will be well with us, when we are all as careful to come ourselves worthily and bring our children to the table of the Lord, as we are to secure the benediction of His heavenly washing. In the mean time it is no small mercy, that here at least, among us, the enemy has not been able to make Baptism little thought of. In some other places, especially in large towns, I fear it is far otherwise: I fear that thousands are born, bred, and sent out into the wicked world with the foul stain of their original sin upon them; no holy name pronounced over them; no cross on their foreheads to drive away the evil one. Whatever becomes of you, and wherever you go, never, I beseech you, be partakers of this sin: never be at all slack, nor encourage others to be slack, about Holy Baptism. Never defer it without cause: some have done so to their great grief. Let those who belong to the family make it a matter of earnest prayer, both before and after an infant is born, that he may live to be baptized: and when he has been so, let them remember it in earnest thanksgiving. It would be well if we all made a point of acknowledging God's great goodness in having us baptized, at least as often as we join in the general thanksgiving, and praise Him for giving us the means of grace. For of all the means of grace Baptism is the first: and it is the way to all the rest.

But neither, on the other hand, may we ever safely forget that, although the guilt of our birth-sin was blotted out in our Baptism, yet the sin itself remains like a spark from hell-fire within us, which may be fanned into a flame, and the devil is always trying to fan it. The lust of the flesh—evil desire—abideth ever in them which are regenerate, and is not entirely subject to the law of God. Good Christians are aware of it, and are always trying to tread it out by holy discipline, prayer, and self-denial: they are never satisfied, until every thought be reduced to the obedience of Christ; i. e. they never in this world feel as if their work was done: the hidden spark, they are too well aware, is still lurking within them: sin is there; and their very soul shudders at the thought, "what if some day or other it should be mortal sin? and surely it will be so, if I become careless in prayer, if I do not cherish the grace given me in Baptism." Or it may be likened to an inveterate ulcer, by God's mercy in process of cure, yet still imperfectly cured: subdued, but not entirely healed: if not attended to, it will soon begin to grow worse, and will spread afresh, no one can say how far. Or again, the remnant of birth-sin in the heart, may be fitly compared to the root of an obstinate weed, which lingers in the ground, when most of the plant has been cut out. You must keep on noticing, vexing, persecuting it, as constantly as ever you can, if you would make sure of its never growing to a head in your ground again. Remember all this for yourself, and remember it for your children also, and for others who are under your care. Be always owning God's mercy in having you and them baptized: be always using the grace then given to destroy the remnant of evil then left within you. So shall it be found, when you come to die and rise again, that the spark, the root, the infection of Adam's sin, has quite wasted away from your heart and your body. So will there be good hope, that the baptismal days of yourself and your children will be feasts and good days to you for ever. And if places known on earth are recollected on high, the Font in which you were baptized will be to you as a bright spot, not fading, but more and more gladdening to think of, as you go deeper on in Eternity.

SERMON V.

Ezekiel xxxvi. 25.

"Then will I sprinkle clean water upon you, and ye shall be clean."

As meat is by nature necessary to cure hunger, and drink to allay thirst, and sleep to remove the weariness of watching, and fire and clothing to keep off the cold, and shelter to protect us from ill weather, so is Holy Baptism necessary, by the rules of God's heavenly kingdom, to allay and cure, to keep off and remove, the sin and misery in which we were born. So the Priest proceeds to tell us at the beginning of the Baptismal Service. He tells us first of our misery: "all men are conceived and born in sin:" and then he tells us of the remedy which the merciful God has provided. "None can enter into the kingdom of God, except he be regenerate and born anew of water and of the Holy Ghost;" as if he should say, Were we left as we are by nature, all would be lost; but the good God has provided a remedy: besides the kingdom and power of Satan under which we are by nature, there is the kingdom and power of God, in which is entire happiness, perfect peace, complete deliverance: and how are we to enter into that kingdom? The King Himself hath told us very plainly. Our Saviour Christ told Nicodemus; it was one of the first lessons He taught, after He began to teach and tell of His Own approaching kingdom. "Verily, verily, I say unto you, except a man be born again, born of water and of the Spirit, he cannot see," i. e. he cannot enjoy, cannot enter into "the kingdom of God." Baptism therefore is necessary in both its parts: as our Church teaches also in the Catechism, it is "generally necessary to salvation:" so necessary that, when it may be had, no one may reasonably hope to be saved without it. We cannot be saved without being in Christ's kingdom: and Baptism is the way into the kingdom. We cannot live the heavenly life, except we be members of Christ: and Baptism makes us members of Christ. We cannot be in the Church without going through the door: and Christ, given in Baptism, is the Door. We cannot please God whilst we are in the flesh, i. e. in our natural state, all fallen and corrupt: but the Holy Spirit, entering into us at Baptism, takes us out of our natural state, mends our fallen and corrupt nature, so that we are no longer in the flesh but in the Spirit, and may please God if we will. All this our Lord teaches, and the Church after Him, in saying that "none can enter into the kingdom of God, except he be regenerate and born anew of water and of the Holy Ghost." When you hear the Priest say these words, you are to listen, as if it were the Voice of our Lord Jesus Christ Himself. For indeed it is His Voice. His minister speaks but by His commission and by the power which He gives him, and the words which he speaks are our Saviour's own Words: "Except a man be born again, born of water and of the Spirit, he cannot enter into the kingdom of God."

Do you not hear how very plain the words are? He says, Holy Baptism is necessary generally, necessary in both its parts: there is no coming into the kingdom of God without it. The water must be there, and the Holy Ghost must be there. He names the one as expressly as He does the other. He joined them together; it is not for us to part them. What He then told Nicodemus secretly, in that retired room by night, He hath since proclaimed in the light and upon the house-tops, bidding His apostles go and make disciples of all nations by baptizing them in the Name of the Father, the Son and the Holy Ghost. He taught it by the same apostles, inviting all who cared for their souls to "repent and be baptized, every one in the Name of Jesus Christ for the remission of sins," and so they should receive the gift of the Holy Ghost. It is Christ's own Truth, plainly taught in the Scriptures and faithfully delivered to us in the Creeds and offices of the Church, that there is "one Baptism for the remission of sins," the way into the kingdom of Heaven, viz. to be "regenerate and born anew of water and of the Holy Ghost."

I say it over and over again, because, although we all know it as a thing to be said, we are apt to pass it over a great deal too easily and unthinkingly, as a matter of course, a thing done for us, a thing practically gone and past, with which we have now little to do, but to be thankful when we think of it. With respect indeed to the outward part, Baptism by water, persons are commonly ready enough to allow that it is necessary. If a child is ill, they make haste to go for the minister; they are grieved and shocked at the thought of the child's passing out of the world unbaptized: and it is very right, and we ought to be very thankful that Christians should be so minded in regard of Holy Baptism. But then ought we not to consider far more deeply than we commonly do, *why* we take all this care for the child, and how deeply we are concerned in it ourselves? What is the sense and meaning of sending for the Clergyman in a great hurry, perhaps in the middle of the night, to baptize a sick infant? Is it not in order to the good of the child's soul, for fear it should die in its original sin, and lose the blessing prepared by Christ for His members? Of course, that is the reason, and a very great and deep reason it is. But what if the person, who is thus anxious for his child or it may be for his neighbour's child, should be all the while neglecting his own soul? What if, while he is really anxious that Jesus Christ should come and take the sick infant in His Arms and bless it and make it His Own before it die, he have no anxiety, no wish at all for the same Jesus to be with him, to bless him and keep him in the Kingdom of Heaven, when it shall be his own time to be sick and to die? Must not this be a sorrowful and a wonderful sight to the blessed spirits and souls of the righteous, so far as they know what is done on earth? Must it not amaze our guardian angels and fill them with something like a holy anger, to see persons so very thoughtless, so very negligent of their own immortal souls, even in the very act of waiting on other men's souls? May we not fancy them whispering in our ears; "you are going, or sending to the man of God in behalf of this little child, that it may not die unbaptized: would it not be well if you said a word to him on your own behalf also, lest you should die impenitent? Consider: that sinful nature which will make it so great a calamity if the infant should die as it is—that same nature is in you also: the grace of your Baptism did not cure it entirely, it only put it in a way to be cured: if you have not made much of that unspeakable gift, if you have since been grieving and vexing that holy Spirit, how can you be at all easy about yourself?" Surely, my brethren, if we would listen to the good counsels and friendly whisperings of the blessed angels around us, we should sometimes be aware of such thoughts and misgivings as these; and, as we feel uneasy if any little child belonging to us is left unbaptized, so should we long to confess our own sins, which may have brought us perhaps into a worse than unbaptized condition. We should feel no comfort, until by true confession we had made our peace with God, and received from Him absolution and remission of our sins.

We must be regenerate and born anew; how great, how thorough a change do these words signify! They lead us to think of an entirely altered state of things: we expect to see what was seen in vision by the Prophet and Apostle St. John; a new Heaven and a new earth; the first Heaven and the first earth having clean passed away. We expect to see the old things departed, and all things become new. As Heaven is altogether unlike this earth; as the life of a child, born into the air and light of day, is utterly unlike the life of the same child so long as he was shut up in the womb; so ought the life of a Christian to be unlike that which the same person would lead, if he were still in his heathen state. This is what we should expect, if we considered our Lord's words only in their natural meaning; if we did not look out upon the world around us and see what passes there. And whereas, the Lord saith by His Prophet in the text, "I will sprinkle clean water upon you and ye shall be clean;" would not one naturally look to see great purity, great cleanness of heart and life, in the Christian people to whom that promise is made? We should expect them to appear, to our eyes at least, undefiled, without spot or blemish, as a flock of sheep just going up from the washing. But alas! my brethren, how do things really appear to us! We dare not deny it; it is a sad truth: sin is even now so reigning and prevailing among us; the cares of the world and the lusts of the flesh have so great dominion over us; that to speak of being delivered by Baptism appears to many a hard and impossible doctrine. They say in their hearts, "such and such an one cannot have been born anew and made a member of Christ: I cannot have been so myself; there must be some mistake; for if we have been new-born, how should our temptations continue so strong, and our goodness so very very weak?" And so they come to think little of the grace which God has given them; and, thinking little of His grace, they think little of their own sins; and are in a way to go down to the grave without even seriously abhorring and forsaking them.

This is a fearful and dangerous snare. It is, I fear, the ruin of millions. I pray, that you all, my brethren, may have grace to be kept from it: and you will be kept from it, if you simply and lovingly believe God, that it was even as He had said, that when He was pleased by His minister to sprinkle the clean water upon you, you were indeed made clean. Believe this in earnest; and consider with yourself what a thing it is to have been once clean, so clean in God's sight from the deadly stain of your birth-sin, that if you had then been taken from the world you would surely have been taken into Paradise,—and then by your own sloth or wilfulness to have brought yourself back in any degree to the foul and miserable uncleanness of your first condition.

There is, in the 16th chapter of Ezekiel, an account in most deep and touching words, of the Lord's mercy shewn to Jerusalem, how she forfeited it by her sin and uncleanness, whereby she made herself far worse than the heathen; how, notwithstanding, in the latter days He would make a new covenant with her, receiving her again to be His own, when she should remember her ways and be ashamed. Doubtless, in so speaking to Jerusalem the Holy Ghost is speaking to every soul amongst us, who hath unhappily fallen away from baptismal grace.

First, there is our sad lost condition through Adam's sin; "Thou wast cast out in the open field to the loathing of thy person in the day that thou wast born." Next, there is God's free mercy, electing us to the Heavenly life. "When I passed by and saw thee polluted in thine own blood," the blood which came to thee from Adam, corrupted with sin, "I said unto thee when thou wast in thy blood, live." Then it speaks of Holy Baptism, "I sware unto thee and entered into a covenant with thee, saith the Lord God; and thou becamest Mine; then washed I thee with water; yea, I thoroughly washed away thy blood from thee, and I anointed thee with oil." O well and happy were it for us, my brethren, if our history stopped there: but alas! too truly may we know our own sin in what follows, even as we may know God's goodness in what has gone before. "Thou didst trust in thine own beauty," saith the Lord to Jerusalem, "and playedst the harlot. Sodom hath not done as thou hast done—neither hath Samaria committed half thy sins." The sins of the heathen and unregenerate are not to be compared with the sins of Christians: because the love shown to Christians is so much greater than that shown to the heathen and unregenerate. But great as our sin is in falling away after Baptism, it is not so great as His Love. For mark what is said to Jerusalem, after all her backslidings and treachery, "I will remember My covenant with thee in the days of thy youth, and I will establish unto thee an everlasting covenant: that thou mayest remember and be confounded and never open thy mouth any more because of thy shame, when I am pacified towards thee for all that thou hast done, saith the Lord God."

Let us all take particular notice, what was the beginning of the sad fall, which we have just been recollecting. Jerusalem trusted in her own beauty. That was what gave her tempters such advantage of her. On the other hand, the sign of her recovery is, if she be confounded, and never open her mouth any more because of her shame. So if any of us, my brethren, get into a way of thinking ourselves good enough; if we begin to take liberties, and scorn the the advice and warnings of those whom Christ sends with messages to our souls; what can happen, but that we too shall be led astray? we shall break our vows and forfeit our baptismal innocence. If on the other hand any is so happy as to retain that innocence to the end, it will be by walking daily before God in reverence and godly fear—fear of sin, and reverence of Christ's Inward Presence. He who is once thoroughly washed does not therefore think he has no more need of ablution: on the contrary, if he loves to be clean, he will carefully renew his washing from time to time; so the thoughtful Christian, once purified, will nevertheless be every day purifying himself, as Christ is pure. By daily self-examination and prayer, confession and penitency, he will bring his sins late and early to be washed away in his Saviour's Blood. He will do his best to return to his baptismal purity every morning and evening of his life: his regular washings and cleansings will remind him of it. Instead of vainly trusting to have all done for him, he will think thus with himself: "When I was a child in my original corruption, I had clean water sprinkled upon me and I was clean; now if I do not wash myself continually, I shall lose all the benefit of that first sprinkling: I shall lose it by my own fault! and I wonder who will pity or befriend me? Such an one therefore will keep his conscience tender, he will be very much on his guard against what are called lesser faults, pardonable sins, as they are called. For why? he will sadly feel that every such fault, every idle word and imagination will go some way, more or less, in polluting his soul, and making his Baptism void. Therefore he will watch, mistrusting himself; he will lose no time in ridding his soul's garments of the faintest speck of what he knows is hateful to his God. He will never neglect nor slur over his prayers, because he has settled it in his heart to believe that he cannot go on for a moment without God's special grace. He will think, say, do all, with the deepest reverential fear of the Great God dwelling within him. He will pray to know more and more of the Blessed Son's infinite condescension in coming so very near to him, and to be more and more afraid of dishonouring Him by wilful sin. Taught by St. Paul, he will say to himself continually, " shall I take the members of Christ and make them the members of an harlot? Shall I steal with the Hand of Christ, tell lies with the tongue of Christ, look proudly with the eyes of Christ? God forbid." May we find grace and help thus to remember our Baptism in all things: so shall we never lose the blessing of it, and if we seek that grace in sincerity, we surely shall find it.

SERMON VI.

St. John vi. 44.

" No Man can come unto Me, except the Father which hath sent Me draw him.

There are two very great mistakes which are apt to haunt us as it were, and trouble us, because of our sin and frailty, all our way through this world: the one, that we can do nothing at all, nothing, I mean, towards our own salvation; the other, that we can do anything without God. According as men are slothful or presumptuous, they are apt to take up with one or other of these. He who is spiritually slothful, and had rather not take any trouble about his soul, too readily takes up with the notion, that Almighty God, when He pleases, will touch his heart and bring him to a better mind, and that in the mean time he can but wait; it is no use for him to take any special pains; that, if he keeps from sin one day, he will fall into it the next, and so he may as well let things take their course. Such an one as this, will too commonly neglect his prayers, because, not finding that he takes delight in them, he will fancy they do him no good.

On the other hand, there are some who neglect their prayers as well from a habit (not distinctly known to themselves yet really lurking in the bottom of their hearts), that they are well enough as they are; that, on the whole, they are in a good way, and need not be so earnestly calling upon God for special help so very often or on every sort of occasion. Such persons do indeed say their prayers; but too often they allow themselves to think of something else all the while.

But all who in earnest care for their souls, and especially all dutiful children of God and of His Holy Church, having learnt of our Lord to pray always, and of the Apostle, to pray without ceasing, will neither leave out any of their prayers, nor say them over carelessly, as though they could do as well without them. Whereas our Saviour said, "No man can come to Me except the Father draw him:" they will own and feel, that in everything, little or great, we have need of His special grace, to go before, to accompany, to follow us; without it, we cannot move one hair's breadth towards Heaven. Again, whereas the same Saviour complained, "ye will not come unto Me, that ye might have life:" they will understand that to all, unto whom He makes Himself known, He offers so much grace, as that they may come unto Him and have life, if they will. There are two things, then, which should always go together, if our souls are at all to prosper. Those two things are, prayer and work. All good prayer is in order to good works: no work can ever be good without good prayer. As the meat which God has not blessed will do us no good, so the plainest undertakings, which we enter on apart from God are sure to fail. It is vain to expect a blessing on them.

All good Christian works must be begun with prayer, with earnest prayer. No wonder if the work of baptizing a child or person, which is in one sense the greatest of the works which God calls us to do here on earth, should be ordered by the Church to begin with very earnest and special prayer, since "no man can come unto Christ except the Father first draw him;" none can enter into the kingdom except by God's free gift in Baptism—" except he be regenerate and born anew of water and the Holy Ghost:" no wonder if the priest, at the very entrance of the Service, beseeches "us to call upon God the Father, through our Lord Jesus Christ, that of His bounteous mercy He will grant unto this child that thing which by nature he cannot have, that he may be baptized with water and the Holy Ghost, and received into Christ's Holy Church, and be made a lively member of the same."

Consider, my brethren, what a great idea these words give us of Holy Baptism. To our outward ears it may seem a very simple thing for the priest to take the child in his arms, to pour the water on it and say the words; but you see here that it is a work so high and so serious, that the whole Three Persons of the Blessed and glorious Trinity are called in, as it were, to bring it about. Even as they consulted together in the first creation of man, saying, "Let *Us* make man in Our Image, after Our likeness," so they are to be prayed to for their heavenly grace and Blessing in the new-making, the new creation of the soul of every poor little helpless infant, brought here to receive It. Observe, how all the Three Holy Persons are named; the priest says, "I beseech you to call upon God the Father through our Lord Jesus Christ." As if he should say; Here, as we stand round this Font, we see only a few weak and sinful mortals like ourselves, the infant, the nurse, the sponsors with the rest of the congregation, and within the Font we see nothing but ordinary water; but Faith, if we have but ever so little of it, tells us of a great deal more here present, which we do not see. By faith we know that God the Father is here; God, Who made all things in their season and ordered the times before appointed and the bounds of their habitation. He did from all eternity predestine this little child to be born, not among Jews or heathen, but here among His own people; not to have unbelieving parents who might scorn and blaspheme Holy Baptism, but such as would send it here into the Church to be christened. His merciful Providence has caused this child to be born alive, and He has preserved it hitherto: (whereas so many little ones are caught away before they can be brought to the Font.) He is here, prepared in His unspeakable mercy to bless what He has put in our hearts to do, and give this child the new and heavenly birth, as He has already given him the first birth from Adam. The Great King is here; the gift is ready; but He expects that we should humbly ask Him for it.

And how are we to ask? In the name of God the Son. We are "to call upon God the Father through our Lord Jesus Christ." For He too is here, doubt it not: the Saviour of us all, and of this little one also, is with us by this Font, around which we are gathered together in His Name: and He is ready to receive the prayers of this congregation now humbly to be offered up, and to present them to His Father, in union with those of His whole Church in heaven and in earth and with His Own mysterious Intercession. Through Him, all the petitions we shall now offer for this little one will be favourably heard by the Great Eternal Father.

He will intercede: He will be this child's Advocate and Mediator: for to this end was He born and for this cause He came into the world, to save this child among other sinners. As He had us all in His Heart, when He took the Body prepared for Him and said to His Father, "Lo! I come to do Thy Will, O God," so did He, at that time and all along since, know and foresee all concerning this particular child also. For He was made Man and born into the world, to be poor, helpless, tender, as this child now is: for him, as for us all, He was baptized; by the Touch of His Sacred Body giving virtue to all the waters of the world, and among the rest to that water which is now in this Font, to the mystical washing away of sin. When He was baptized, He had us all, and especially this child, in His Heart; and so He had when He was dying; He poured out His Divine Soul unto death, He gave His Body to be torn and pierced, with distinct purpose to redeem this little one whom we see now here in his nurse's arms, just as much so as if there were no other but this one child to be redeemed; and ever since, in His Work of Mediation in Heaven, this same infant has been in like manner present to His All-knowing Mind. And now since He is here with us, doubt not but He will both hear our prayers and intercede for this child to His Father, that it may receive the fruit of His ancient undying Love, and may be truly made a member of Him Who hath loved it.

And then, whereas the priest adds further, that the particular grace now to be asked of "God the Father through our Lord Jesus Christ," is that "this child may be baptized with water and the Holy Ghost;" you see what a very special place the Third Person also in the most Holy Trinity graciously takes in this assembly of ours. For He too is present, ready to come down as on the Day of Pentecost, and overshadow these waters, so that they shall be apt to bring forth living creatures, souls full of heavenly life. He is present; ready, when the Sacrament is given, to enter into the soul and body of this child, as He hath entered into the souls and bodies of all who have been rightly baptized hitherto: to make him "a member of Christ, a child of God, an inheritor of Heaven:" to destroy the old Adam, the power of sin within him, and make him for ever, (if he fall not wilfully away), pure and free, holy and happy.

By this you see, what a solemn thing it is in the account of our holy Mother the church, whenever an infant is baptized, and how much we ought to think of it. It is in fact no less than the Day of Pentecost over again, so far as that infant is concerned. It is Jesus Christ Himself coming down to baptize that child with the Holy Ghost. The Whole Sacred Trinity, as you have heard, is called to the work. No wonder that the priest goes on, in speaking of the Baptismal gift, to declare it to be " that thing which by nature the child could not have." For being by nature conceived and born in sin, the child of the old Adam, heir of God's wrath and damnation: how could it ever redeem or sanctify itself, any more than a dead carcase, thrown to the bottom of some loathsome pit, could raise itself up and make itself an angel? The baptismal gift cannot be had by nature; it cannot be given by any created being; it is such a gift and such a work, as only the Most High Himself can accomplish for us. For who but God can make one partaker of God?

To make us understand this the more thoroughly, the priest goes on to give some account of what the child is presently to receive. The great and good gift, too high for nature, which will go along with the simple pouring of water on the child in the Name of the Trinity, is, first, that he will be baptized with the Holy Ghost; secondly, that he will be received into Christ's Holy Church; thirdly, that he will be made a lively member of the same.

He will be baptized with the Holy Ghost, i. e. as I just now said, the same Spirit, Which came on the Apostles on the first Whit-Sunday, will descend upon him, to change his heart and soul, to give him a new nature after the likeness of Jesus Christ, to renew in him that Image of God, in which Adam was at first created. And hereby he will be admitted into Christ's Holy Church; he will be made a member of that Body, of which Christ is the Head; one Christian more, among all the millions of Christians who make up the holy family in earth and in Heaven. Now this may seem to many a very simple thing. We all profess and call ourselves Christians;

and so do all, or almost all, with whom we have ever been acquainted: therefore to be made a Christian may appear to us no great thing, no extraordinary work, no special favour. Moreover, we see with our eyes that both good and bad are members of the outward Church. A great many, almost all, fall very short of their profession. Some forget or renounce it entirely: and so people come to think, "after all, it signifies very little whether I belong to the visible Church or no." But think it once over again, my brethren, and think of it in this way; that the sheep who stays quietly in the pasture has not the less to thank his shepherd for, because there are a great many others enjoying the pasture, if it be abundant, with him; nor yet, because some are so foolish as to wander from that pasture or to neglect it, not knowing when they are well off. Neither ought the blessing and favour of God towards each Christian to be at all the less thought of, though all the world were Christians as well as ourselves: nor yet, though ever so many should prove hypocritical unstable Christians, and in the end fall away. Still to each one of us the offer of mercy is the same: our own souls are equally precious, and ought to be equally dear to us, whatever happens to the souls of others: and besides, who would not find it a joy and an encouragement to know, that, in every right thing he does, he has with him all the blessed spirits and souls of the righteous, all who go to make up the whole Church? He is never alone: there are always more for him than there ever were against him. This is an exceeding privilege, to be really one with all the saints and martyrs, all who at any time have served Christ faithfully; and this we could have in no other way, than by being united to Christ and through Him to all Christians.

And, thirdly, this again depends on one thing mentioned before, that we be *lively* members of Christ's Church: lively, i. e. living, not dead, having life and spirit within us. That is, as we are limbs of Christ's Body, we may never become dead and palsied as to the doing of what God commands us, but all of us be always quick, earnest, and alert in performing it: that we may not be like withered hands which will not, or cannnot obey the Head, that would fain stretch them out to do good: nor yet like feet that are benumbed and useless, and unable to go where He, Whose they are, would send them.

This is the Prayer that our Church instructs us to make over every child that is to be christened, that it may become a lively, or living, member of Christ's Holy Catholic Church. Observe that, " of Christ's Holy Catholic Church." Our Prayer-Book has no thought of any salvation or regeneration, any union with Christ or interest in Him, apart from the Holy Church thoughout all the world, His Mystical Body, to which all His Promises are made. Of Christ's Holy Catholic Church we are to be members, not dead but living members: we must be so when we come to die, else we are surely lost for ever. We had need be so all our lives long; for we may die at any moment. O Lord, can we ever think enough of it? Simple as it may seem, and a mere matter of course for a child to be brought here and christened, it is indeed the greatest of all changes. It places that child ever after in a supernatural and miraculous state, with God for his Father, the Church for his Mother, angels to wait on him, Christ's Body and Blood to be his nourishment. He belongs from that hour to Christ in a nearer and more awful way than he belonged to Him before: as the children of Israel were the Lord's people in a different sense from all other nations, though the whole earth is His. This is our condition, as many as have been baptized; we cannot be as the heathen, though we wished it: we cannot give the heathen's account; our account, whenever we give it, must be that of members of Christ. God grant, it may be the account of true and living members, that we, and all who are concerned for us, may render it with joy, and not with grief.

SERMON VII.

1 St. Peter iii. 20, 21.

"The long-suffering of God waited in the days of Noah, while the ark was a preparing, wherein few, that is, eight souls, were saved by water. The like figure whereunto, even baptism, doth now save us."

We have now done with the priest's exhortation, in which he tells the people the need of Holy Baptism, and asks their prayers for the child now to be baptized. They kneel down; and what are the words in which the Church instructs you to pray? "Almighty and everlasting God, Who of Thy great mercy didst save Noah and his family in the ark from perishing by water . . . We beseech Thee, for Thine infinite mercies, that Thou wilt mercifully look upon this child: wash him and sanctify him with the Holy Ghost, that he, being delivered from Thy wrath, may be received into the ark of Christ's Church."

You see, in the very first prayer, we are put in mind of the ark of Noah: how that, when we read of it, God would have us think of Christ's Church, and how that, as the ark and all that were in it was in God's providence saved by water, so the Church, and each Christian soul in the Church, according to the law of the kingdom of heaven, is saved by Holy Baptism. The flood in the time of Noah was really and truly, in the purpose of Almighty God, a type of Christian Baptism. The Church has known this, ever since the time of St. Peter. For he, speaking by the Holy Ghost, saith, that Baptism, being the thing represented by the waters of the flood, saves us, bearing up the Church of Christ, as the flood bore up Noah's ark. Then he gives us to understand, that, as that old world of the ungodly, being overflowed with water, perished, so the heaven and the earth that now are, shall one day perish in a flood of fire; and as nothing escaped that destruction, but only Noah and those who were with him in the ark, so nothing will escape the fire of the last day, but only those who shall be found in the ark of Christ's Church. As the flood came not without warning (for God gave one hundred and twenty years' notice of it, commanding Noah to prepare the ark); so likewise of the Day of judgment, ample notice has been given beforehand, seeing that for eighteen hundred years every Christian child has been taught to prophesy of it, repeating his creed and saying, "From thence He shall come to judge the quick and the dead." But as then they made scorn of Noah and his forebodings, and went on just as they had been used to do; so it will be in the last days: "they will eat, they will drink; they will buy, they will sell; they will plant, they will build; they will marry wives, or be given in marriage, until the day that the Son of Man is revealed; and the flood will come and destroy them all." They only who believe what the Church teaches, of a judgment to come and everlasting life, and who therefore have entered into Christ's Church by Holy Baptism, and have remained there, they only will be saved; just as all, who did not with Noah go into the ark and abide there, were drowned in the flood. And as the ark was a long time preparing, even one hundred and fifty years, so is the Church of Christ a long time building up. For all this eighteen hundred years that work has been going on; Noah, i. e., Christ and His apostles, have been preaching, and the ark, i. e., the Church, has had daily additions made to it. As the ark was framed, it is said, of incorruptible wood, so is the Church made up altogether of the Cross of Christ, and of those who by faith are nailed to it. As the ark was builded under the Almighty's particular direction, so also is the Church. For we know that our Lord, during forty whole days, was teaching His Apostles after His resurrection; and what things did He teach them? the things pertaining to the kingdom of God. And when they went out and preached everywhere, gathering disciples into the Church, this was Noah's building up the ark according to all that God commanded him. There were clean and unclean in the ark, so there are in the Church of God: some faithful and some hypocrites. Of all that whole generation, only seven besides Noah were saved in the ark; and we know that our Lord's way of life is narrow, and the gate is straight, and few there be that go in thereat. And as it might be truly said, that all those who were in the ark were saved by water (for the water bore up the ark, and it went upon the face of the waters); so, and much more, may it be truly said, that all Christians are saved by Baptism. The water which joins them to Christ is the means of their salvation: not of course in itself, but in that it joins them to Jesus Christ by the power of the Holy Ghost going along with it.

Thus you have heard some of the chief points of resemblance between Noah's deliverance and ours. Now what should be the thought of a good Christian going over these things in his mind?

First, he cannot fail to perceive how great, how unspeakably great is the gift given and the work wrought in Holy Baptism; seeing it is compared to the two greatest deliverances of God's people in the Old Testament. He will say to himself, When I see a little child christened, I see an instance of God's power and goodness, of which the preservation of Noah in the ark was but a faint image and shadow. The preservation of Noah in the ark, and the passage of Israel through the Red Sea, were the two greatest and most wonderful miracles whereby God delivered His ancient people; the one kept all mankind from perishing, the other the holy and chosen seed; and both these were by water, and were types and tokens of the Holy Sacrament of Baptism; both these great deliverances, the wonder of the world, were but types and tokens of what Almighty God did for me, when He by His Spirit came to me in my Baptism, and made me a member of His Son. This is our deliverance, my brethren, your's and mine; it has been really wrought for us: let us not cast it away. Think how it would have been with

Noah, or with any of his sons, if they had refused to go into the ark, or had cast themselves out of it, after they had been admitted. The ark, as we read in Genesis, was finished, and Noah and his sons invited to come into it, full seven days before the flood was upon the earth. We are not told that to the eye there were any signs of a great storm, any gathering of dark clouds, any lightning or thunder, or other such tokens; we are told that everything around went on as it had done before. Whichever way Noah looked about him, he might see people building houses, planting forests, making bargains and sales with one another, contracting marriages, and doing everything else, just as if the world were to last for ever,—as if God had never said a word of His anger against it for its sins. There was no sign of a flood, and nobody thought there would be one; or, if they did ever notice what God had said to Noah, they made sure it would not be in their own time. Well! what if any of Noah's sons had said, "After all, I see no sign of a flood, and I see that nobody but my father believes there will be one; I am sure there must be some mistake; I am not going to make myself foolish by entering into this ark before there is any occasion; it will be time enough when it begins to rain; till then at least I will enjoy myself as other people do." I say, if any one of Noah's family had reasoned in this way with himself, and in consequence had stayed out of the ark, refusing to know and consider until the flood came, we know what the consequence would have been. The ark, as we read in Genesis, was closed, after Noah and his family went into it. That was a full week before the flood began.

They went in, and the beasts and the fowls which were to be preserved with them; and the Lord shut them in. The Lord shut and fastened the door of the ark, when all had gone in, who were obedient to His call; it might not open again to receive any more. If then any of Noah's sons had waited, as I said, till the rain had actually begun, and then had come to the ark, intending to go in, he would have found himself too late; he would have been in the condition of those foolish virgins who came knocking at the bridegroom's door, after he and the wise virgins were gone into the wedding, and found it shut, never to be opened unto them.

This would have been the condition of any person who had put off going into the ark. And would it not be very like the condition of any of us who should wilfully delay his entering into Christ's Church, because he saw not yet with his eyes the horror and misery, from which the Church would save him? Yes! I am sure you perceive at once that a person refusing to be a Christian casts himself away in a manner infinitely more fearful, than if he had been unbelieving in Noah's time, and had refused to enter into his ark.

But you may be tempted to think, "What is all this to me? I am a Christian. I am no unbeliever. I have been in the ark long since, ever since I was baptized in my infancy." True, my brother, you have been so; it is your great privilege, and you cannot thank God enough for it. But think of this again with yourself, that it is not enough to have been once in the ark; no, nor even to be there at present; but the thing is, to be there when the flood shall come. For suppose either one of Noah's sons to have gone indeed into the ark when God bade him, seven days before the flood, but to have grown tired of waiting there; suppose, when he looked out through the window, he had seen his neighbours and acquaintances, and thousands besides, enjoying themselves, just as they had been used to do, or rather more; some of them perhaps mocking at him for shutting himself up where he could have no such pleasure; and suppose therefore he had grown restless and uneasy, and had first in his foolish heart longed to be with them, and then at last contrived to get out of the ark, and join them, and had been caught in that condition by the great waters when they arose. I say, such a miserable person as that would not be half so miserable as you, baptized as you are and born again in Christ, if you so go after the things which you in Baptism renounced, as that, when the Judge comes and the fire goes out before Him, you shall be found out of His Church, and among His enemies. And this will be, if you either die in your sins, or be caught by Him living in them.

You, having been baptized, think you are safe in the ark. God grant it may be so! It surely is so, if either you have kept your robe pure from grievous sin, or, having fallen, have truly repented and received our Lord's absolution. *Then* you are not only in the ark, but are safe in it; for in that case it would be well with you, were you to die this very moment; but if you are going on in carelessness, or any other known sin, you may indeed be in the ark, I don't deny that, but you are by no means *safe* in it. If the storm were now to arise, you would find yourself suddenly cast out and exposed to its fury. Do not say, "I have plenty of time, I see no storm as yet." That was the very saying which the sinners of the old world had in their mouths, when the flood came and took them all away. Do not say, "Why should I be strict and particular? they will all laugh at me, and I cannot bear this laughter." Look on a little while: imagine the flood come—the flood of fire which shall drown all sinners, and consider, how such an excuse will appear to you then.

Neither, again, can it be safe for you to say (as the manner of some is), "why make so much ado about my being in this ark, the Church? why cannot I be saved without that? I see in this Church clean and unclean together; surely God's mercy is not limited to such a company." Nay, but what should you have thought of Noah, if he had scrupled about trusting to the ark, because beasts and fowls, as well as men, were to be in it; and because it was to hold for a time the clean and unclean alike?

Sometimes the evil one puts it into our minds to think less of Christ's Church, because even outwardly it has been received as yet by much the smaller portion of the sons of Adam, and because at the last it would seem that but a few of many will be saved in it. But do you not observe what is written of the ark? "Few, i. e., only eight souls were saved in it;" yet it was God's way of salvation, and those who slighted it brought ruin on themselves.

Much less will any person, who has faith as a grain of mustard seed, stumble at what Holy Church and Holy Scripture tell us of Baptism, for want of understanding how such great good should come by water.

This would be no wiser, nor more dutiful, than if we had lived in Noah's time, and had despised the ark, because it was merely wood; or if, living in our Lord's own time, we had despised the Cross for the same reason.

But let us all, who by His great mercy have been, before we could know it, saved by water; whom His Fatherly hand has so far brought in safety over the waves of this troublesome world, outwardly at least within the ark of His Church; let us put away once and for ever all thoughts of doubting, indifference, or scorn as to the high privileges of our baptism; and having seriously confessed and amended our sins, let us with earnest and thankful hearts contemplate what is prepared for us, when the flood shall have finally abated, and the ark should have settled on the mountain of God. The raven, i. e., the unclean and the heretic, will have been turned out of the ark for ever; the dove, i. e., the spirit of prayer, will have brought the olive leaf, the token of peace. The rainbow of our Lord's forgiving mercy will be all around Him on His Judgment Seat, and Noah and his sons, all good Christians (God grant we may be there) will come out of this earthly ark, to glorify Him in His nearer Presence with a sacrifice of eternal thanksgiving.

Then, and not till then, shall we know what He did for us when He had us baptized.

SERMON VIII.

1 Cor. x. 1. 2.

"All our fathers were under the cloud, and all passed through the sea: and were all baptized unto Moses in the cloud and in the sea."

In considering our Church's baptismal service, we are come to that sentence in the first collect, which makes mention of the Israelites' deliverance from Egypt. "Almighty and Everlasting God, Who of Thy great mercy didst save Noah and his family in the ark from perishing by water; and also didst safely lead the children of Israel Thy people through the Red sea, figuring thereby Thy Holy Baptism—look upon this child,— wash him and sanctify him with the Holy Ghost, that he, being stedfast in faith, joyful through hope, and rooted in charity, may so pass the waves of this troublesome world, that finally he may come to the land of everlasting life."

Here we see, as I have pointed out before, how great a thing Baptism is; seeing that the two chiefest and most wonderful deliverances in the old Testament are but shadows and figures of it :—the ark which saved the race of Adam, and the passage of the Red sea which saved God's own favoured people. And we know that what happened at the Red sea, as well as what happened about the ark, was meant to be a figure and type of Baptism. We do not only guess it, but we *know* it; for it is expressly taught us by St. Paul, as the other is by St. Peter. "All our fathers were under the cloud, and all passed through the sea: and were all baptized unto Moses in the cloud and in the sea." Now these things were types and *figures* of us ... "all these things happened unto them for types."

As therefore we considered, not long ago, how the ark and its safety was a type of Christian Baptism, so it falls to-day to be considered, how the passage of the Red sea by the Israelites is another type of the same great reality. And of this you heard a good deal in the Catechising: how that the profane and heathen land of Egypt, in which God's people were slaves, answers to this wicked world, in which by nature we are all born. Egypt is the world, and Pharaoh the king of Egypt is Satan, the prince of this world, who boasts to have all its kingdoms and the glory of them made over to him, to bestow them on whom he will: and who will never cease to do his worst against the faithful people of Christ. Pharaoh is Satan, and his work and bondage is sin—those foul dark miserable ways, in which he compels his unhappy subjects to walk against their own judgments and better will. Canaan, on the other hand, is the better country, of which the Israelites had heard and to which they looked with faith: for none of them had seen it. Canaan was the type of Heaven, our eternal rest. And the wilderness, through which they had to pass in making their way into Canaan, is the type of our condition here as Christians; the Church militant here on earth, our state of trial intended to prepare us for Heaven. The passage then from Egypt to the wilderness is the passage from the world to the Church: and that is none other than Holy Baptism. For our Lord's own Word is, "Verily verily I say unto you, except a man be born of water and of the Spirit, he cannot enter into the Kingdom of Heaven." You see then, how aptly the water of the Red sea, through which God's people had to pass in order to be delivered from Egypt— you see how aptly that water represents the water in our Fonts, the water of Holy Baptism; the water, through which we passed out of Satan's kingdom into the Kingdom of Christ. And as the sea represents the water, so the cloud represents the Holy Spirit coming down upon the water, to quicken and bless it and make it effectual to the good purpose for which God's providence has set it apart. And so St. Paul's saying is, that they were all baptized unto Moses in the cloud and in the sea: even as we all are baptized unto Christ in water and the Holy Ghost. And, in this our Baptism, whosoever outwardly performs it, Christ is the real Baptizer. It is He that baptizeth with the Holy Ghost: much in the same way as none but Moses might lift up his rod over the waters of the sea, and cause them to go back for the people. And as Moses did this by his rod, so our Lord by the Virtue of His Cross. He did not ordain His Sacrament of Baptism, He did not begin to baptize with the Holy Ghost, until after His Saving Passion and Resurrection. The water of Baptism saves only by the power of Christ's Cross, as the Red sea parted to save the Israelites, only at a token from the Rod of Moses. And lastly as Pharaoh and all his host, all the might and power of Egypt, essaying to follow Israel through the sea, were drowned, so that all Israel saw them dead upon the sea-shore and they could never again do them any harm for ever:—so when one is rightly baptized the body of sin is destroyed within him: i. e. the power of sin, which it naturally has over us: so that we are made free to keep the Commandments, if we will. That is one deliverance: just as it was Israel's deliverance, to be released from the heavy burdens and painful and irksome labours imposed by Pharaoh's taskmasters. The Son, the Eternal Son of God, the Great Master and Owner of the family, has made us free; and we are free indeed! It is a great, a high, a blessed, yet fearful thought; *very* blessed, and therefore *very* fearful. Let us try and think it well over; let us turn it this way and that, in our minds. We were all, one and all, baptized unto Christ with water and the Spirit. We have all been made free indeed: we have been admitted to the glorious liberty of the children of God. What follows?

In the first place, this is most evident; that now we are without excuse, if we any more serve sin; if we make ourselves slaves to it. What would you have thought of those Israelites, if, as soon as they were safe on the farther side of the Red Sea, they had again set about their hard bitter slavish work? Gathering stubble, and making bricks, and building cities for their severe unpitying master? If they had forgotten God their Deliverer, and had taken pride and pleasure in being again servants to Pharaoh? Should we not at once say, that they were mad? But their madness is nothing to our's, as often as we, being baptized, give up ourselves anew to serve sin. The foulness and noisomeness of their dirty work is nothing, compared to inward uncleanness and corruption of heart and body. The pain and toil and weariness of making bricks is not to be compared with that of making money by dishonest and irregular ways. The task-masters, who kept the Jews to their work, were not half so hard and severe, as the evil spirits driving us on ever in mischief. Think, my brethren, but for one moment; think steadily on the wretched condition a man's heart and mind must be in, who actually chooses to say with the heathen, "The good that I would I do not, but the evil which I would not, that I do," rather than to say with S. Paul, "I can do all things through Christ which strengtheneth me. Think on it, you who unhappily allow yourselves to give way to anger, or lust, or any other evil habit. Say in your hearts; "it need not be so: I am free, I am not in Egypt; the Holy Spirit has been given in Baptism, to help me: why should I do this great wickedness and sin against the Lord, and bring back upon myself the chains which He mercifully brake, and bind them for ever?" For, although you are not a slave now, yet be sure that every known sin brings you some way backward towards a state of slavery. Every time you tell a lie, or say knowingly any other kind of bad word, you help to make a sort of chain for your tongue, a chain of evil and accursed habit. If it be continued long enough, it will seem as if it left you no choice, as if you were under a perfect necessity of lying, or otherwise sinning with your tongue. This is the kind of thing, of which the apostle warns all Christians, when he says, "stand fast in the liberty with which Christ hath made you free, and be not entangled again in the yoke of bondage." Assert this freedom, my brethren: claim it wheresoever you go, as St. Paul claimed the privilege of being a citizen of Rome. St. Paul told the Roman officer who would have used him disgracefully, "I was free-born;" do you make the reply to the enemies of your soul, when they would fain get you to disgrace and pollute yourself with sin. When the evil spirit of lust comes near you with a tempting thought—when he whispers; "all men give way sometimes, and you cannot be perfect; you of course must have your faults as well as other people, and it may as well be now as any other time, just this once, now that the temptation is so strong;"—when you perceive such whisperings as these in your frail heart, you may know for certain, from whom they come, and how you ought to treat them: you should reject them at once, and say "I am free-born; I am born anew, by God's great mercy, of water and of the Holy Ghost; I am a member of Christ, Who is my life; I have or may have such thoughts, that for me to indulge this sin is quite inexcusable: I cannot, and I will not; Get thee behind me, Satan." Do this once with a firm purpose of heart, and pray to do it better the next time: and, when that next time comes, do the same again: oppose the remembrance of your Baptism, and faith in its privileges, to each temptation as it arises: and you will find that, like a mighty shield, it will shelter you against all bad thoughts, all the fiery darts of the wicked one: it will quench them, as the Apostle says, before they have laid hold of your mind, and kindled it into any flame of evil desire.

But, in order to get this benefit from the remembrance of your Baptism, you must have it always at hand, always in use, as a soldier, who would catch on his shield or buckler all the darts of the enemy, must not lay it by, but must wear it constantly on his arm, to accustom himself to turn it every way at a moment's warning. Therefore the good thought should be renewed every morning: every morning the distinct acknowledgement of our baptismal blessings should go along with our prayers, and also of our baptismal vows: as in Bishop Ken's morning hymn, well-known to many of us; "Lord, I my vows to Thee renew." Surely it would be well, in saying or thinking over those words, to recollect for a moment what the vows are, by which as Christians we are bound: to say unto God solemnly, every morning, for ourselves what our godfathers and godmothers said in our baptism once for all, "I renounce &c. I believe &c. &c. and I will keep &c." Do this in the morning with devout prayers, and you will find help, I doubt not, to do it in the day from time to time, as often as you are aware of temptation coming near you; and so the Rock will, as it were, follow you; Christ the Rock, and the Water which flowed from His Side, will be in a manner always at hand; and there you will quench all impure and unholy fires, and go on your way, like Israel in the wilderness, not indeed without hardships and trials, but with a sure and certain trust that you are free at least from your Egyptian slavery; that the Red Sea, Christ's Holy Baptism, is between you and your enemies; and if we believe this, we cannot but be very thankful, even as we read of Moses and the children of Israel, that, when they had passed over as on dry land and they saw the Egyptians dead on the sea-shore, they presently brake out into hymns and triumphant singing: "Sing unto the Lord, for He has triumphed gloriously; the horse and his rider hath He thrown into the sea." Christians! if we truly call ourselves Christians, we are partakers of a deliverance as much more awful and wonderful than that of Israel, as hell-fire is worse than Egypt, the devil more cruel than Pharaoh, and the Kingdom of Heaven purer and happier than Canaan: and shall not we, as Christians, be joyful and glad in our Lord? Shall we suffer any temporal affliction, much less any passing annoyance, slight or disappointment, to ruffle our temper, make us cross and unthankful, cross towards man, unthankful to our gracious God? Ought we not rather to use the recollections of this deep baptismal Love, breathing over our hearts like fragrant airs of a summer morning? ought we not to be refreshed by them, especially on a Sunday morning and most especially on days of Holy Communion—so that, all our earthly cares and sorrows being soothed and turned into pledges of His Love, we may approach His Altar with all fervency and gratitude? Yes, surely, so it ought to be, and so by His grace it will be with us, in such measure as we are sincere and constant in our devotion. We shall not be so grievously put out, as most men are, when news comes to us of our having lost so much money, or of a friend's illness, or of the ill behaviour of some one whom we trusted. None of these things, not even the sudden death of a dear friend, will disturb the thankfulness of that man's heart, whose joy is in God, made his own God in Holy Baptism.

And if we are thus thankful, we shall, of course, be sincerely obedient. Little good would Israel have obtained by the passage of the Red sea, had the people, then landing in the wilderness, refused to follow the guiding cloud. And little good will even our Baptism do us, good and holy and perfect as it is in itself—if we will not follow on through this life, where that Holy Spirit shall lead us, Who was present in our Baptism—Who alone made us Christians—He is our Sanctifier and guide as well as our Comforter. If we will let Him, He will be to us more than a pillar of a cloud by day and a pillar of fire by night: only we must make up our minds to go where He guides us: no great thing surely to ask, when the guide is God Almighty, and the end to which we are guided, everlasting Life.

Moreover, as we know that the Israelites in the passover always kept up the special remembrance of their deliverance from Egypt by the blood of the Paschal Lamb, as the Lord had said, "remember this day;" so it is good and wholesome for us Christians to bear in mind, as well as we can, the day of our baptism, and to make it a day of solemn thoughts and good resolutions, a day of deep penitence for our many sad breaches of our vows: a day, wherein to sacrifice ourselves, our souls and bodies, more devoutly than ever to our Lord. More particularly is it good and useful to think of our Baptism, when we are preparing to draw near the other Sacrament. For how shall we examine ourselves thoroughly, if we do not go back to our first vows? They are the very rule, by which we are to be tried: by them, accordingly, we must try and judge ourselves. How again shall we be sorry and ashamed, as we ought, for our sad transgressions of God's law and our own engagements, except we duly bear in mind the abundant grace which was given to help us in keeping them, and against which we have sinned? how shall we stedfastly purpose to lead a new life, but by reliance on the same merciful Spirit Who gave that first grace? how shall we be thankful enough in our remembrance of God's "mercy through Christ," and of His saving Death, without bearing in mind always, how we ourselves have been made partakers of that Death and those mercies in our Baptism which joined us to Him? Thus you see, the recollection of our Baptism should always go with us to Holy Communion. Finally and above all, since without it all would be void, it behoves us, as baptized children of God, to walk on our way through life with a deep sense of His aweful and peculiar Presence, in Baptism first imparted to us, His presence in our very hearts: wherein also the children of Israel may be an example, going on their way through the wilderness in company with that pillar of fire, that guiding cloud, under which they all were in the sea. Ought not they to be full of reverence, having God so nigh unto them? and if they, much more we! O my brethren, what shall we say? For it is even now our own case. We, you and I, and all of us here present, are under that miraculous cloud; all our ways, our words, and our thoughts, good, bad, or indifferent, are immediately and specially before Him, and, as such, are noted down by His angels. What shall we do? We must fly to His mercy, which is over all His works. We must try to serve Him, as well as we can, in our poor and low way, and He will reward us in His rich and overflowing way. If *we* remember the covenant of our baptism, be sure *He* will never forget it.

SERMON IX.

St. Matthew iii. 15.

" Thus it becometh us to fulfil all righteousness."

When a child is to be christened, the Priest, as you know, puts God in remembrance, as it were, of the great mercies, which in old time He had wrought for His chosen people by water. First, in that He delivered the whole world by the ark; next, in His bringing the children of Israel, His people, safely through the Red Sea. These two, even to the outward eyes, even to the eyes of unbelievers, were very great things indeed. They were events, which it was quite impossible for any one to pass by. But there is a third type, greater than either, which to the eye of man was, in comparison, very obscure and insignificant; yet in itself far greater, far more wonderful, far more miraculous and heavenly, than these deliverances of Noah and the children of Israel. This was the Baptism of our blessed Lord; concerning which the collect in our service says, that "by the Baptism of His well-beloved Son Jesus Christ in the river Jordan, Almighty God sanctified water to the mystical washing of sin."

I say, that our Lord's Baptism was outwardly and visibly, and according to what the people of that time knew, a far quieter and more ordinary thing than either the flood or the passage of the Red Sea. For what was our Lord's Baptism, measured by what men's senses shewed to them? How may we draw the picture of it in our own minds? We may imagine a very still and solitary place, the river Jordan flowing quietly on, and St. John the Baptist, in his well-known dress, the raiment of camel's hair, the leathern girdle about his loins; and Jesus of Nazareth, in Whom the world saw no great difference from other men (as it is written, " There is no form nor comeliness, and when we shall see Him, there is no beauty that we should desire Him "). Him, I say, we may imagine coming up to the holy Baptist, and offering Himself to be baptized, as multitudes had been before. But St. John, who knew our Lord well to be the Holy Son of Mary, of Whom so great things had been promised, forbade Him at first, in deep humility, saying, "I have need to be baptized of Thee, and comest Thou to me?" Dost Thou, who art so much holier, come to me, who am not worthy to wait upon Thee? Our Lord however goes on, and tells St. John, how necessary it was for Him to be baptized, though He had no sins to be forgiven. "Suffer it to be so now, for thus it becometh us to fulfil all righteousness." Upon this, St. John gives way, and in deep fear and reverence baptizes his and our Lord. Jesus goes down into the river, and St. John pours some of the water upon Him, as the manner is in baptizing;

and then He goes up out of the water; and, whilst He is beginning to pray to His Father on the bank, this great wonder happened, the heavens are opened, and the Holy Spirit descends in a bodily shape like a dove, and lights upon Him, and there is a voice from heaven, "This is My beloved Son, in Whom I am well pleased." It was an unspeakable wonder, even to the outward eye and ear. But it does not appear, that any one besides the Baptist himself was a witness to it. His own account is, that he had received before from Almighty God this notice, "Upon Whom thou shalt see the Spirit descending and remaining upon Him, the Same is He which baptizeth with the Holy Ghost. And I saw, and bare witness, that this is the Son of God." He speaks, as if he himself were the only witness; and if so, only think how very quiet and secret were the doings of God in this great matter. How truly was the saying here fulfilled, "Verily Thou art a God that hidest Thyself, O God of Israel, the Saviour; the Wonderful, the Counsellor, the great God, the Everlasting Father, the Prince of Peace!" Behold, He is here, as the son of a poor carpenter, to be washed by another poor man in a lonely river. What is there here outwardly, for the world to be amazed at, and adore? And yet, inwardly, it is so great an event, that the heavens were opened; and we read not, as at other times, that angels came and ministered unto Him; but the heavens were opened, and the Spirit of God descended in a bodily shape like a dove, and abode upon Him; and there was no voice of the heavenly host, singing, "Glory to God in the highest," but the Eternal Father Himself spake from heaven, and said, "This is My beloved Son, in

Whom I am well pleased." And thus, as the Psalmist had sung years before, "The Voice of the Lord, which is a glorious Voice, was upon the waters, the great and many waters." The glory of the Lord was seen, and His Voice heard upon the waters of Jordan; but it was only seen and heard by St. John the Baptist.

Now the Prayer Book informs us, that this event, so simple in man's account, so full of majesty and wonder to saints and angels, was altogether a token and a pledge of the blessing given to Christians in Holy Baptism. For it says, that "by the Baptism of His well-beloved Son Jesus Christ in the river Jordan, God did sanctify the element of water to the mystical washing away of sin." For to this end was God the Son made Man, and for this cause did He take to Himself a body in the womb of the blessed Virgin, of her substance, that He might not only offer Himself up as a sacrifice of atonement for our sins, but also might cure our sin and misery by causing us to be partakers of Himself. By His touch, when He was upon earth, He healed diseases, and restored sight to the blind. By His spiritual but real Touch in Holy Communion, He from time to time renders "our sinful bodies clean through His Body, and washes our souls in His precious Blood." And so, by His touching the waters of Jordan, in that solemn and mystical way, when St. John baptized Him, He gave, not to Jordan only, but to all earthly waters generally, His heavenly blessing, so sanctifying them all, that, when duly applied in the name of the Father, the Son, and the Holy Ghost, a person, yet heathen and unregenerate, has his sins so washed away by the power of the Holy Ghost, that God will remember them no more. They are in His sight as if they had never been; as it is written, "I will sprinkle clean water upon you, and ye shall be clean;" I mean of course, unless we make void the blessing, and bind our sins on us afresh, by continuing in them, or returning to them. This virtue Christ gave to the waters of this fallen world of ours, when He permitted Himself to be touched by them in His Baptism by St. John. In Jordan, all water was sanctified by the touch of Christ; it has been sanctified, to be a pledge and means of our sanctification; and, that we may know that we have been so favoured, observe what followed on Christ's touching the water. Immediately the heavens were opened, and the Holy Ghost descended upon Him; that we may know, that as in Jordan, that day, all water was in a manner sanctified, so in Christ at the same time, all believers were made partakers of the Spirit of adoption. For the Person of our Lord Jesus Christ is, in a manner, all believers in one; all are members of Him, all are branches graffed into Him, the True Vine. So that what was done and suffered by Him is, in its measure, a type and token of something to be done and suffered by each one of them. The Holy Ghost, poured on Him at His Baptism, was a figure and pledge of the same Holy Ghost poured on His apostles at Pentecost, and on each one of us when we receive the Sacrament of Baptism. He wanted no fresh gift of the Spirit, Himself; for He is One God with that Spirit for ever and ever. And God giveth not the Spirit by measure unto Him; but on our behalf He received that Spirit. It came all over His blessed Body, like the oil of gladness mentioned in the Psalms—" like the precious oil upon the head that ran down unto the beard, even unto Aaron's beard, and came down to the skirts of his clothing." So was Christ, our Head and Priest, anointed for us, and we, His members, are every one anointed in Him. By His Holy Spirit, received in Baptism, we are made righteous and holy; and, if we die without grieving the Spirit, we shall remain righteous and holy, and so happy with Him for ever. And this, perhaps, was part of our Lord's meaning, when, on St. John's being loth to baptize Him, He said, "Suffer it to be so now, for thus it becometh us to fulfil all righteousness." As if He should say, "you *must* baptize me; for I, the Head, am in all things to be a type to the members; and this, that is, Holy Baptism, is the way in which it is appointed for them and Me to fulfil all righteousness." To be baptized with water and the Holy Ghost, and so made members of Christ, was to be the ordained cure for men's natural unholiness and unrighteousness; therefore it was requisite that Christ Himself should be baptized. For He was to show us in His own Person all things needful to our justification and salvation through Him.

See then, my brethren, what we ought to think of the gift and blessing of our own Baptism. It is so very great, that our Lord condescended to be baptized, for a type and token of it. For John indeed baptized with water, i. e., with water only, but Christ baptizeth with the Holy Ghost. As a token whereof, the Holy Ghost, in our Lord's Baptism, did not come down immediately as St. John poured the water upon Him, but afterwards, when He had gone out of the water and was praying. But He Himself baptizes, through the ministers of the New Testament, with both at once, with water and the Holy Ghost; as the Apostle plainly teaches, "As many as have been baptized into Christ, have put on Christ." Of these two things then we, by God's mercy, are quite sure; we need have no doubt of them at all; viz. that when a little child is brought here and baptized, first it is baptized by Christ Himself; and, secondly, it is baptized with the Holy Ghost. Now of Christ Himself being the Baptizer, I hope to say more another time; but at this time I would ask you a question about the Holy Ghost, wherewith our children are baptized. I would ask you every one, (O that you would but put your minds to it), what if, at the moment of the little child's Baptism, just as the consecrated water is being poured on his face, you were to look up and see the heavens opened, a great light and glory from God, and His Spirit descending in a bright cloud, in a bodily shape like a dove, and resting upon that little child, as He rested on our Lord presently after His Baptism? What if you could see this? would it not fill you with unspeakable thoughts of the high place and dignity to which that child was called, and of God's mercy and grace towards him? Would it not come strong over your mind, how shocking, how intolerable it will be, if this child should fall into grievous sin, and drive away the good Spirit thus graciously taking possession of him? Should you not have thoughts of this kind, if you had seen the Holy Ghost descending like a dove, and abiding on any little child which you have just seen taken from the Font? I am sure you would; you could not help it. Well then, try, as near as you can, to have the same thoughts now. For whether you have them or no, the thing is true. The Holy Spirit has really come down upon the child, though not in a bodily shape like a dove. He has entered into him, and is yet abiding in him. *We* see it not; but that surely makes no difference. The Divine Spirit is dwelling in that infant's soul and body, and God the Father, for Christ's sake, is for the time at least well-pleased with that infant. God hath adopted him, for Christ's sake, to be His well-beloved son. Of all this we are certain by God's word concerning every infant that is baptized; we are certain it was our own case, just after we were baptized. If we had died then, we should have been undoubtedly saved. If now it is not so with us, whose must be the fault?

And even should it prove that, by His continual mercy, we are not lost in wilful sin, but yet retain some reasonable hope of pardon, yet surely it is a serious thought, how very unlike our doings are to what we should expect from one on whom the Holy Ghost had gloriously descended. I have read sometimes of Saints, who, when they were infants, had a bright light shining round them in their cradles. What should you think their parents and nurses expected of them, when they came to grow up? That they should only tell a *few* lies, when the temptation was very strong? only help themselves dishonestly to a *little* at a time, according to what they supposed other people did? only indulge lust and sinful desire, when it came *urgently* upon them? only swear seldom, and less coarsely perhaps than some others? Would this satisfy you, as an account of the behaviour of one who had been miraculously marked out for a saint? I know it would not; neither would you be quite content, were you told that he only kept clear of notorious wilful sin. You would look for more than this; you would say, the glory of God was around this child from his birth; his goodness surely was meant to be more than common; it will be a pity and shame, if we do not find him unusually pure, self-denying, humble, charitable, devout, never forgetting his Saviour, but doing all to His glory. This exalted goodness, I say, you would naturally look for in a child, which had had God's glory around him in his cradle. Well; but we have all had God's glory around us in our cradles. He Who came down visibly on our Lord, He, the very same Spirit, is invisibly among us, and within us. In good truth, then, we ought all of us to be saints. Let us at least be ashamed and confounded to think, how far, immeasurably far, we are at present from that glorious name; how great a work remains for us, and how short a time to do it in. Yet let us not fear to attempt it; for " greater is He that is in us, than he that is in the world." As for temptations, we know they must arise. Jesus Himself, immediately after the descent of the Holy Ghost and the Voice from heaven, was led up into the wilderness to be tempted of the Devil. Temptations will come; and, that we may be armed against them, we must prepare for them as our Lord did, by prayer. His prayer after His Baptism is mentioned, as having much to do with that wonderful descent of the Holy Ghost. "Jesus being baptized *and praying*, the heavens were opened, and the Holy Ghost descended in a bodily shape like a dove upon Him; and lo, a voice from heaven." Therefore we, being baptized, must pray; we must pray every morning and evening on our knees, and all day long in the purpose of our hearts; that the sin which it has washed away may never return and defile our souls again. If we have grieved the Spirit by serious sin, we must pray Him to return, and to grant us, as it were, a second Baptism in tears of penitence. We must pray without ceasing; for the Evil One will not cease to tempt us. Thus having been baptized and praying, we too, like our great Head and Pattern, may hope one day to see the heavens opened, and the Glory of God revealed, and the Voice from heaven owning us for His well-beloved sons, and saying, "Come, ye blessed children of My Father." O God, grant that these words may be spoken to us through Jesus Christ, Thy well-beloved Son, our only Saviour and Redeemer.

SERMON X.

1 Cor. vi. 11.

"*But ye are washed, but ye are sanctified, but ye are justified, in the Name of the Lord Jesus, and by the Spirit of our God.*"

WHEN the Priest in the first collect has put God in remembrance of His great deliverances, wrought for His people in old time by water, and of the mysterious Baptism of Jesus Christ, he goes on and beseeches Him to apply the same mercy to the particular infant who is now brought to the Font; "We beseech thee, for Thine infinite mercies, that Thou wilt mercifully look upon this child." The goodness and bounty, which is offered to all the world, is here attracted as it were to the soul and body of that one little boy or girl; as when the lightning, which is mysteriously and invisibly floating all above us in the whole Heaven, is attracted to a particular point, and strikes upon it. The prayer of the Church does as it were attract it. The little child in its nurse's arms by the Font is, as it were, one called out of all the millions of people that are on earth, to receive an especial favour of God: as if some great king, having before him all the people of his kingdom, should call out one of them singly and apart, and, in the presence of all the rest, shew himself ready to grant him some great favour. In such a case we may well imagine, how attentively all the Court and the king's whole army—all the people, rich and poor, would watch and listen, to know what special favour was going to be conferred on that person. So, no doubt the Saints and Angels from Heaven are round the Font, though we see them not, and watch when a child is christened; and so do all good Christian people who are present; they try to join, with all their heart, in the petitions which the Church puts up, remembering at the same time with a thankful heart, that they have, by the same mercy, been made partakers of the same blessing, and, with a penitent heart, how they have trifled with it, or abused it.

Now, what the Church prays for is this; " wash him and sanctify him with the Holy Ghost." Grant that, when his body is washed with water, his soul may be washed by the power of God's Spirit in the Blood of Jesus Christ, which cleanseth from all sin. So St. Paul told the Corinthians, that they, even those among them who had sinned most grievously while they were heathens, were nevertheless washed, sanctified, justified, in the name of the Lord Jesus and by the Spirit of our God. If they were washed from their grievous sins, much more are little children, who as yet have done no wilful sin, washed in Baptism from the guilt of their birth-sin, which they had from Adam. And we have no doubt that, by God's mercy, they are so washed; so that, if they die before they commit actual sin, they are unquestionably saved for ever. For being washed, they are sanctified; i. e. they are made holy, made holy to the Lord, by the gift of the Holy Ghost, the good Spirit sent into their hearts. And God will not part with His own. What is once His, He means it to be His for ever. It cannot be lost, except it lose itself by sin. O what a happy condition is this, and what a fearful thing to deal carelessly with it, or to put ourselves wilfully out of it! But let us consider it more particularly; for so the Collect goes on to describe it.

The fruit and effect of Baptism is this first; that the child or person is delivered from the wrath of God. It was born, as the Catechism says, a child of wrath, but now it is made a child of grace. It was born in original sin, and in the wrath of God; but as soon it shall be made partaker of the laver of Regeneration in Baptism, it will be received into the number of the children of God, and heirs of everlasting life. God is naturally so far angry with that child, as He discerns in it that taint of Adam's sin, which is against His holy will, and is sure to bear evil fruit. Therefore we pray, that the child, as the first good effect of Baptism, may be delivered from God's wrath.

Christian Fathers and Mothers, have you ever tried to think worthily of this? If you saw your child exposed to a roaring lion, hungry and furious, and seeking whom he might devour, and knew at the same time that you could do nothing of yourselves to take him out of the lion's reach, and that the only person who could help him was for some reason angry with him, would it not be enough to break your heart? and would you not look on *him* as the best of friends, who should reconcile that person to you and your child, and teach you how to obtain protection and favour, so that the little helpless creature might not be the prey of the cruel beast? Now, this is just what happens in Baptism. The devil is a roaring lion, seeking to devour your child. Your child, because of his sinfulness which he has from Adam, is out of God's favour; yet no one can help him but God: and Jesus Christ the Son of God has taught and invited you how to bring your child to God, and obtain that gracious help. Surely He is yours' and your child's best friend; surely this is a favour never to be forgotten, never to be out of our minds all day long; surely you cannot do less in return, than serve Him truly as long as you live, and teach your children, whom He has saved so wonderfully, to do the same.

The Collect goes on, and prays that the child, being delivered from God's wrath, may be received into the Ark of Christ's Church. Now we are used to consider it as a matter of course for every child that is born among us to be baptized; so that it is hard, very hard for us to understand, how it should be a special favour; and thus, unhappily, too many of us take no pains to be thankful, when children are baptized, nor to remember our own Baptism with thankfulness. But let us carry back our thoughts again to the time which the Church here puts us in mind of. Let us remember Noah and his Ark. Had you been a father or mother when the flood came on, should you have thought it a small favour then, to be admitted into the Ark? Should you have counted it a matter of course? You would not, because you would have seen with your eyes, that only eight persons, Noah, with his three sons, and their four wives, were there admitted. O what a favour would you then have thought it, how would you have looked and longed for your children and yourself to be, if possible, among that happy number who were admitted into that vessel of God's own building, and whom the Lord shut in there with His servant Noah! And yet that flood of water could but drown the bodies of men; but the flood to which we look forward, the flood of fire, will in some mysterious way inwrap and torment both the souls and bodies of those who are so miserable as not to be caught away from it. All who shall not then be found in Christ's Church will perish; and Holy Baptism is the ordinary way into Christ's Church; and when we come to think it over, though we ourselves may know but few unbaptized, yet the whole number of the baptized, taking all the world over and all ages of it, is small, I fear, in comparison with those who are not so. Why, it was 4000 years before there was any Baptism, any Body of Christ on earth at all; and, for the 2000 years or near it which have since passed, few in comparison of the nations of the world have been Christians. At this present time it is believed that not more than two or three out of eight even call themselves such. The rest, being born among Turks or Heathens, continue without God in the world. So, you see, the Church goes on as it began, and as St. Paul says God's people always have gone on—not taking in the whole world but in the manner of a remnant, and by way of election—as a few out of many: and those who belong to it, or have their children belonging to it, ought to own it as a special favour; as it is written, "He predestinated us unto the adoption of children through Jesus Christ unto Himself." And if we fall away, so much the greater is our misery.

But the collect goes on to pray for those graces which still secure us against falling away: that the child may not only be received into the ark of Christ's Church, but also may be "stedfast in faith, joyful through hope, and rooted in charity." What good and gracious and beautiful words are these, my brethren, to be spoken over young children in the first days of their tender life; spoken by God's ordinance, in His own special Presence, and to be sealed presently by Christ's Holy Sacrament of Baptism. How sad to think of their being slighted, as they too often are, at the time: and of the kind of lives afterwards led by too many of those, over whom that Prayer has been said. For consider what it is, to be stedfast in faith. It is, to look to the great things out of sight, not only now and then; but continually and regularly. It is, to remember every morning, you have an account to give and every evening, that you are so much nearer that account; and all day long, that your doings are being put down there. It is, to turn your heart to Jesus Christ, God and Man, crucified for you, and to refrain from sin for His sake; not merely to speak affectionately, and to be at times touched with the thought of Him. To be stedfast in faith is moreover, to believe our Lord when He says, that *we* must take up our cross, *we* must lead strict lives, we must be zealous and repent. It is, to part with our worldly wealth gladly for Christ's sake and the Gospel's, looking forward to the treasure in Heaven. It is, to turn away our eyes from improper sights, because we know that those eyes shall one day have to look upon Jesus Christ. It is, to believe that, in Holy Communion, we verily and indeed take and receive the true Body and Blood of Christ, which is the life of our souls, as bread and wine of our bodies; so we cannot do without it. And he who believes this, will of course be earnest to come often to it. All this and more the Church prays for, when it prays that the baptized may be "stedfast in faith." But alas! how unlike is all this to the ordinary course of those, over whom the Prayer has been said. To be tolerably decent and respectable; to go to Church once on a Sunday, when it is not too much trouble; to be no worse than other people—this is the religion of many in this Christian land. But is this being stedfast in faith? is this walking by faith, and not by sight? is this setting our affection on things above, not on things on the earth? O my brethren, think better of it; and you, my younger brethren especially, remember that the Prayer made over you was, not only that you might believe, but that you might be "*stedfast* in the faith;" that, having begun well, you should not suffer yourselves to be hindered; having been confirmed, you should be Communicants; and, having communicated once, you should go on doing so regularly. If you let yourselves be moved from such good rules for fear of men's opinions or ridicule, or for love of the world's pleasures, where is the stedfastness of your faith? and how are you to continue in the ark of Christ's Church? Only think how sad it will be, if these loving prayers, which were made over you at your Baptism, should be remembered at the Last Day, only to add to your shame and reproach for having lived so unsuitably to them.

You know the next thing asked for you at the Font was, that you might be "joyful through Hope." Hope naturally makes men joyful and glad of heart. One reason, I suppose, why young persons are commonly merrier and more cheerful than old ones is, that they live more upon hope; they look forward to many pleasant things. So now the Church, in praying that the new Christian may be joyful in hope, prays that he may continue all his life long in the freshness of early youth, with joy and comfort looking on to pleasant things. But in order to this, there is but one true way; he must abide in the innocence also of his early youth; he must keep the good thing, which God gave him at the Font, unpolluted by grievous sin. Or, he must so truly repent that he may, according to Scripture, hope that God remembers his sin no more. Either way there must be a reasonable trust in God's Pardon. Otherwise any joy which you feel, any notion of things going well, is a mere dream, not the joyfulness of Christian Hope. But if prayer, the Church or the Sacraments, be wilfully neglected, there can be no reasonable nor Scriptural trust in God's Pardon. Let those look to it, who think it enough to say an earnest prayer or go to Church now and then; to have communicated once or twice in their whole lives. I do not imagine they would themselves say, that they thought they had such faith and hope as was asked for them at their Baptism.

But perhaps they may think they have charity, since they do not bear malice. I hope few or none do so, and are glad in some sort to help a neighbour in distress. Reflect, however, for one moment, what the charity is, which the Collect speaks of, when it says, "rooted in charity." It means the true love of God, the Father, the Son and the Holy Ghost; such a love, as our Saviour meant, when He said; "If ye love Me, keep My commandments. And this, not to come and go, as one might chance to be minded at the time, but regularly, as a matter of course; much in the same way as dutiful children love their parents, and do as they bid them. This is being "rooted" in the love of God, when we have hold of it, and do not waver about; as plants that are rooted have constant hold of the ground. And this is so necessary, that, as you well know, the word steadiness is very often used, as if it meant all manner of goodness in a young person. "Such an one is very steady," is accounted one of the highest characters that can be given. And indeed what can be higher, provided it be truly spoken of any one, not by men only, but by the inhabitants of Heaven also? What higher praise than to say, he is steady, he is rooted in charity, he has fast hold of the true love both of God and of his neighbours, it is what he lives upon; in charity he has struck deep root; his leaves and fruit, his words and actions, are ordinarily such as Charity only can bring forth.

There is no higher praise than this to be given to the sons of men; nor is there any other way to their final blessing. Hear the end of our Collect. It prays that, being stedfast in faith, joyful through hope, and rooted in charity, he may so pass the waves of this troublesome world, that finally he may come to the land of everlasting life, there to reign with Thee, world without end, through Jesus Christ our Lord."

Our life, my brethren, is a voyage. We are all embarked on it, whether we will or no. So far we have no choice. But Christ, that we may voyage safely, has put us in His ark, the Church. The rest is all at our own choice; whether we will abide in that Ark, by practising faith, hope, and charity, or whether we will wander from it, and be shipwrecked for ever. This is our choice; we sealed it once for all at our Baptism; we are called upon to renew it every day and hour. Happy, through God's grace, if our daily and hourly choices do not contradict our first and most solemn choice.

SERMON XI.

St. Matt. vii. 11.

"If ye then, being evil, know how to give good gifts unto your children, how much more shall your Father which is in heaven give good things to them that ask Him."

As the first collect in the Baptismal Service pleads with God by His mercies to His ancient Church, so this second Collect puts Him in mind of His gracious ways at all times, and especially of His Son's promises, whereby He encourages the Church to pray. We do not now mention the Ark and the Passage of the Red Sea, and the Baptism of our Lord, but we call Him "the aid of all that need, the helper of all that flee to Him for succour, the life of them that believe, and the resurrection of the dead." And we put Him in mind of Christ's sayings in His sermon on the mount, "Ask, and ye shall have; seek, and ye shall find; knock, and it shall be opened unto you. For every one that asketh receiveth, and he that seeketh findeth, and to him that knocketh it shall be opened." All these mercies and promises are drawn down, as it were, by Holy Church in this prayer upon the head of the little child just coming to Holy Baptism.

She seems to plead with her great Maker and say, "Thou art the aid of all that need, and behold this child is in grievous need; 'born in sin and the child of wrath,' stripped of the Robe of original Righteousness, and lying half-dead by the wayside, like him who had fallen among those cruel thieves. Be Thou to him a good Samaritan, and bind up his wounds, pouring in oil and wine. Take him up in Thine Everlasting Arms, bring him to Thy Holy Church, and there have him taken care of, till Thou comest again."

Again, the Church says, "Thou art the helper of all that flee to Thee for succour" against the enemies of his soul. For, though he cannot yet come of himself, nor feel, nor understand why he should wish to come, yet his very sobs and cries are a plain token what he would do, if he could know. Did you ever observe this, my brethren? Did it ever strike you, how children crying as they do is a token from Almighty God, how much they need a Saviour? Think, when you hear the little voice in such distress at the Font—think, what is indeed the truth, that you hear the poor helpless one crying out to Christ for succour: and lift up your hearts to discern and acknowledge, that he does not cry in vain. The Almighty and Immortal God, the Helper of all that flee to Him for succour, He has promised to be there: and there, you may be sure, He is. As surely as ever you hear the child cry, so surely, depend on it, is Jesus Christ at hand to answer that cry: to take the babe up in His Arms and quiet him with more gentle nursing than ever did mother or nurse on earth. What pity, that our sad transgressions should ever make such care void!

G

Again, we call upon God by His title, The "Life of them that believe;" because Christ is our Life, and the Holy Ghost, since He joins us to Christ, is called in the Creed "the Lord and Giver of Life." As in God, our Creator and Preserver, all men, whether Christians or no, live, move, and have their being—their being and life in this world; and not only men, but the lower creatures also; so in God Incarnate, that is, God the Son, the Second Person in the Blessed Trinity made Man for us, Christians live by a special life; a heavenly and spiritual life; a life which they have, as members of Him. God is the Life of all: but Jesus Christ, God made Man, is especially the Life of them that believe. Observe that last word, my brethren. In order to keep the life which He has given us, we must in good earnest believe. The little child indeed, who is brought to be christened, cannot actually at the time believe—at least it seems as if he could not: and therefore our Lord mercifully accepts the faith of the Church presenting him, as if it were his own faith, and gives him life in Himself accordingly. But as soon as he is old enough, he must believe with a faith of his own; else the heavenly life that is in him will wither and die away. Now you know what we mean, when we talk of *believing*, and Faith. We mean persons looking always to the great things out of sight, which are to last for ever. And by unbelief and unbelievers, we mean people caring only for the things in sight, the things of this world. Such persons, although our Lord did actually give Himself to be their Life in Baptism, yet must not expect to live by Him, any more than they may expect to be warmed by a fire which they have wilfully allowed to go out. The fire was really lighted within them; they could not do it for themselves, it was kindly done for them; but whether they would feed it and keep it up or no, *this* did depend on themselves. I pray God, we may all look well to the fire which God Almighty graciously lit up in our hearts, when He made us members of Christ. Deadly indeed is the chill which will come upon us, if we once suffer that fire to go out; if, as St. Paul says, we "quench the Spirit." And it will go out, if we are not careful to feed it with Holy Communion, and to fan its flame, if I may say so, with prayer and good works.

Once again, we plead with God for the child which is going to be Christened, how that He is "the Resurrection of the dead." Because the young child, being naturally Adam's flesh and blood, is dead in sin, and cannot of itself do works pleasing to God, any more than a dead body can do the acts of a living one, therefore we put God in mind, that He has promised to be the Resurrection of the dead; as our Lord said over the grave of Lazarus, "I am the Resurrection and the Life." And as Lazarus, presently after, arose from the grave at our Lord's call, though he had been buried four days, so we trust and pray, that He will presently put forth His quickening power to raise this child from the state of spiritual death and helplessness in which it was born, and in which it is brought to the Font: that it may live with Him, and by His Spirit do works well-pleasing to Him. This is part of what we mean when we call upon God first before a Baptism, as being the

Life of them that believe, and the Resurrection of the Dead.

And what is it we are going to ask of God, that we so earnestly and solemnly remind Him of all these His glorious attributes? Our Prayer is, this time, not at all for ourselves, but wholly for the little helpless child whom we are bringing to the Font. "We call upon Thee for this Infant that he, coming to Thy Holy Baptism, may receive remission of sins by spiritual Regeneration." Remission of sins, we know, is given in Baptism. For St. Peter invited the Jews to "repent and be baptized every one of them in the Name of Jesus Christ, for the remission of sins," and Ananias invited St. Paul to "arise and be baptised, and wash away his sins," and the Church teaches us all in the Creed to acknowledge "one Baptism for the Remission of sins." But what sin has this Babe to be forgiven, which is only perhaps a few hours old? You know, my Brethren, it has the stain and guilt of Adam's sin born in itself, which is sure, like a plague-spot, to spread over soul and body, and ruin both, except it be forgiven and cleansed. How can we be thankful enough— any of us who care either for our own souls or for the souls of these little ones —to Him Who has provided so sure and merciful a way out of that sad condition, which is the beginning of all sin and misery. You know, if there were any frightful infectious disease in the place, and some one came, provided with a sure and easy way of guarding all your children against it, so that it should never take hold of them to hurt them, how earnestly you would seek that man, and thank him when he had made your children partakers of the benefit. Something like this you will do, if you are wise, next Friday. For the very fatal disease, though not yet in the place, is, we know, not far off; and we trust that, next Friday, One will be here, Who has both the power and will to cure or keep it off. Our Lord Jesus Christ will be here, to see what use we are making, in Church and out of Church, of the call which He has favoured us with by His servant the Bishop, to humble ourselves before Him in earnest. O let Him not find us cold, careless, indifferent, little caring for them and for our own souls! That would be a very likely way to provoke Him to let the pestilence loose upon us, which He has so long kept off. At any rate, were it actually here, I am sure you could not be careless about it; you would hasten to the bodily Physician at least. Why then are any of you cold, unthankful, indifferent about Baptismal grace, which Jesus Christ has Himself brought hither from Heaven for your children to be a sure safeguard, if you and they will so take it, against the far deadlier infection of sin?

And then observe how this remission comes. Not simply by passing over the sin but by overcoming, and as it were overwhelming, it by an unspeakable free gift of goodness. For thus saith the Church: "That he, coming to Thy Holy Baptism, may receive remission of his sins by spiritual regeneration." Not only are his sins forgiven, but he has the root of holiness put into him. Not only is the Evil One driven out, but the good Spirit has come to dwell in his place. Not only is he put in a better outward condition, as one of God's kingdom and family, but he is inwardly and spiritually regenerated, new-born unto righteousness and made a new creature. Henceforth One abides in this child, greater than he that is in the world. A spark of holy fire is lit up in him, which, if it be duly attended to, will consume all that is gross and earthly, and purify him altogether in the likeness of Jesus Christ. What a great thing is this to ask! And yet we dare ask it; for, besides all that is gone before, we have the great and precious promise of which the Collect next speaks.

"Receive him, O Lord, as Thou hast promised." Here we bring our Saviour's Words before God as our warrant, to receive without fail the blessing we ask for, great as it is; much in the same way as a person might present a ticket of admission to a hospital, or an order to receive a little bread or money or clothing, and, if signed by the proper person, it would ensure him the gift. Our Lord's promise, in like manner, is our pledge and warrant which we bring before God in prayer, with a sure and certain hope to be graciously received. See what a full, what a bountiful promise it is: three times repeated, that we might have no doubt at all about it. "Ask and ye shall have; for every one that asketh receiveth." We are to ask, because, even as the world goes and according to the ways of men, there is no good thing to be had but for asking. And if these earthly matters, which last but for a day, are yet counted worth the trouble of earnestly begging for them, well may it be expected of us that we should ask for heavenly things. Again, "seek and ye shall find; for he that seeketh findeth." Do you not see when people have lost any thing, let it be ever such an ordinary thing, how they presently begin to search after it, and, if they will not take that trouble, nobody expects them to find it? We and our children have lost no ordinary thing. In Adam we lost the happy innocency, the Image of God, in which our God at first created us. But Almighty God tells us where we may find it again,—in His Church, at His Font: only we must seek it with the eye of persevering faith.

Again, Christ has said, "knock, and it shall be opened; for to him that knocketh, it shall be opened." He only that knocks in earnest at a door has any right to expect, that the Porter within will hear and attend to him, and open the door as he wishes. If he only waits loitering about the door, now and then looking towards it but never knocking, never seeking an entrance, who can believe that he really desires to get in, or who will take the trouble of opening to him? So with Baptism, which is the Door into the Kingdom of Heaven. Almighty God loves that those who are seeking an entrance there, should knock at the door with all humble earnestness: that they should pray to Him again and again with all their hearts for the fulness of the blessing: as it is written, "The Kingdom of Heaven suffereth violence, and the violent take it by force:" i. e. there is a kind of holy violence, an earnestness in devotion which God greatly loves, and by which men shall make their way, in spite of the worst difficulties and fiercest opposition, into His Kingdom with all its Blessings. As therefore you see, that we could not be too earnest in asking and seeking baptismal grace for ourselves, if we were not yet Christians, so you see that our wishes and prayers should be *very* fervent, when any one belonging to us has to come to Christ in Holy Baptism. Devout persons have always been used, even before a child is born, to make it matter of special prayer that it may be spared to receive that Holy Sacrament of Regeneration; so that this prayer of the Church at the Font is only the summing up, as it were, and the last solemn rehearsal of the petitions which have been continually made by parents, kinsfolk and friends at home. And indeed this may be one chief meaning of the petition, put up in the Litany for young children. When those words are said, we may well think in our hearts of the little ones who are yet unbaptized, especially of any that we know of, and charitably help them with a kind wish and prayer that they may not be unbaptized long.

It is a prayer meet for all good Christians, but for good parents more especially: for our Lord, in this promise, is speaking especially to Parents. For He goes on and says, "If a son shall ask bread of any of you that is a father, will he give him a stone?" As parents, He here teaches us to pray. Parents have a key to His full meaning, which others, perhaps, in some measure want. Therefore He adds again, "If ye then, being evil, know how to give good gifts unto your children: how much more shall *your* heavenly Father give the Holy Spirit to them that ask Him?" Christian fathers and mothers, to you the word is spoken: as parents, you were encouraged by our Lord to pray for your children: and He encourages you, moreover, to pray to Him as to a better and more real parent than yourselves. He is that Father of us all, from Whom Alone our fathers and our mothers too learnt all their love for us. They may think it came of itself, or, as the saying is, by nature; but, in deed and in truth, it comes direct from God. Pray then, fathers and mothers; pray for your children more earnestly: be sure that He Who fills you with love to them, will not reject your prayers for them. And He is that Father, Who has not only what you can give them, bread and fish and the like, to keep their bodies awhile from starving, but His Holy Spirit to make them partakers of His Son. Pray for that: which is indeed worth praying for. And pray that it may never pass away: "that they may receive the *everlasting* Benediction and come to the Eternal Kingdom;" and, when you rise up from your prayers, do not forget those words. Go home, full of the thought, that these children's souls will last for ever, and that you are entrusted with them. So may you save, by God's mercy, both *yourselves* and *them*.

SERMON XII.

ST. MARK x. 14.

"Suffer the little children to come unto Me and forbid them not, for of such is the Kingdom of God."

We may consider the Introduction of the Baptismal Office, that which prefaces the way for the rest,—as coming to an end after the second Collect: and the Office itself as beginning, when the people stand up and the Priest gives out the Gospel. This, I say, may be regarded as properly beginning the Baptismal Office, inasmuch as in Holy Baptism there are two things to be considered: It is both a covenant or agreement between Almighty God and the person baptized; and also a mean, whereby God bestows on that person a very great and unspeakable gift. Now, in our Prayer-Book, as soon as the Collects are over, the covenant or agreement is set forth. It has of course two parts, as all covenants and agreements must have. For no person covenants and makes agreements with himself. To such a transaction, there must be two parties at least. And you plainly see, that in Holy Baptism the two parties are, on the one side Almighty God, the Father, the Son, and the Holy Ghost; on the other the little infant, who is now for the first time brought nigh unto God. Wonderful it is, that the great God should so condescend to treat with such a helpless little creature, made out of a little dust, and soon to return to dust again, and, what is more, polluted all over with the taint and infection of Adam's sin. Wonderful, yet most assuredly true. But because it is so greatly beyond what a sinful mortal might have to expect, therefore in setting forth the covenant God's part is rehearsed first, as is meet and natural; for, without such express invitation, how could anything so frail and unclean safely draw near or be brought to the God of all Purity? God's part therefore of the Baptismal covenant is first set forth and rehearsed out of the Gospel of St. Mark, and afterwards the child's part, when the promises are made in his name by the godfathers and godmothers.

And in both there is one thing very particularly to be observed; viz., That as Holy Baptism and its blessings are entirely matters of faith, not of sight, so in the Covenant, which seals those blessings, neither party is so present as to answer and speak openly for himself. Both are indeed present, yet for both the agreement is spoken and made by another person—or as it is sometimes called, by proxy. On the one hand, our Lord, we know, is especially present at the Font, not only because He is God and therefore is present every where, but also by virtue of His special promise, "where two or three are gathered together in My Name, there am I in the midst of them." He is present, but we see Him not; He hides Himself, to try our Faith, and commissions His Priest to speak for Him; which the Priest does by reading the appointed words out of Christ's gospel. Again, the other party to the covenant, the child, is indeed present, and we see him: but then he is so young, that he can neither speak, nor in any other way signify that he agrees to the covenant, and will be bound by it. Therefore the Church speaks for him by the godfathers and godmothers whom she appoints: and it is his own covenant just the same, and he is equally bound by it, exactly as if he had promised it with his own lips, and set his own hand and seal to it. However, in both respects it is, you see, more or less a trial of people's faith, of their putting their minds in good earnest to things out of sight, and making very much of them. It is an act of religious faith, to feel sure that our Lord is there speaking to you, though you see and hear only the clergyman and the Book. It is another act of religious faith, to believe that the young child does really, before God, make the promises, though to our eyes and ears it would seem to be only the godfathers and godmothers. I wish we thought more than we do of both; both of our Lord's Presence and of the promise being our own.

But let us now consider the words which contain our Lord's own part of the covenant: the words themselves, and the manner in which they were spoken. They were spoken very solemnly, in the hearing of the assembled Apostles, and they are carefully set down in three out of the four gospels, St. Matthew, St. Mark, and St. Luke. It seems that, when He was very busy, certain women brought to Him their infants, that He might lay His Hands on them, and bless them: and His Disciples, as many would have done in their place, rather checked them, thinking it was troublesome. But when Jesus saw it, He was much displeased and said, "Suffer the little children to come unto Me, and forbid them not; for of such is the kingdom of Heaven. Verily I say unto you, Whosoever shall not receive the kingdom of God as a little child, shall in no wise enter therein. And He took them up in his arms, put His hands upon them, and blessed them." Here we see, Providence so ordered things, as that the doubts and scruples of the disciples should help us to an end of all doubts and scruples in this matter. Their complaint it was, which drew from our Lord the remarkable saying, "of such is the Kingdom of Heaven;" by which we know that not these children only, but all infant sons and daughters of Adam, have a right to Holy Baptism, as soon as they can well be brought to it. For He said expressly, "Of such is the Kingdom of Heaven," i. e. the Church—the condition of baptized persons. The Church, which is Christ's Body, pertains to such as they are: they were made for it, and it for them: and what right they have to the Church, just the same, of course, they have to the way into the Church, i. e. to Holy Baptism. For if God calls them to come into His house, of course He calls them to go through the Door. If the Kingdom is theirs, so is the entrance into it. And so, as the Jews knew for certain that all their boys were to be circumcised, so Christians know for certain that all their children are to be baptized: not only that they *may* be, but that our Lord is very earnest, very desirous to have them all so brought to Him. See how many tokens He gave, at that very time, of this His desire and wish. First, He was much displeased with those who were for sending away the children. He took it very much amiss of them. He complained, as a man might do, who counted himself ill-used. Not above once or twice in His Ministry do we read of His expressing the like feelings: and each time it was in behalf of some one who had been ill-treated. That displeasure of His was one token of His special love for young children. Another was His express command, "Suffer them to come to Me." As if He should say, "There is something in them which will cause them, if let alone, to come to Me: do not you hinder them. They cannot do without Me, and I in a manner cannot do without them. They want Me for a Saviour, and I want them for members. Who dare take on him to hinder us from coming together?" Thus our Lord's saying, "Suffer them to come," is a second and most clear token of His love. A third is, His adding, "Forbid them not." For when a master not only commands his servants to do a thing, but adds, Take care you leave it not undone, the servant understands that his master's heart is more than usually set upon that thing. But again *our* Master gives the reason, why He is so earnest upon having the little ones brought to Him: and this is another and an unspeakable token of His Love. For what is the reason? "Of such is the Kingdom of Heaven," i. e. the blessed condition which I came into the world to provide for men, belongs as it were by right to them: to them and to such as they are, children and those who are become like children, are the very persons for whom that Kingdom is provided. Instead of being unfit, they are the very measure and standard of fitness for it, so that by comparison with them shall be known, who are true children of the Kingdom. "Verily I say unto you, Whosoever shall not receive the kingdom of God as a little child, he shall not enter therein." Instead of keeping them out, know that you must become like them, in order to enter in yourselves. And He confirmed His gracious words by three most merciful signs, actions of love which no one who beheld, certainly I suppose no mother, could well ever forget. He took the children up in His Arms—one by one, the babes which were brought to them—that was His preserving, nursing care—He took them in His Arms, and their mothers knew that they were safe in His care from all the powers of evil and spirits of darkness. But He did more. He laid His hands on them; He touched them, as a father his children, or a Pastor, when he would most earnestly desire to shew his anxious and tender love for them. He touched these children, as He was used to touch those who came to Him for healing, or who were vexed with unclean spirits: and no doubt virtue went out of Him, to do them unknown, unthought-of good: no doubt each one of those was the better for our Lord's touch, (unless he threw away the gift) as long as he lived.

But there is yet one thing more—"He laid His Hands on them, *and blessed them.*" To His gracious Touch He added words of Blessing: as His Bishops and Priests do in their solemn Benedictions; and as He doth Himself continually in His holy Sacraments. All these tokens of love are, as it were, gathered and bound together in that one minute of our Lord's life, in that one sentence of His gospel. So that we can no more doubt that, whoever else have Him for their Saviour, surely He is in a special way the Friend and Saviour of these little ones.

This then, as I said before, is our Lord's part of the covenant made at the Baptism of any child; the words being "Of such is the Kingdom of heaven;" the sign and seal, His taking those children up in His Arms, and so lovingly laying His Hands upon them, and blessing them. It is His part of the covenant: and, as such, it is taken up afterwards in the Priest's instruction to the sponsors—"Ye have heard that our Lord Jesus Christ hath promised in His gospel," i. e. in this place just read out of the gospel of St. Mark, "to grant all these things which ye have prayed for: which promise He for His part will most surely keep and perform." That is, those few short words, "Of such is the Kingdom of God," are a promise, that Christ will receive the Infant presented to Him for Holy Baptism—will release him of his sins, will sanctify him with the Holy Ghost, will give him the Kingdom of Heaven, and everlasting life. O great and glorious Promises! how can we ever think enough of them? We never can think enough: but we may, by God's mercy, be in a way to think rightly: and I will endeavour to shew you how.

When one who is a parent stands by and hears with his own ears Jesus Christ standing to His covenant; when he hears out of the gospel read over a little Babe, "Of such is the Kingdom of God:" surely if he have a parent's heart, it must overflow with love towards the Saviour of his child: surely he must wish and long to know what he can do, by way of shewing forth some small gratitude to Him. You may talk of loving your children; but how is it possible you can truly love them, if you are not very full of love towards Him Who so chooses out and blesses them, Him Who is even now taking them up in His Arms to save them from Hell. And if you love Him, you will try to please Him. You will not pass slightly over any of His Commands, especially His last dying Command, "Do this in remembrance of Me." Your love to your child, if you really believe in Christ's blessing given to that child in Baptism, will be enough, by God's grace, to make you a good Christian.

Next, let us suppose a child or young person listening to the baptismal service, thoughtfully listening to the saying, "Of such is the Kingdom of Heaven." Of course it will come into his mind, "not so very long ago I was received in this way, and God made His covenant with me to enter me in the Kingdom of Heaven: of which I have ever since been an Inheritor. He made it at that time *with me*: with me and with no other: I did, as it were, stand on the one side of the Font, and Jesus Christ stood on the other, and we pledged our troth either to other, as people do when they are married,—and He for His part will most surely keep His word—but what shall I do for my part? how will it prove, in the end, with me? Oh, it is a serious thought, a heavy burthen: but no need to sink under it: He is so good, that He has even promised to help me effectually to do my part: I have but to put myself in earnest to the work, and He will give me His Holy Spirit to perform it. Therefore I will not listen to the busy tempter, who is even now whispering to me, 'It is too

H

much—you cannot do these great things—neither you nor any man can keep the baptismal engagement.' Nay, I will say, 'get thee behind me, Satan.' By the help of my God I can and I will keep my vows: Christ promised me as much at the Font, and I dare not doubt His Promise."

But what if one has already fallen; fallen into grievous sin; into a course of neglect and forgetfulness towards God? what is he, then, to think of God's part in the covenant sealed to him in Baptism? Alas, his thoughts must be very sorrowful, they cannot and they ought not to be otherwise; yet it may be a sorrow, mingled with joy and hope. Sad indeed it is to think of Christ's most true and loving Promise, "Of such is the kingdom of Heaven"—dishonoured and met on one side by a broken vow and an untrue profession: sad to think, how very unlike one has become to the pure and guileless babe, over whom the gracious words were uttered. But never mind the sadness: encourage and welcome it: let it sink into your mind: only keep on all the while, beseeching God inwardly to turn it to your good: so by His infinite mercy it may prove the commencement of a true penitence. And, for your comfort, you may take this thought home with you, and may He cheer and establish your heart with it: that, although your sharing in your Lord's baptismal promise, of course, makes your sins more intolerable, yet, on your *truly* repenting of these sins, part of that promise is to grant you a free pardon and cleanse you entirely. Only take care that you *truly* and sufficiently repent, and do not abuse yourself with a vain shadow of penitence. So when the last day comes, and the account begun at the Font will have to be finally closed, you with those who have kept their first vows, the Innocent and the Penitent together, will praise Him for His great and precious Promises, wondering to find them accomplished in yourselves.

SERMON XIII.

Deuteronomy xxxiii. 27.

"The Eternal God is thy refuge, and underneath are the everlasting Arms."

WE saw last Sunday, that after the first prayers the Church in the Baptismal Service begins to set forth the terms of the covenant which God vouchsafes to make with us in Baptism; and that God's part of course is declared first; that is, the free gift which He bestows upon the child, and how plainly and mercifully He has promised it. This is contained in the Gospel, i. e. in the account of our Lord's receiving the little children, declaring that "of such is the Kingdom of Heaven," taking them up in His Arms and blessing them. After those words have been read, the Priest, as you know, makes a short discourse upon the words of the Gospel, saying, "Beloved, ye hear in this Gospel the words of our Saviour Christ, how He commanded the children to be brought to Him," i. e. when He said, "Suffer the little children to come unto Me;" "how He blamed those that would have kept them from Him," i. e. when He said, "Forbid them not;" how He exhorteth all men to follow their innocency, i. e. when He said,

"Of such is the Kingdom of Heaven," and verily I say unto you, "whosoever shall not receive the Kingdom of God as a little child, he shall in no wise enter therein." Having thus put you in mind of our Lord's words, the Holy Church next goes on to put us in mind of His doings at the same time; "Ye perceive how by His outward gesture and deed He declared His good will towards them; for He embraced them in His Arms, He laid His Hands upon them, and blessed them." Then we are encouraged to apply what He said and did to the little child who is even now to be baptized; "Doubt ye not therefore, but earnestly believe, that He will likewise favourably receive this present infant, that He will embrace him with the Arms of His mercy, that He will give unto him the blessing of Eternal Life, and make him partaker of His everlasting Kingdom." These surely are great, unspeakable things; far greater than if one should say, Doubt ye not, but earnestly believe that this child will be a rich and fortunate man never out of health, never failing in what he undertakes. If a person made you such a promise, as he stood by your child's cradle, you would with reason doubt it; you would not believe it at all. Why are you then not to doubt at all, but earnestly to believe, these promises, infinitely greater, and more precious? Because these are Christ's own promises, and He is the unchangeable God, "the Same yesterday, to-day, and for ever;" and, being God, all things are at all times present to Him. When He did and said the things, which have been just read out of the Gospel, He did, in His mind and purpose, do and say them to this child, and to all who should at any time be brought to Him for Holy

Baptism. For every one of them was in His mind; He knew and thought of every one. In encouraging those mothers to bring their children, He encouraged you Christian mothers, coming here from time to time with your children to the Holy Font. In blaming His disciples for wanting to keep them back, He was blaming all who in any time should carelessly or mistakenly keep a child back from Baptism. In taking them up in His Arms, He was taking up you and me, and all who have had the unspeakable privilege of being baptised as Infants in His Holy Church. When He laid His Hands upon them and blessed them, Virtue went out of those Divine Hands to bless us all, even every child who is brought to Him to be christened.

For indeed this is the manner in which we are taught by the true Faith to look upon what passes when a child is baptized. As I am often telllng you, what we see then, is nothing in comparison of what is there present unseen. The Priest is but a shadow and token of our Lord Jesus Christ, as the water is but a shadow and token of the cleansing and sanctifying Spirit. It is Christ Who baptizes; only He does it by His servant's hand; for so we have been taught by St. John Baptist, "This is He that baptizeth with the Holy Ghost. There may have been hundreds of thousands of Priests and Deacons, since the Church began, but all along there has been only one real Baptizer, viz. our Lord Jesus Christ. When therefore you see the nurse or godmother, coming to the Font with the child, and lifting it to the Priest, try and imagine that you see one of those women in the Gospel, bringing an Infant to our Saviour. When the Priest takes the child in his arms, think you see Jesus Christ doing so; think of the words, "Jesus beholding him loved him;" and remember also those other words, "The Eternal God is thy refuge, and underneath are the everlasting Arms." For all these things really are so. Jesus Christ is really then and there especially present, taking the child up in His Arms, which are the everlasting Arms; only let us have faith to see it.

Now supposing our eyes and ears for once opened, so that we were able to see and hear what we can now only believe, what would our thoughts be of it all? how should we feel? Surely our hearts would be very full of exceeding deep and earnest thoughts, both concerning the little child, and concerning ourselves.

First, as concerning the child, we should, as the Church teaches us, not doubt but earnestly believe that it was receiving all these blessings. Far too great a thing were it for us to believe upon any reasoning of our own, any thing which we saw or made out for ourselves. But now the Word of God, as declared by His Church, is so plain, that we are not to doubt it at all, but simply to believe it. Fathers and mothers, are you in care for your children? Do you love them very much? are you always, night and day, longing, wishing, labouring for their good? O then consider it well, and bring it home to your hearts, that, when they received Holy Baptism, Christ, the Friend of little children took them up in His Arms, and that He is the Eternal God, His are the Everlasting Arms, so that if they have not changed, you may be sure He has not. "His gifts and calling are without repentance:" He is "the Lord and changes not." If they are still young children, too young for actual sin, He is still bearing them up; the world is very bad and dangerous, there are thousands of evil spirits abroad, but *your* little ones, so far, are safe: and if He should take them as they are, they are safe for ever. O fathers and mothers, and all who care for these little ones, what a comfort is this for you to carry about with you through all the changes and chances of this mortal life! Come what will, you may say to yourselves over and over, " my child, if it please God to keep him as he is, is safe." " The Eternal God is thy refuge, and underneath are the Everlasting Arms." Jesus Christ hath taken him up and blessed him, and none can take him out of his Saviour's Hand. I say, as long as your children are very young, before they are of age to commit known and actual sin, so long you have this unspeakable comfort, whenever you think of them; and especially if it please God to visit them, as He does so often in those tender years, with pain, sickness and death. It is said, I believe, by those who are skilful in reckoning the chances of life, that more persons die before they are two years old, than in the whole remaining years of man's life. What a mass, what a quantity is here of deep distress and sorrow! but then what a consolation too! "not to doubt, but earnestly to believe" that each one of these tender Babes, cut off, as to us it may seem, so untimely, is but removed to a brighter room in God's House, from earth to Paradise, from its cradle to Abraham's Bosom, from its nurse's songs to the chanting of the Holy Angels. What a wonder of love to think on such a tender Babe getting the victory over all the spirits of darkness, and especially over the Evil one, the Prince of them all; passing unhurt through the midst of them, in the Name and through the power of Jesus Christ! Well may we thank our Father in Heaven for His good will towards this Infant, declared by His Son Jesus Christ, and for His favour to us also, in looking graciously on what we do, and counting it a charitable work, when we bring the child to His Holy Baptism.

But besides these thoughts, relating to the child to be christened, a serious person, when present at a christening must needs have many thoughts concerning himself; he will say in his heart, "not long since, I too was a little infant, I too was brought to the Font, a child of wrath; and by God's mercy went from it a child of grace; that great and marvellous work was wrought in me, which we are now beseeching God to work in this Infant. Surely I ought to be very thankful for myself as well as for this child. Surely, when I see him taken up in his Saviour's Arms, I feel how good it is for him to be there; I cannot but remember that I too, not so very long since, was embraced in like manner by the Arms of the same Mercy, and made partaker of the same blessings. Surely if I do not feel very thankful, at least I may be ashamed of being cold, heartless and unthankful; and I may beseech Him Whom I know to be especially present to receive those little ones, that He would make Himself present to me, to kindle in my dull, lukewarm soul one little spark of that earnest adoring love, wherewith the Saints in all times have been ever used to think of their Baptism." If we have but one grain of faith, something like this must be our wish and prayer, as often as we are by when a child is baptized; and it is the very wish and prayer which our Mother the Church puts into our mouth. She says, "Let us faithfully and devoutly give thanks unto Him, and say, Almighty, everlasting God, heavenly Father, we give Thee humble thanks, for that Thou hast vouchsafed to call us to the knowledge of Thy grace and faith in Thee." In these words every fresh christening is made an occasion of thanking God for all the christenings which have gone before; for each person to call to mind the blessings of his own Baptism—the Election and calling out of the world, whereof, as I have shewn you before, a small portion only have been even outwardly called: the knowledge of the grace of God, while so many lie in darkness; the faith in Him, while so many disbelieve. The sight of an infant brought to the Font is to remind us of these favours; and if we have them really in our mind, we cannot but be very than ful; for we must needs feel that these mercies are everything to us, and that without them our life would do us no good, and it were better for us that we had never been born.

But along with this deep thankfulness, must go also another feeling, more or less, of deep anxiety and fear. The more thankful we ought to be for the great grace bestowed on us in Baptism, the more keenly, alas! may many of us fear, whether we have not sinned it all away; and he who has least to reproach himself with, may yet be humbled in the dust to think, how very much more he might have made of it than he has. Therefore to the words of thanksgiving are presently added words of prayer, "We give Thee hearty thanks for that Thou hast vouchsafed to call us to the knowledge of Thy grace and Faith in Thee; increase this knowledge and confirm this Faith in us evermore." We began in our own Baptism to know this Thy regenerating grace; increase, we beseech Thee, that knowledge; help us to grow more and more in it; order our hearts and our lives so, that we may daily and hourly set a higher value upon the good thing given us in our Baptism, and shrink from all that might rob us of it. Confirm also our faith, to which Thou didst at the same time call us; grant that we may go on until the very hour of death, believing more thoroughly, and minding more steadily the great things out of sight, and most especially Christ on His Cross. This is the prayer for ourselves, which the Church puts into the mouth of every one of us and teaches us to mingle it with our thanksgivings, when we assist at the Baptism of a child; "Increase this knowledge, and confirm this faith in us evermore." I beseech you, my brethren, if we have but a little remnant, but one faint spark of care for our own souls, let us try to say at least this one prayer in earnest. Let us try to know more of God's grace to have our weak faith strengthened; not to be left to grow quite like the beasts that perish, with hard hearts and unbelieving minds. Who knows but his earnestly endeavouring to join in such a prayer as this, may by God's mercy do great things for him? It may be the turning-point, the salvation of his soul. It may win for him that precious and powerful look of Christ, such as when the Lord turned and looked upon Peter and Peter remembered the word of the Lord. Therefore, whatever we do, let us strive to be quite in earnest, when we say, "Increase our knowledge, and confirm our faith."

And if in that Petition we are ever so little in earnest, we shall of course be earnest also in the other petition which follows and concludes the Collect; wherein we leave off praying for ourselves, and present the child to God, interceding for it, that it may be baptized with water and the Holy Ghost. "Give Thy Holy Spirit to this infant, that it may be born again, and made an heir of everlasting salvation through Jesus Christ." Then we lay down the tender babe in a manner at the foot of God's throne, beseeching Him to receive it, and deal with it as He has dealt with us, and with so many who, since the Day of Pentecost, have been made Partakers of His grace. And then in a manner we leave it, until the other part of the Covenant, its own part, has been transacted for it; to which the Priest immediately goes on, in what he proceeds to say to the godfathers and godmothers.

To this we shall go on by God's Blessing another time. For the present how can we do better, than endeavour to go away with *this* consideration deep in our hearts, That what prayers and thanksgivings we say, or have had said over us, here in our baptismal Services, have by no means passed entirely away? They are set down in God's Book; they sound continually in God's Ear; they will be remembered to our honour or to our confusion at the Day of Judgment. We have prayed that God would increase in us the knowledge of His grace. How, if on that Day it be read out of the Book concerning us, "This man wilfully neglected prayer; he never came to Holy Communion; he cared not to know more of God's grace."

Again we have prayed to have Christ's faith confirmed in us. How, if we be found to have gone on, from week's end to week's end, without ever saying the Creed, or thinking on the great truths contained in it? If we have sense to think of ordinary matters, I do not well see what we can say for such neglect of the greatest of all. Lastly we have prayed for the child, that it may be born again, and made an heir of everlasting Salvation. What, if any one of us by our bad example shall be found to have led or encouraged that child, directly or indirectly, in the way of sin and ruin? What if we have made void our prayers by going on in our sinful ways: perhaps as soon as ever we come out of Church? How should such prayers as those do any one good, himself or his children? God grant us for Christ's sake, and for the sake of Christ's little ones, to be in earnest when we call on Him!

SERMON XIV.

Psalm cxix. 32.

"I will run the way of Thy commandments, when Thou hast set my heart at liberty."

WE treated last Sunday of that portion of the Baptismal Service which concludes our Lord's part of the Covenant, and also of the Prayer and Thanksgiving, in which the whole Church joins, acknowledging God's mercy in calling them, and asking it for this child. After this it is directed that the Priest shall speak to the Godfathers and Godmothers; putting them in mind of God's part, and telling them what is the child's part; as who should say, "Here is this agreement to be signed and sealed; behold, the one party has signed and sealed it, and now it is your turn, who are the other party, to do the same. Our Lord Jesus Christ hath given you His assurance, in answer to your prayer and to the prayer of the whole Church. He hath declared Himself ready to receive it, by causing His gracious words to be said over it, in which He encouraged the little children to come to Him. It is just as much His own declaration, as if He were here in sight, to say the words to us concerning this child in particular." Then whereas the Priest says, "Ye have prayed that our Lord would release the child of its sins," we may remember that in the second collect the petition had been, " That he, coming to Thy Holy Baptism, may receive remission of his sins by spiritual regeneration." And this too Christ had promised, when He said, Let them come to Me; for He hath told us Himself, "Him that cometh unto Me, I will in no wise cast (out);" now the Blessing and Embrace of Jesus Christ cannot be without forgiveness of sins.

Also it is said here by the Priest, "Ye have prayed that our Lord Jesus Christ would vouchsafe to sanctify this child with the Holy Ghost." That was, where in the first collect it was said, "We beseech Thee for Thine infinite mercies that Thou wilt mercifully look upon this child; wash him and sanctify him with the Holy Ghost." This prayer our Lord promised to hear, when He said, "Of such is the kingdom of Heaven;" seeing that to enter into that kingdom of Heaven we must be regenerate and born anew of water and the Holy Ghost. Thus you see how Justification, which is being made a member of Christ the Righteous, (as all little children are at their Baptism), brings with it both pardon and peace. Pardon for sins past, and for original sin, and grace to do well for the time to come. How great is this gift! can we be too careful of it, or too penitent for our many sins against it?

Further; the Priest reminds the Godfathers that they had prayed God to give the child the kingdom of Heaven; that was, when they prayed that he might be received into the ark of Christ's Church; for the Church of Christ is the kingdom of Heaven.

And to this our Lord, as you all know, has pledged Himself in so many words, saying, "Of such is the kingdom of Heaven."

And observe; this means not only that God will make the child one of His Church, a Christian, in this world; but also that He means him to go to heaven, and to be happy in God's Presence with the Saints and Angels for ever. "The kingdom of heaven, *and everlasting Life*"—this we had asked in our Prayers for the Child; "that we may so pass the waves of this troublesome world, that finally we may come to the land of everlasting life," and again, that he "may come to the eternal Kingdom which Thou hast promised;" and once more, "that he may be made an heir of everlasting salvation." And as we had prayed, so Christ had met us with His Promise, "Of such is the Kingdom of God." "Whosoever will not receive it as they, he shall not enter therein," meaning not only the church in this world, which is the beginning of the Kingdom of God, but much more the Church triumphant and glorious in Heaven, which is the perfection and fulness of His Kingdom.

Thus you see that the prayer of the Church, and the Promise in the Gospel said at baptism, provide for the Child's entire salvation, both in time and in eternity. They take him up, if I may so speak, just as he is; and they never leave him; they carry him on for ever. Christ having once taken him up in His Arms, will never let him drop, you may be sure. I pointed it out to the children last Sunday in the Catechizing, how seldom it happens that children are let fall on the ground, considering how many are being constantly nursed by persons more or less weak, ignorant, and careless; and if helpless mortals can do so much for those little ones, how much more may we make ourselves certain that the Everlasting Arms will not fall from under us; that Jesus Christ will never, of His own accord, cease to bear us in His loving Embrace. We may break away from Him; *that*, alas! we know too well: but He will never of His own accord leave us or forsake us. As the Priest goes on to say, "This promise He for His part will most surely keep and perform." It cannot be broken, because He is True, and not only True but Truth Itself. "If we believe not, yet He abideth faithful; He cannot deny Himself." His Word endureth for ever in Heaven. Well may we doubt or fear for ourselves; but we may not, we must not, in any wise doubt what He hath told us, or fear lest He should prove untrue.

Now you know what a satisfaction and comfort it is, in any matter of this world, any covenant or bargain we have to make, to be quite sure that we may depend on the other party: when he is so honest, prudent, and punctual, that we may without hesitation take his word, and settle all our matters accordingly, knowing that whatever he has promised, (be it to pay money, or to bring home work, or to render an account, or to meet us at any time or place,) *there* he will be, God willing, and *that* he will do. O then, if we only cared for the things of the eternal world as much as we care for a sum of money to be paid us, a piece of work to be done for us, the bringing of some business to an end—how great to us would be the joy and blessing of having for our souls a friend and helper, of whom we can say with absolute certainty; "His Promise He for His part will most surely keep and perform." And consider this too, my brother, whoever you are, who have been baptized to be a Christian. If you had to do with such a friend as I am speaking of, and knew that he was continually putting himself out of his way for you, that he spared no pains to keep his engagements, and to bring your business to a good and comfortable end, should you not feel a little bound to save him what trouble you could, to meet his wishes and convenience, to put him to no unnecessary pains or expence, to shew how entirely you trusted in him, and how you thanked him from your very heart? Yes; I am sure you would have some feelings of this kind; you would not be so entirely cold-hearted and selfish, as to take all the benefit of your friend's kindness and punctual trouble to yourself, without at all thanking him, or putting yourself out of the way to be exact and punctual as well as you could in your turn. Now apply this to the great agreement, the covenant made in Holy Baptism between God Almighty and you His unworthy helpless creature, His promise He for His part will most surely keep and perform. There is no doubt of it; "one jot or one tittle shall in no wise pass from His Gospel until all be fulfilled." And can you find in your heart to receive all this good at His Hands, and take no pains to please Him? Can you forget Him morning by morning, not even trying always to say your prayers to Him in earnest? Will you take your meals like the beasts that perish, without begging a blessing beforehand, or offering praise to God afterwards? Will you, all the day through, let things have their own way, never stopping to consider what will best please Him, but only pleasing yourself, and seeking your own profit? O my brethren, be ashamed of such ingratitude.

And if you are not ashamed, be afraid. For now I must put you in mind of the other part of the Baptismal covenant, your own part; what you promised and vowed immediately after you had heard God's part. As the Priest, taught by the Church, said to your godfathers and godmothers: "After this promise made by Christ, this infant must also faithfully for his part promise by you that are his sureties, until he come of age to take it upon himself, that he will renounce the devil and all his works, and constantly believe God's holy Word, and obediently keep His commandments." As much as to say, though it is a free gift, yet it is given you in the way of a Covenant, and may be forfeited if you break what you promised in the Covenant. He will keep *His* word, you need not fear about *that;* only do you take care to keep your's.

The whole transaction appears to me very like the verse which I read to you for the text out of the cxixth Psalm, "I will run the way of Thy commandments, when Thou hast set my heart at liberty." God has set our heart at liberty; we were in sad and hard bondage, born in slavery to the world, the flesh and the devil; and He has come down to be our Saviour and mighty Deliverer; He hath broken our bonds in sunder; the snare is broken, and we are delivered. He has set our heart at liberty, so that it need no longer be led captive at the will of the Evil One. It is no longer forced to lust after evil things, as the Gentiles which know not God. He is ready to set this child's heart at liberty; and then what will the child have to do but to run the way of His commandments? Mind, the Psalm says, not "walk" but "run"—not go slowly and lazily, as if it had no pleasure in the work, but make haste and put forth its strength; doing God's will heartily and thankfully, as to the Lord, and not as to men; coming forth as a bridegroom out of his chamber, and rejoicing as a giant to run his course. This is what Christ expects of us, that, He having delivered us out of the hand of our enemies, we should serve Him without fear, not fearing nor doubting to trust ourselves with Him, in holiness and righteousness before Him, all the days of our life. This is, in substance and meaning, the vow by which we bind ourselves at our Baptism, as the Priest goes on with his instruction: "Wherefore, after this promise made by Christ, this infant must also faithfully, for his part, promise by you that are his sureties, until he come of age to take it upon himself, that he will renounce the Devil and all his works, and constantly believe God's holy Word, and obediently keep His commandments."

Now concerning the particulars of this promise, there will be something to be said another time; now I will add a word concerning the part which the Godfathers and Godmothers have in it. It is plain that, if the child is to make the covenant, he must do it by another, since he cannot yet speak or write, nor make any sign at all of himself. That other is his surety, he becomes bound, as it were, to Almighty God and His Church, for the child, that he will keep his covenant; just as in earthly matters, in the case of an estate for instance ; If a rich man die while his child is under age, there are trustees ordained to manage the property for the benefit of that child, any bargains and engagements they make in the child's name are held binding on him when he comes to age, being made entirely for his advantage. And of course such trustees are bound in duty, when the heir comes of age, to get him to fulfil such engagements, so far as he can; still, if he will not, the loss and the disgrace must be his own. So it is with the sureties of our souls in Baptism. We are bound by their words, bound before God and man to all eternity, and *that* at the peril of our souls. The Covenant of our Baptism is one from which we can never be discharged, and they are bound, as they have opportunity, to put us in mind of our duty, and see us to do it. Being then so far in the place of parents, they should have something fatherly and motherly in them; however young they may be, they ought to feel as if God had put into their hands something of a father's or mother's trust. The least they can do is to wish and pray in their hearts, that the little one for whom they answer may keep his vow. But this they cannot do, they cannot really wish and pray for the child's soul, except they be really in care for their own souls also. Now the Church well knows, that no one whatever, who in earnest cares for his own soul, will live in wilful neglect of Holy Communion, and therefore she has ordained, that no person be admitted to answer for a child before he or she has been admitted to receive Holy Communion, and although, in this sad condition of things, we find it hard to keep to this rule, and sometimes think it more charitable not to insist on it, yet I am sure you must all feel how reasonable and proper it is; and that nothing can be quite right, while Communion is neglected.

But as for such as really endeavour to be regular and worthy Communicants, I most earnestly recommend it to them as a real work of Charity, to answer for their neighbours' children without making too many difficulties; intending of course to do their duty according to the best of their power. If Godfathers and Godmothers were always so minded, then our gatherings round the Font would oftener prove, by God's mercy, unfailing tokens of so many meetings in Heaven.

SERMON XV.

PSALM l. 5.

Gather My saints together unto Me, those that have made a covenant with Me with sacrifice.

AFTER rehearsing God's part in the Covenant of Baptism, the Priest speaks thus to the Godfathers and Godmothers, setting forth what part the child has in the same Covenant. "After this promise made by Christ, this infant must also faithfully promise for his part, until he come of age to take it upon himself, that he will renounce the Devil and all his works, and constantly believe God's holy word and obediently keep His Commandments."

We hear this very often, as often as we are present at a child's christening. I wish we as often reflected on the very serious and awful account which these words give us of our own condition. They tell us that we are every one under a Covenant with God, bound to Him by a promise and vow. You see in the Psalm, God accounts this as the very mark of His own people, His Saints. For the word Saints does not always mean really good and holy persons, but sometimes it only means those who especially belong to God. People are not seldom called Saints in Scripture, whether they be good or bad, if God have called them to be His own in any special way, apart from the rest of the world. So here, He makes proclamation, "Gather My saints together unto Me," and in the next words He explains whom He means to call saints, those namely who have made a Covenant with Him with sacrifice: not those only who have kept their covenant, but also those who have at all made it: bad Christians as well as good ones. For all Christians, good and bad, are alike in this, that they are under covenant with God; and also in having that covenant sealed by sacrifice. We make the covenant, the engagement, here at the Font; and having once made it, we never can at all unmake it: we never can be, as if it had not been made. We may go on sinning, until we wish it to be so: we may wish that we were not at all in covenant with God: but it is a wish which cannot be granted. As the prophet Ezekiel said to the Israelites (in the first lesson this very morning), "that which cometh into your minds shall not be at all, that ye will be like the heathen, the families of the countries, to serve wood and stone:" so it is with us. We are baptized, and do what we will, be as wicked as ever we may, we cannot unbaptize ourselves. We may turn our Baptism into a curse, but we cannot get rid of it altogether. We cannot be, as if we had never made any promise and vow to God. His mark is set upon our foreheads, and although, by wilful sin unrepented of, we wear out all its beauty and glory, all its saving grace and virtue, we cannot altogether wear out the Mark itself. It will be there, to be our worst condemnation, if it is not there to save us.

Thus you see, that we are, once and for ever, in

covenant with God, we cannot be like the heathen and unbaptized who never heard of Him: and consider also what the Psalmist tells us, that this covenant was made with sacrifice. It was signed and sealed with the Precious Blood of the Son of God, God and Man. In fulfilment of God's mysterious Will, He in due time offered Himself up a Sacrifice and Sin-offering for us. He offers to His Father continually the same Sacrifice on our behalf; and we, on earth, offer and present the perpetual memory of it in Holy Communion. He sealed His gifts and promises with His Own Blood poured out on the Cross, and we seal our offerings and promises with the same Blood poured out and received in Holy Communion. Thus you see how our Covenant is with Sacrifice.

It will be all the plainer perhaps, if we recollect what we are told of God's covenant with His ancient people the Jews, which was so ordered as to be throughout a type and figure of this covenant of ours. The Israelites, we know, made a covenant with God, and He made a covenant with them in Mount Sinai. He agreed to be their God, and they agreed to keep all His commandments. And this covenant was made with sacrifice; for, when Moses had written it in a book, he took the blood of rams and goats which he had sacrificed to God and sprinkled it both on the book and on all the people, saying, "This is the blood of the covenant which God has enjoined you." Thus the first covenant was made with sacrifice, and sealed with blood as the second Covenant is: only *that* was the blood of bulls and goats, *this* is the Precious Blood of Christ, Who, as a Lamb without spot or blemish, offered Himself without spot to God.

And thus we, as well as the Jews, indeed far more truly and really than they, may be said to have made a Covenant with God by Sacrifice.

Now here are two thoughts, two certain and undoubted truths, which we ought surely to have ever before our minds: the one, that we have made a Covenant with the Most High, the Almighty Everlasting God, the other that we made it with Sacrifice. It was sealed by the Blood of Christ Crucified.

We are all of us in covenant with God, you, I, every one of us. It is not as if He had made a general rule, and then left us to ourselves; for He *has* made His agreement with each of us, one by one. You know what kind of difference it makes in the Priest's way of speaking to you and telling you anything for your good, whether he only says it in Church to the whole congregation together, or takes an opportunity of mentioning it to each one of you privately at home. It may be God's Word just as much in the one case as in the other, but we naturally feel it as brought more home to us in particular, when it is addressed to us ourselves privately. It is so much the surer proof of God's kind and watchful care of us. Not exactly like this, but something like it, is the difference between our case as it is now, and as it would have been, had God made no Covenant with each one of us separately. Our duty and our Blessing is brought more home to ourselves, we are the more utterly without excuse, if we give ourselves up and forget God. For instance, take any person who is most poor and miserable, most forlorn and neglected among Christians. Suppose his friends all dead or departed, no one in the world, that he knows of, to take care of him; let him be all ragged and hungry, and without any certain prospect of maintenance even for a single day: yet if he knows and believes and will earnestly remember that he is in covenant with God and God with him, surely he will look up and lift up his head, and he may say to himself, "Jesus Christ Who is the Truth has taken me up once for all in His Arms, He has promised to be my God; I am sure He will not forget me, nor let me drop; for not even a sparrow which is worth but half a farthing, is ever permitted to fall on the ground without His and His Father's leave." And so it has been always; as saith the wise Son of Sirach, "Look at the generations of old, and see; did ever any trust in the Lord and was confounded? or did any abide in His fear and was forsaken? or whom did He ever despise that called upon Him?" Therefore be of good cheer, O thou afflicted and poor Christian. If such were God's promises even before the Gospel, be sure that under the Gospel they are far more bountiful. Never for a moment allow yourself to think, that our Lord has ceased to be your Father, and to care for you, though the times be never so hard, and your pains of body and mind never so grievous. Complaining thoughts, I dare say, will come into your mind; but never do you let them stay there. Put them away by the remembrance of your Baptism, of the Holy Covenant then and there made. Say in your heart over and over, "My flesh and my heart faileth;" I have nothing at all of mine own, whether within or without, to lean upon: "but God is the strength of my heart and my portion for ever." Do you think there is any forlorn beggar, any person incurably sick, any one outcast or forsaken of those who ought to be kindest to him, any sufferer at all among men, who might not find comfort in such thoughts as these, if he really and steadily tried to have them in his heart, as often as ever the distress and anguish came on him? But the misfortune is, that we do not steadily and regularly try this: such thoughts, it may be, come sweet to us now and then, and seem to do us good for a little while; but we do not endeavour and pray to have them *always* at hand for our relief. We suffer our poor frail hearts to be carried away by earthly things far more entirely than they need be: we willingly forget God for a long time together: too often alas! we do things which we know will vex and grieve Him; and then, when the trouble is again strong upon us, and we try in some measure to go back to our Baptism for comfort, it seems as if the good thought would not come, or as if, though it came, it did us no good. This is most sad: but the remedy for it is plain, and by God's great Mercy it is in our own power. We must use ourselves to think of our Baptismal promises, not now and then, but regularly and always. We may pray and try for this: and if we go on doing so, and fighting in earnest against all known sin, the good thoughts will by degrees come oftener, and stay longer, and give us more help.

It is much the same in our fighting against sin. As the covenant of our God, truly remembered, would be our greatest comfort in trouble, so would it be also our greatest help in temptation. Joseph, when the wicked woman would have led him astray, repulsed her with this plain and earnest saying, "How can I do this great wickedness and sin against God?" So may we fellow sinners and fellow Christians, as often as we are tempted. We may say to the lawless and unclean Spirit which would cause us to look where we ought not, or to take any other improper liberties, "How can I do this great wickedness and sin against God, Whose I am and Whom I serve? I am not my own; I am bought with a price; I am to glorify God both in my body and spirit." So to the devil that would tempt us to indulge anger we may say: "All my strength, courage, and spirit is made over in a manner to my God: I must not waste any of it upon those provoking persons and their ill behaviour. To Him I belong, and Him I am to serve: therefore for His sake I will keep my temper; I will not let others' ill behaviour hinder me from serving Him with a quiet mind." Thus you see how that, if we would constantly remember our being in covenant with God Almighty, it would furnish us with direct helps against two of the worst sins, anger and unchastity: and it is just the same with all other wicked ways. The covenant of Baptism, well and dutifully remembered, will sufficiently set us at liberty from them all.

Particularly if we remember always that we are not only in covenant with God, but also that our covenant was made with Sacrifice. Christ laid down His life to purchase us. He bought us by His Own Blood that He might set us free. When we read or hear His Commandments, " Thou shalt not take My Name in vain, Thou shalt not kill, Thou shalt not commit adultery," and the like, we may set ourselves earnestly to consider what we are bound to, and how awefully. These commandments are to us written, as it were, with the Blood of the Precious Lamb without spot: if we wilfully break them, we scorn and make void His Blood. Oh! then let us hesitate no more: let us shew to the tempter, when he next assaults us, the Commandments of God written on our hearts, written in the Blood of His Son our only Saviour: when the Evil one sees God's Word so written in the hearts of His People, he will go away dismayed: and the words of the Psalm will be fulfilled in us: "God will arise, His Light will arise, and shine over us, and His enemies will be scattered and they also that hate Him will flee before Him." O how happy is that Christian, who has so regularly used himself to obey the Voice of God's Spirit reminding him of his Baptismal Covenant, that every new temptation is a new Victory: he is the better and the happier for every thing that the devil does to make him wicked and miserable. This blessedness shall be yours, my brethren; it is promised even to the simplest and meanest among us, if we will but look back, as we go on in life, on the Covenant of our first beginning: if we will rightly and dutifully call to mind, that we stand before God, bound by a promise which can never wear out, "To renounce the devil and all his works, constantly to believe God's Holy Word, and obediently to keep His Commandments." This is our three-fold Covenant, the triple cord of our Baptism, our Catechism our Confirmation: most of us know it well, so far as repeating it goes: most of us account themselves bound to pay to it some regard, more or less, but observe, I pray you, what kind of regard we promise, even in the very letter of what we say. We promise to "renounce the devil and *all* his works:" not *some*, not the *most*, not the *worst* of his works: but *all*. We are "constantly to believe His holy Word:" not at times only, as in sickness, in leisure or in devotion, but *always;* giving up our fancies at once when He teaches us better: our favourite fancies as well as any others. Lastly, we are *obediently* to keep His Commandments, i. e. as I suppose, in the *temper* and *spirit* of obedience, doing things with joy and delight because He bids them, this is our Covenant and vow, one and all of us. How are we keeping it? May God give us grace to ask ourselves this question seriously this night and every night before we lie down to rest: that we may not have to ask it of ourselves with seared hearts and bewildered minds when we shall be taken for death, and the time for keeping our vow will have passed by for ever.

SERMON XVI.

2 Cor. vi. 14.

"What communion hath Light with darkness?"

SINCE it has pleased Almighty God to give us His unspeakable Blessings, freely indeed, for we never could deserve them at His Hands, yet by way of an agreement, signed and sealed, the Baptismal Service goes on next to declare the terms of that agreement: as if one who knew should read over to another the terms of any lease or covenant before he had to sign it. And whereas in earthly covenants it happens sometimes, that people set their names in a hurry to what they do not well understand, here in God's agreement with us, what we are to do is so plainly expressed, that no one can fail to understand and know it, when once plainly set before him. It consists of three parts, as every child knows; for it is taught near the beginning of the Catechism. The first condition of the Covenant is, that we renounce the Devil and all his works, the pomps and vanities of the wicked world, and all the sinful lusts of the flesh: the second is, that we believe all the Articles of the Christian Faith: the third, that we keep God's Holy Will and Commandments, and walk in the same all the days of our Life. Or, to put it in a shorter form, first we are to renounce what God hates, secondly to believe what God teaches, and thirdly to do what God commands. For since Baptism makes us members or parts of Christ, living by a life from Him, of course we must have the will and mind of Christ. The members must agree with the Head, and not go contrary to it. Therefore we must love what Christ loves, and hate what He hates. And because we are naturally in a bad way, in a way to do the very contrary of this, to love what Christ hates, and to hate what He loves: therefore the renouncing part is the *first part* of our three-fold vow. We are as people who have their faces turned away from the Light, and looking towards darkness: if we would come to the Light, the first thing is to turn our backs on the darkness. For what communion hath Light with darkness? The two are contrary, the one to the other, and we cannot look towards both at once. God is our Light, and all that is against God, all that God hates, is utter darkness. If we would come to God in Holy Baptism, we must first of all turn away, in the purpose of our mind and heart, from all that God hates.

For this reason, there being, as you know, three engagements, which the priest requires the child to make by his sureties, the first is as follows: "Dost thou, in the name of this child, renounce the devil and all his works, the vain pomp and glory of the world, with all covetous desires of the same, and the carnal desires of the flesh, so that thou wilt not follow, nor be led by them?" And we read in old books, that in very ancient times this renunciation was made, not in words only, but in action also, at the Baptism of every grown person. He stood with his face towards the West; because that is the region of darkness; looking Satan as it were in the face: and then, while he repeated the words, "I renounce Satan and his works and his pomps and his service," he was bidden to stretch out his hand, as though he were putting something very disagreeable away from him: whereby all that saw might understand that he was pledging himself to have no more to do with Satan, his pomps and his works.

And this shaking of the hand at the enemy and ordering him, as it were, away, with some other expression of abhorrence, was ordered to be done three times, perhaps because of the three enemies, which we renounce. For we have three enemies, as you know, the devil, the world and the flesh, all banded together for our ruin. First, there is the devil, the malicious and subtle spirit who has hated man from the beginning, because God loved him; and is never far off, never off the watch for occasions of hurting us; as the Psalmist, you know, describes him. "He sitteth lurking in the thievish corners of the streets, and privily in his lurking-dens doth he murder the innocent; his eyes are set against the poor. For he lieth waiting secretly; even as a lion, lurketh he in his den, that he may ravish the poor." This enemy is without us, just the same as any wicked person among men desiring our harm: only he is so much the more dangerous and dreadful, as he is out of sight. We never can tell at any time how near he is to us, or what encouragement we give him by the slightest word look or gesture of known sin. We know that, when he is near us, he is very sharp-sighted and watchful: nothing escapes him: he never lets the moment pass for putting what he knows will most tempt us full in our way. He contrives so to bring the wicked world before us, as that it shall most effectually tempt our frail and corrupt hearts. Still he can do us no harm, except by our own fault. His only way of really hurting is by making men sin: and he cannot make them sin against their will. Therefore we may be bold to defy him. Holy Scripture encourages us to be so: as David with his sling and his stone was bold to defy Goliath with his full armour. "Resist the devil," it says, "and he will flee from you." Say to him in the Name of Jesus, " get thee behind me, Satan:" and he will by and by depart. This is in effect said to the Evil one at every Baptism; and though it is but a little child who says it, and he is a great and strong and wise spirit, an Archangel, though a fallen one, yet he trembles and departs when it is said to him, and the saying is sealed with Holy Baptism: he is forced to let that little child go, having no power at all against it, until it shall have grown older and shall have given him power by wilful sin.

But we renounce not the devil only, but likewise all his works, that is to say, all sin; for all sin in man is originally the devil's work, as we know by the account of the Fall. However, those sins more especially are reckoned works of the devil, which are practised, as Scripture teaches, by the devil himself: not what are called carnal sins, for he, being a spirit and having no body, cannot be guilty of such. For example, he cannot be a glutton or a drunkard, but he can and doth abound in spiritual sins, such as Pride, Envy,

Malice, Aversion to God: he was a murderer from the beginning: he is also a Liar and the father of it. Thus, then, in renouncing his works, we put away from us all pride of heart, all setting-up of ourselves against our God: we draw back also from the thought of envy, or of grudging our brother any good thing which God has given him: for this was that very sin of Satan which caused Adam's fall and all our misery. He could not bear to see our first parents so happy as they were in Paradise, and so he contrived how to tempt them and get them turned out; and in doing this he told most fearful lies, saythat sin would not bring death: so that whenever men lie, whenever they indulge envy or malice, they are but rehearsing over again the great sin of our great enemy. Remember this, when you are next tempted: especially when you are tempted to tell a lie: and say to yourself, "It is the devil's work: I have renounced it and can have nothing to do with it."

Next, we renounced "the vain pomp and glory of the world with all covetous desires of the same:" i. e. all things around us, so far as they draw off our heart from Heaven, and make us to be in love with this present world: such as money, or things that are money's worth, beauty, dress and fine clothes: skill and strength in bodily labour: the praise and honour and good opinion of men: satisfaction in being admired, and in feeling that we ought to be. All these things are "the world;" they are "pomps," when the world sets them before us in any remarkably subtle and enticing way; as when Balak tempted Balaam with the promise of promoting him to great honour: and they are "vanities," because they are vain, and have no soundness in them : they are sure, before long, to pass away as in a dream. Whatever they are, and on what side soever they tempt us, we have renounced and must renounce them : we must not, for money nor for beauty nor for pleasure nor praise nor amusement, go near any of the things or places which we know to be hateful to God. For these things, vain as they are, have a wonderful power to attract and dazzle our poor frail spirits. Gold and silver, jewels and embroidery, take a great hold upon some minds: praise and honour, and seeming to be of consequence, upon others : it is not easy to turn away from them undazzled, and to make up our minds to do without anything of the kind ; especially since the malicious Adversary is ever putting things in our way, shewing to us, as he did to our Lord, the most tempting objects in the most seducing way, and causing us, even if we can *do* nothing, to sin in covetously desiring such things.

And even if we had no world without us, no evil spirit to put the bad world in our way, there is an enemy in the very fortress, a Serpent lurking in our own bosoms: "the carnal desires of the flesh," which are therefore mentioned to be renounced in the last place. To see how these desires are distinct both from the world and from the devil, consider the first sin, that of Adam. There was the devil, standing beside the Tree, pointing to it, and saying the false words. That was one enemy. There was the Tree itself with its forbidden fruit within a near distance of Adam. That was as " the world," a second enemy ; and both these were without the man. But there was also the frail and evil desire within his own heart, whereby he consented to the wickedness suggested to him : that was the third enemy, "the lust of the flesh:" and so this last, having conceived, brought forth sin, when Adam ate of the fruit.

If then the mischief wrought in us by that first sin is to be cured, we must renounce all three: as we do renounce them in our Baptism. We must neither listen to the unseen Tempter, nor look greedily at the outward and visible world, nor indulge the evil craving within our own heart. So we have promised. God grant we may be keeping our promise! If not, we know the consequence.

But there is another thing which we had need observe very particularly in this first parcel of our Baptismal vow. We promise concerning these our three enemies, and especially concerning the sinful lusts of the flesh, to " renounce them, so that we will neither follow nor be led by them." To be led away by temptation, in either of these kinds, is bad enough; to follow after temptation is much worse. It is not so very hard to perceive the difference. David was "led away" by temptation coming in his way, when from the roof of his palace he beheld his neighbour Uriah's wife, and all that sad and mournful history followed. That was being "led by the carnal desires of the flesh." *That* was bad enough, so bad that all his life after was spent in the deepest penitence; but it would have been still worse, had he gone up to the housetop, foreseeing the mischief, on purpose to put himself in the way of it: which kind of thing, following after enticement and seeking to be tempted to sin, is alas! but too common even among Christian people, though they have all so expressly renounced it. However David in this instance, as it appears, was *led* by the sin, he did not *follow* after it; but it came in his way, and he was too frail to resist it. The Prophet Balaam, on the contrary, seems to be an instance of one who wished to be tempted, who, as it were, went out of his way to get near temptation, i. e. in the words of our Baptismal Service, he *followed* after evil desires. His covetousness was so strong on him, that, although God had forbidden him most plainly to go to Balak and curse the people, yet, when the messengers came to ask him, he would not send them away at once: he said, "lodge here this night, and I will see if God will permit me to go with you:" that is, he would not send the temptation away, he kept it as near him as he dared, he sought somehow to persuade himself, that, if he sinned in strong temptation, God would be merciful to him and forbear to punish: and so he went on following his covetous fancy, making his own temptation strong, and came at last to that miserable end.

Do you seek a plain example of what I mean, on the difference of "following" and being "led by" sinful lust? Suppose then—a common case, alas! that there are two persons in the same parish or family, alike in this respect, that both are apt to sin in the matter of strong drink: but suppose also this difference between them, that the one has to pass the public-house every day, going and returning from his work: the other we will suppose to have his home quite in another direction: so that he, if he go to the alehouse, sins more wilfully, he follows after the temptation; the first does but permit himself to be led. Do you not see that the one of these is at the beginning *so far* worse than the other? But if the other use himself to give way, he will soon be just as bad as the first: he will be contriving excuses to put himself in the way of mischief. It is just the same with regard to all other sins. The course of them commonly is, that, men being overcome by surprise and strong temptation in the first instance, the false and miserable sweetness of the sin haunts them afterwards, corrupting their minds, and if they have not a real fear of God, and sense of His presence, this will tempt them to sin again; they will be rather glad to have the sin come in their way: and when they have sinned a second or third time, they will even follow after the temptation, and try to make themselves opportunities of sinning: each time, perhaps, saying to themselves, "only this once," but alas! it comes over and over, until by degrees they are past feeling and give themselves over to their sin, committing it with greediness. O fearful, but too true history of thousands of redeemed and regenerated souls! And there is no security, no recovery from it, without our earnestly and constantly remembering this our solemn and sacred vow, "neither to follow nor be led" by such things. Especially let young people, who are as yet happily ignorant of many sins, draw back from seeking even to *know* any thing about them, except so far as they are warned against them in Holy Scripture and by such as have care over them. To look after sin, except just so far as is useful in order to avoid it, is in some measure "following after" it—tempting ourselves: and we shall be so much the more easily "led by" it. Therefore "stand not in the way of sinners:" say not, "*How* do such and such transgressors go on? I will just look on and see:" nay, my brother, but rather give ear to our Lord's warning; "Turn away your eyes lest you behold vanity:" let not the evil way, if possible, be "once named among you;" be not ashamed to be entirely ignorant of it; much less dwell upon it in your thoughts: for why should you go out of your way to corrupt your new-born soul, and put such a stain upon your white baptismal robe, as will either make your life anxious by a sad and careful repentance, or what is infinitely worse, being found on you at the Last Day, will cause you to be cast into the outer darkness?

SERMON XVII.

Acts viii. 36, 37.

" The Eunuch said, see here is water; what doth hinder me to be baptized? and Philip said, If thou believest with all thine heart, thou mayest."

THE first part of your baptismal vow or Covenant is, we saw last Sunday, to renounce what God hates; because we cannot be His own, His servants and children, as long as we are in league with His enemy. Therefore we turn at first as it were towards the West, the land of darkness, and say to Satan, the prince of darkness, " get thee from me, with all that take thy part, whether they are openly in the world around us, or inwardly in our own wicked hearts." And then we go on in a manner to turn the directly contrary way towards the East, the region of light, the side on which the Day-Spring from on high hath visited us. Whether we do so with our bodies or no, we assuredly turn towards the East with our souls, when we make answer about believing. We make it of course, i. e. the godfathers and godmothers make it, in the child's name; as the promise before was made. Before, it was said, "Dost thou in the name of this child, renounce the devil and all his works; now it is said, "Dost thou believe in God" and the rest. You see plainly that we are still to understand it, as it was before expressed. The Faith is accepted in the child's name, as the world, the flesh, and the devil had been renounced in his name. And he is bound to it; the child from that moment is bound to be a sincere, constant, complete believer, in things whereof for the present it seems as though he could not know anything. He is bound to believe what God teaches; all of it; all the days of his life; and that, most seriously. You heard the engagement just now; you heard when the Priest asked the sponsors,

"Dost thou believe in God the Father Almighty, Maker of heaven and earth?

"And in Jesus Christ his only-begotten Son our Lord? And that he was conceived by the Holy Ghost; born of the Virgin Mary; that he suffered under Pontius Pilate, was crucified, dead, and buried; that he went down into hell, and also did rise again the third day; that he ascended into heaven, and sitteth at the right hand of God the Father Almighty; and from thence shall come again at the end of the world, to judge the quick and the dead?

"And dost thou believe in the Holy Ghost; the holy Catholic Church; the Communion of Saints; the Remission of sins; the Resurrection of the flesh; and everlasting life after death?" And you heard the Sponsors make answer, "all this I stedfastly believe." There were three of them at least, and yet they said, *I*, not *we*. Why was that? Because they were speaking altogether in the child's name. They were speaking, not for themselves, but for that little one.

And though that little one cannot as yet have any understanding of what they said, yet he is bound by it and will be so all his life long. That you know very well. You know that he will be called to a strict account, as to how he has kept that engagement. He cannot be as if he had never been so near God. You feel and are sure of it concerning that little child, concerning each child that is brought here to be baptized. Can you help reflecting, that you are no less sure of it as concerns your own self also? For over each one of us also, when we were first brought to Church, were the same holy words rehearsed. *We* too, in our sureties, had the same question put to us concerning the Creed, "Dost thou believe" &c. and we, by the same sureties, made answer and said, "All this I stedfastly believe." We are in covenant then to believe all this, and if we do not really believe it, we have broken the covenant; and what will become of us, if we die in that condition?

Wherefore the very least we can do, in order not to slight this covenant, is to consider it very often over, and see how far we are going on stedfastly in it. The covenant binds us, you see, to believe something. What is believing? We all have a notion that we believe; we should all be angry to have it made out that we were unbelievers. But can all of us be truly and really said to believe? Nay, consider, as I said, What is believing? It is receiving something, which God Almighty tells us or teaches us, not in our eyes or ears only, but in our minds; and not in our minds only, but in our hearts. I will try and shew you what I mean. There are little boys and girls here, aye and grown people too, who can say the Belief, every word of it, who could read it quite exactly out of a book, and would do so presently, if you asked them; and yet they cannot well be said to *believe*, because, with or without their own fault, they know not the meaning of what they speak; they only say it over, like parrots; they are too young or too dull to attend, or they will not take the trouble to do so. Now of these it may be said, they believe with their eyes ears and tongues, but they do not believe with their minds, much less with their hearts. Others again do believe with their minds, i. e. they not only say or mark the words of the Creed, but they really attend to its meaning, and being perhaps quick of understanding, they see how it all comes out of the Bible. So far as it is a lesson to be read, thought over, and answered about, they have learnt it well; they receive it with their minds and understandings. But is this Christian believing? is this true Faith? No; for they do not yet receive it with their hearts. What is receiving it with their hearts? You will know this better, if we stop for a moment to consider what sort of things we, as Christians, are to believe, and why it is so needful we should believe. They are the great things out of sight; What and Who God is, and the wonderful course of His doings towards us sinful children of men. And it is quite necessary we should know and receive them, in order to overcome our enemies, which are also the enemies of God. Those enemies we have just renounced; we have promised to have nothing to do with them, to be altogether on God's side; knowing that to be against God is certain ruin. But they are not easy to renounce; they are all three close at hand, and one of them, the flesh, is even within us, we carry it about with us wherever we go; our three enemies are close at hand; the false goods wherewith they would tempt us are full in our sight, and seem often within our reach, and we are naturally very weak and frail. Therefore the gracious Lover of our souls, earnestly desiring that we may never perish, has provided us, in His holy Book and in the Creeds which are taken out of it, with the knowledge of a world out of sight, and of wonders unspeakable wrought for us in that world, on which we may set our hearts, and carrying the remembrance of them everywhere about with us, may be able to overcome God's enemies, near and powerful as they are, and to keep the Commandments, though contrary to flesh and blood. Thus, Faith comes second in our baptismal vow; for it is receiving God, and the things which God hath done, into our hearts, clinging to the thought of them, having them ever before us, and by their mighty presence and power driving away the devil, overcoming the world and the flesh, and really keeping the Commandments both in will and deed. Believing what God teaches is the only way to have power and will to renounce what He hates and to do what He commands.

Observe, it is said, *constantly* believe and *stedfastly*, "All this I *stedfastly believe.*" Our faith must not come and go, according as the fancy takes us, now *in* the heart and now out of it; but it must stay and abide with us day and night. This is meant when it is said, "Do all in the Name of the Lord Jesus," and "whether ye eat or drink or whatsoever ye do, do all to the glory of God." Since we cannot for one moment be safe without our Lord's blessed Presence, since the world the flesh and the devil are always at hand to do us harm, therefore we had need have Christ dwelling in our hearts by faith, like a shield ready to turn every way, to quench all the fiery darts of the wicked. Therefore God's Saints and those who have learned of them have been used to begin every serious work in the Name of the Father, the Son and the Holy Ghost; in that Name to rise up from their beds, in that Name to kneel down to their Prayers, in that Name to make all solemn gifts and engagements; as a token that, wherever they go, they carry with them by Faith that Holy Trinity into which they were baptized, as a shield against all enemies, visible and invisible. They do not only believe while they are saying the Creed or thinking it over, but at all times, whatever they are about. When temptation comes, it finds them believing that Christ will judge the quick and the dead; and that faith enables them to resist it. When pride or malice would find room in their souls, there is none; for their souls are filled with faith in God made Man, and crucified for His enemies. When a thought would come over them, I am so very weak and frail; surely I shall be forgiven if I do for once give way to this strong temptation; Faith says to them in the depth of their conscience, "you believe in God the Holy Ghost, you know that He dwells in you; greater is He that is in you than he that is in the world;" and so they put away the bad thought. This is constant and stedfast Faith, the Faith whereby good Christians shall be finally justified, the Faith by which people *walk* on the way towards Heaven, and do not only *gaze* on it, and *wish* they were in it. And it is of this faith, I suppose, that so great things are spoken in Holy

Scripture. The faith of the heart, not of the mind, much less of the tongue only, is what we promised in Baptism.

As for example; when St. Philip the Deacon met that Eunuch on the road, as he was sitting in his chariot, and reading the fiftythird chapter of Isaiah, and when the Saint, beginning at that Scripture, had preached unto him Jesus, and, on their coming to some water, the Eunuch said, "What doth hinder me to be baptized?" St. Philip's answer was, "If thou believest with all thine heart, thou mayest." He was not simply to believe, but to believe with all his heart. When St. Paul on his conversion was invited to "arise and be baptized, and wash away his sins, calling on the Name of the Lord," it was that he not only believed in Christ, but so believed in Him, as to cry out heartily, "Lord, what wilt Thou have me to do?" When the prison doors at Philippi flew open at midnight, God having sent a great earthquake to deliver His servants Paul and Silas, and the keeper of the prison, moved to repentance, fell down before the two Saints, and asked, "Sirs, what must I do to be saved?" St. Paul's answer was, Believe; "Believe on the Lord Jesus Christ, and thou shalt be saved." Did St. Paul mean that the jailor should merely agree in his mind to the Gospel which he was preaching; that he should say as so many do, "yes, it is all very true, very good," and should go on in other respects as he was before? Did he mean that the heathen jailor, continuing in his heathenism or in any other known sin, might and would be saved, only for a strong feeling which he had, that Christ died to save him, and that He was very good and merciful to do so? Nay, my brethren, we all know better than *that*. We know that when the Apostle said, "Believe on the Lord Jesus Christ," he was requiring of the jailor far more than any such inward conviction and feeling. He was requiring of him that he should give up all, change his way of life altogether, turn his mind day and night towards the great, pure, unseen wonders which the Creed of the Apostles would teach him, and live altogether as one believing in them all. This was the Apostle's meaning when he said, "Believe on the Lord Jesus Christ, and thou shalt be saved." This was also our Lord's own meaning, in those most heavenly and comfortable words, the very Gospel of man's salvation, " God so loved the world, that He gave His only begotten Son, to the end that whosoever believeth in Him, should not perish, but have everlasting life." " Whosoever believeth in Him;" not with any kind of belief, but with constant, steady, hearty, practical belief. That man shall not perish. For he shall conquer the enemies of his soul: he has *that* within him, whereby he shall overcome the world. So believing in Jesus Christ, we shall not pray to Him in vain. He will give us more and more of His Spirit, which will help us to please and obey Him. Thus, believing the Articles of the Christian Faith, which is the second part of our baptismal vow, is the only safe way for us to keep the first, and the third. We must believe rightly; otherwise we shall neither renounce, nor obey quite rightly. The temptations will be too strong for us, and the commandments too hard.

But, this constant, enduring, ever-present faith, which of us, my brethren, has it as he ought to have? It is too true, that many of us permit themselves to be so taken up with the labours, cares, follies, of this short and miserable world, that they hardly think, from week's end to week's end, (even if they do it regularly then) of such high matters as the Creed sets before them. But if they think not of it, how can it help them in temptation? If you go out to your work in the morning without a thought of Jesus Christ Crucified, if you lie down at night without any apprehension of sleeping in death, and of waking afterwards to stand before His Judgment Seat; how can you depend upon His being with you to guard you? What can you expect, but that the Evil one should have power over you, sleeping and waking? Wherefore, I beseech you, beloved brethren, as you have learned your Creed, *use* it. Use it (I know very many of you do so) as a part of your daily devotions; only beware of merely saying the words over. Whilst you speak them, believe them in your heart, and treasure them up against the hour of temptation. The Baptismal Creed, thus put into practice, will by the help of God prove the best help to preserve Baptismal grace; heavenly things will be more and more to you, and earthly things less and less; believing, you will keep the Commandments, and then, whatever happens, you may go on your way rejoicing in Christ.

SERMON XVIII.

St. Luke xiv. 23.

" Compel them to come in."

You will remember, many of you, that these words are part of a prophetic parable of our Saviour's, in which, under the similitude of a great supper, He told His disciples how they might expect men to behave, when His Kingdom the Church should be set up, and all should be invited into it. When those who were first called, the Jews, had made their undutiful excuses, and were rejected, the servants were to gather in, first the poor, maimed, halt and blind, out of the streets and lanes of the city, then those who were scattered in the highways and hedges, the lost and undone Gentiles, wherever they are. They were to be compelled to come in, to be urged and pressed and not let alone, to be constrained with a holy and loving violence, if haply they might be brought to take care of their own souls.

But besides all this, it has been truly said, there is another way of compelling persons to come in, i. e. of bringing them into the Church of Christ, by a sort of compulsion, without asking their leave. I mean, when little children are brought, as the manner is and always has been, to be made partakers of

Holy Baptism. Plainly they are brought to Christ without their own leave; they are, in a manner, compelled to come in. Now this is brought strongly before us in the part of the Baptismal Service to which we are now come. After the Priest has made enquiry about the Articles of the Christian Faith, and has had answer made him in the child's name, "All this I stedfastly believe," he is directed to ask, "Wilt thou be baptized in this Faith?" and answer is made for the child, "That is my desire:" and yet we cannot well think, that the child has any such desire, so as to feel it, in his little heart; it is answered for, and made a Christian, without any permission from itself; very often, as we know, in its sleep: and we need not doubt that all this is right, seeing that our Lord tells His Apostles, and through them all His ministers, not only, "Suffer the little children to come to Me," but "compel, force them to come in." They cannot give you leave in words, but you are to bring them, and answer for them, all the same for that.

And in this you do them no wrong, but the very greatest good you can do them. So that you may truly say in their name, "That is my desire," being so very certain as you are, that if they could know, they would desire it above all things. Just as if one had a humble petition to make to the Queen for any child who was too young to know the meaning of it, to have its property taken care of, or the like, one should present it in the name of the child, and call it that child's petition. Or, if an infant was crying at the door for hunger, though it were too young to understand its own wants, or at all to speak them out in words, yet we should not scruple to say, The child is longing and asking for bread. So here comes a little child to the door of the kingdom of heaven; it comes, partaking of the distress and weakness, spiritual and bodily, in which all children are born; rehearsal is made of those blessed and saving truths, which make up the Creed or Gospel or Faith of Jesus Christ; and the child being asked, "Wilt thou be baptized in this Faith?" well may we answer for it, that such is its desire; knowing as we do most assuredly, that this is the very thing which it wants, the only petition which being granted will do it real good.

For let us consider one by one, but very shortly, the articles of the Faith into which the child is to be baptized. Let us try and look at them with the eye of a parent who is just bringing his child to Baptism; a serious and faithful parent I mean; one who, in presenting his little one at the Font, does not only mean to go through a serious and proper form in a dutiful manner, but who really believes that Holy Baptism is to that child the one thing needful, because it is thereby put into the Arms of Jesus Christ. How will such a parent as that feel when he hears the Priest in our Lord's Name asking his child, if he believes in God the Father Almighty, and in the other articles of the Creed?

I should think that when he hears, first of all, of God the Father, he might very well say to himself, "Yes indeed, thankful may I well be, and I desire to thank God with all my heart, that He invites this my child to be His child; to have the great Almighty Father of all for his own Father by special adoption and grace. Poor child, if he knew his own condition, sinful and born of sinful parents, cast out of the great family for the sin of his first father, and with no chance, if left to himself, of not perishing eternally:—how earnestly would he join in the answer, 'That is my desire,' when asked if he wished to be baptized in the Faith of God the Father."

So again, when the priest goes on to make mention of Jesus Christ His only Son, our Lord, may not a parent well say in his heart, "how great, how aweful a blessing, that our little infant should be thus enlisted on the right side, on the Church's side, before he could believe or know anything." Our hearts sometimes burn within us, when we read of our Lord taking up the little children, embracing them in His Arms, laying His Hands upon them and blessing them, though He presently set them down and departed thence. But here, Christian Fathers and Mothers, here at the Holy Baptismal Font, your children are taken into Christ's Arms, not to be set down again, but to be embraced and blessed and lifted up by Him for ever. The parents know how the child very early begins to cling to them, what pain and tears it very often costs him to go to any one else. Well may they say for him, "That is my desire," when he is asked whether he will go to Christ, and abide with Him, Who is the very fountain of all fatherly and motherly love.

Next the Priest, reciting the Creed, goes on to speak of our Lord's Sufferings; how He suffered under Pontius Pilate, was crucified, dead, and buried; and when, having done so, he asks the child, "Wilt thou be baptized in this Faith?" in the Faith especially of Christ crucified;—what father or mother who believes will not in heart eagerly answer for their child, "That is my desire;" the very desire of my heart; of all things I long to be partaker of Christ crucified? And while you thus answer for your children, you will lift up your hearts in loving thankfulness to Him Who has vouchsafed to be their Saviour. You will imagine to yourselves what misery it would have been for you, the parents of these little ones, who feel as if your very souls were bound up in them, to know that they were doomed to eternal ruin, that they were lost, body and soul for ever. Why, when you hear of any dangerous and frightful disease, such as we have been lately delivered from, it is more than you can well bear to think, What if one's own dear children should be seized and taken away by it, first one and then another? And if this thought is so shocking, how would it be, were there no deliverance in eternity, nothing between them and everlasting death? Set your minds to it earnestly, my brethren; for surely it is quite true, that without Christ crucified these your treasures, so unspeakably dear to you, must have been lost for ever and ever. Well may they, and you for them, desire that they be baptized in the Faith of Him; for so they lay hold of the only Hand which may keep them from falling into the bottomless pit. And when you think of His sad Sufferings, and reflect that He bore it all willingly for the sake of these dear children of your's, surely your hearts cannot be so hard, but that, even on your children's behalf, you will love Him and try to please Him.

And this so much the more, if from His Cross you go on in thought to His Judgment. For so the Faith teaches you, into which your child is baptized; it says that "He shall come to judge the quick and the dead." We have heard it often, may be, in Baptisms as well as at other times, without its making much impression upon us. Yet assuredly it *is* a most solemn thing, to be thus reminded of the judgment to come, when we stand by the Font. It may be, the parties who are there assembled, child, sponsors, minister, attendants, may never meet again in this world; but there will be one day known to the Lord, in which they will assuredly meet. Then the mark, which is now to be set invisibly and mysteriously upon the infant, will be seen openly before men and angels, either to his exceeding glory, or to his incurable shame and torment. This moment of Baptism is a sure pledge and token of that moment of absolution or condemnation. *Now*, we are made God's own for the time; *then*, He will determine whether we shall be His or the prey of the Evil One for ever. O that Christians would so remember, so use, what is given them *now*, that it may be their joy and not their condemnation in that hour!

They may do so if they will. You may do so; you children may do so, every one who is baptized may do so. Do you not hear how the Priest, after the questions about the Father and the Son, saith to your children, "Dost thou believe in the Holy Ghost?" and then they desire to be baptized into the faith of the Holy Ghost, as well as into that of the Father and the Son. Thus their Baptism introduces them to a Comforter, as well as to a Father and a Saviour; and all Three alike Divine, One God in substance, power, and eternity. Thus the hearts of thoughtful parents may be comforted concerning their children, of whom otherwise they might almost despair. Knowing by sad experience the sore temptations which await them, they might be swallowed up with fear, lest their children, after all, should forfeit the mercy so dearly bought for them. But seeing that their little ones are baptized into the Faith of the Holy Ghost, they may take courage; for the Holy Ghost, they know is, Almighty; and where He is, there is liberty, and persons are free to keep God's commandments, and to save their own souls, be their enemies never so troublesome. Thus He, Whose Name is the Comforter, is so in this respect among others, that, in coming to young children at the Font, He comforts and assures the hearts of believing friends and Parents by the certainty, that the infant, come what may, will not be left to himself. He will not be left alone in the forlorn and dangerous world, to wrestle with the evil powers. His father and his mother may forsake him; death or other change may remove them; but the Lord hath taken him up. If ever the thought comes over parents' minds, (as I suppose it must now and then come,) What if we should be called away, and these children be left orphans? what greater relief could they have under such a sad thought, than in remembering how their children have been baptized into the faith of God the Holy Ghost, the Comforter; how He hath taken them under His especial guardianship; how He hath said to them, I will never leave thee nor forsake thee? Surely such a remembrance as this must be everything to a loving parent, when his spirit is vexed with the thought of having to leave his children unprovided for.

Then, my brethren, think of those comfortable truths, which follow the mention of the Holy Ghost in the Creed; the Holy Catholic Church, the Communion of Saints. Is it not a great thing to a parent, to be sure of a home for his child? Now the Holy Church of God is a sure Home to every Christian. Is it not a great thing to have kind, good, near and powerful friends, ready to help your children in need or trouble? Well, here are all the Saints of the Most High, in Paradise and in earth, made your child's friends at Baptism, and ready and willing to help him by their prayers to God. And, O my Brethren, which of us all, that unhappily knows what wilful sin is, how bitter, how noisome, yet how subtle and ensnaring, how hard every way to cure,—which of us, I say, who knows this, but would thank God with all his heart for making the Remission of sins, a part of his own and his children's Baptismal Creed? So that he may yet feel hope concerning those little ones, though in this miserable and naughty world they should be offended, and do things which would ruin their souls: he may hope and pray and labour that they may truly repent; and, truly repenting, he knows that they will be forgiven; for they were baptized into this Faith, of the Remission of sins.

Lastly, since in presenting your babes at the Font, you make them declare that they believe in the Resurrection of the Flesh, and everlasting life after death; ought it not to reprove you, and make you tremble, if your life and behaviour be such as to shew, in God's sight if not in man's, that you care little for such things, that you are wholly swallowed up in minding this body which you now have, and in the business and gain and amusement of this present life? Still, whatever your conduct be, you can scarcely be so blind, so irreligious, as not to believe in your heart that there will be a Resurection, a Judgment, an Eternity of Life or Death. Then you must needs be glad to have your children early brought to that faith; you will wish and pray that they at least may be better than yourself; and who knows but such wishes and prayers may come home to your own bosom, and our long-suffering God in His own good time may give you true repentance, as He has to so many others, shewing charity for His sake?

I have mentioned now the chief heads of the Baptismal Creed, that parents, going over it in their minds, might perceive how comfortable a thing it is to have their children brought early to the acknowledgement of it; and also for the parents' own sake, that they may be ashamed to have set so little store by these greatest of all truths. In conclusion, mark this. We are to be baptized *in this Faith*. We were so, all in our turns; that is, as holding this Faith, as professing it, and saying that, because we believe it, therefore we ask to be baptized. Again, we are baptized in this faith, as it is our state and condition, in which we hope to grow and improve, as we should in any bodily state and condition. Therefore, my Brethren, dearly beloved in the Lord, if we would not renounce our Baptism, and with it all our hope, we must hold fast this faith; we must cling to it; it must be very near and dear to us; we must sooner die than part with it, or any considerable portion of it. Come what will, we must never slight nor deny it.

We must live by it; live as believing it, and then it will be sure to stay with us. Then we shall die in the same holy faith; it will rise with us in the Last Day; it will save our souls; through Jesus Christ our Lord. Amen.

SERMON XIX.

Jeremiah vii. 23.

"*This thing I commanded thee, saying, Obey My Voice, and I will be your God, and ye shall be My people.*"

WE are now come to the last, and in some respects the most aweful portion of the covenant we made in our Baptism. When the person to be baptized has said, I desire to be baptized in this faith, the priest asks, "Wilt thou then obediently keep God's holy will and commandments?" As if he should say, "you cannot be baptized, unless you seriously engage yourself to be a true servant of God, doing His will from the heart, in all respects, as long as you live." Now, this is a great, a wide, and a deep promise, and I have known people before now, who were afraid to make it in the child's behalf; and when they were asked at the Font, have said instead of the two little words, "I will," "I will endeavour myself so to do, the Lord being my helper," or "That is my desire," or some other like form of words. I do not blame such persons, if they do so in a reverent spirit, not as finding fault with the words which the Church puts into their mouth, but simply as expressing their deep sense, how weak and unworthy we all are through sin. I do not blame them; I do not wonder that at first they inclined to shrink from the promise, considering how great a promise it is, and how sadly, alas, it is broken and profaned to their knowledge. For it reaches through the whole of life, childhood, youth, middle age, old age—and it extends to every part of duty, to God, to our neighbour, and to ourselves, binding us both to do what ought to be done, and to leave undone what ought not to be done. And they see and know how many persons, having made this vow, live in open neglect and defiance of it, and (what is still sadder) their own hearts and consciences tell them how many things they have done, and still perhaps are doing from time to time, very contrary to this Christian obedience. For these reasons, some good sort of people, naturally enough, shrink from this solemn promise; saying, they know not how the child may turn out, and how can they engage that he will be good? But they need not so draw back, any more than, if they were grown-up heathens, they would draw back on the same account from receiving Holy Baptism themselves. You know that, if you were born and bred among the Pagans and unbelievers, and Christ had mercifully called you to the true Faith, you could not come to Him without making this profession. By the act of entering into His service and family, you do in reality promise to obey Him, whether you make the promise in words or no. For what is the sense, or use, or goodness of calling yourself the servant of such and such a Master, if you do not mean that you will do as he bids you, or owning yourself the child of such and such a Father, if you do not intend to be dutiful to

Him? Therefore if you came to be baptized in your riper years, you would feel that you must not shrink from this engagement; you must intend, and, being called on by the Lord, you must promise to keep obediently God's holy will and commandments, and to walk in the same all the days of your life. And as you would promise it for yourself if you were grown up, so you need not fear to promise it for the child, who cannot speak for itself. The child is quite entirely bound by the promise, whether you make it for him in words or no, it is only speaking out a duty which would be put upon the child by the very act of Baptism (as indeed it is when a child is privately baptized) without a word being said about it.

If you ask the reason, why the child or person need not shrink from so large and serious an engagement, the reason is, the great help which is given in Baptism, and which is continued to every baptized person, until he has finally cast himself away. You know that I mean; the help of God's Holy Spirit. Suppose a child were asked, Will you engage yourself to be at such a place to-morrow? it being well known that the place was far too distant for the child to reach in the time by its own strength; still, if the child knew that he had a kind and strong father, on whom he might entirely depend, and who had promised to be with him, and carry him in his arms for the whole of the journey that he could not perform alone; there would be no presumption, nothing wrong, (would there?) in the child's promising and making the engagement. So it is with us in Holy Baptism. We have a great, a long, a dangerous journey before us, the journey from this sinful world to heaven. Of ourselves we have no strength to perform it; yet we are called upon to promise that we will perform it. Why are we not wrong in making that promise? Because our Father in heaven has promised, for Christ's sake, to be with us by His good Spirit, and to help us along every step of the way; we being members of Christ, and not breaking off from His holy comfort and guidance. That gracious offer of His makes all the difference. It is no longer presumption nor boasting, but plain faith and duty, for every the simplest Christian to say in his heart, "I can do all things through Christ which strengtheneth me;" without Him I can do nothing, but with Him all things are possible.

I say then, Let Christian people look their own condition boldly in the face. Let us all for once lay to heart this most serious, yet most certain truth, We *are*: Whether we will or no, we exist: we are in God's world, and we cannot resist His Will. We *are*; and in spite of what the Evil One may sometimes whisper to us, we very well know in our hearts, that we shall be for ever. What if a person, having the choice, were to refuse Baptism altogether, and to say, I had rather remain heathen and unregenerate; perhaps I shall have less to answer for? Would that do him any good? Would it save his soul, or abate his punishment? We cannot dream of such a thing; the imagination is too profane; although indeed, my Brethren, it is too fearfully like what many Christians say and do in respect of the other Holy Sacrament, that of the Body and Blood of Christ. They decline coming to God's Altar, in the thought, that perhaps they shall have less to answer for. I am sure they will find one day that they have made a great and inexcusable mistake: I only wish their conviction may come in good time. Yes indeed, I most sincerely wish that all my brethren and sisters who now hear me, and to whom God's Providence has in any way brought the knowledge of His holy Sacrament of Communion, would seriously consider in their hearts, that, having once heard of it, they cannot be as if He had never said anything to them about it. Put it fairly to your own consciences. Would it not be very wicked to refuse to offer your child to Baptism, in order that it might go on by and by with less guilt in sin and ungodliness? and is it not the same kind of profaneness to stay away from the Supper of the Lord, in order that you may yourself with less danger abide in wrong ways? Believe me, my friends, you cannot do so and be safe. You cannot put away from you the yoke and the burthen which your Creator has laid on your shoulders, the yoke and burthen of your duty to Him and to your neighbour. You may, by His grace, cause the yoke to become easy and the burthen light; but you cannot put it away from you. You cannot bury your talent, or hide it in a napkin, and hear no more of it; an account is sure to be demanded of you. You are fairly embarked on the great Ocean of Eternity; you cannot stop, you cannot draw back; on and on you must sail for ever and ever. A great prize is set before you, or a great and unspeakable loss: you have a soul to save or to lose, an immortal soul, and you cannot say, you had rather decline doing either: it is a hazard which *must* be run: your soul *must* be either saved or lost. Make up your mind to this at once, I beseech you. One choice or other must be made. If you say, you had rather not choose yet, this is in reality, for the time, choosing amiss, it is choosing Hell before Heaven. Hear what He says, Who cannot lie; He Who holds you in His Hand, both body and soul, and Who can do what He will with you; though He most mercifully wills only your good, He says, "Behold, I have set before you this day life and good and death and evil; therefore choose life." Choose you must, one or the other; you cannot avoid *that;* therefore choose life. Choose life, my brethren, and lose no time in choosing it; for why should you pour out the best of your cup on the ground, and offer the dregs only to your God and Saviour? Why should you of set purpose affront Him by giving Him only a few of your latter years, the years of which it is said, "There is no pleasure in them;" whereas He counted nothing too much for Him to give up to you? Why should you wantonly throw away so much of this life's sweetness and comfort? For, depend on it, all the days and years that we put off turning to God, are so much sweetness and comfort thrown away. O believe this, now while you have time. Wait not to learn it by bitter experience. Fear not to devote yourself at once. Now, without waiting any longer, turn towards the bright and glorious Light which freely and graciously offers to shine in your hearts. You ought to have done so, on the very first ray which you perceived; your not having done so is your great loss, and may be your loss for ever. The good Angels, we may well believe, did so at once. On the first moment of their creation, they turned themselves in adoring love towards Him Who made them, and began that glorious exercise in which they now go on, and will go on to all Eternity. They began at their first Creation, and since then they have never rested, day nor night, saying, "Holy, Holy, Holy, Lord God Almighty, which was and is, and is to come." Is not their's all perfect happiness? Is not the Lord infinitely gracious, Who allows your children, in their measure, the same happiness, by inviting them to meet Him at the Font at the beginning of their life? He invites them to turn to Him, He will not have them forbidden. You would think it cruel to keep them back, and you are right in thinking so. But how are you behaving to the same gracious goodness, no less freely offered to yourself? On you too that glorious Light has risen, and is even now waiting to shine into your heart, if you will let Him, if you will at once obediently give yourself up to the fulfilment of *all* His holy Commandments. How can you think you should lose anything by this? Is it not what the most affectionate parents have always most longed for in their children? Remember what Hannah did for Samuel, her only and dearly beloved Infant, when she was most earnestly bent on making him happy. She even parted with him herself, that he might appear before the Lord, and there abide for ever. Why should it be so very hard to get Christians to care for their own souls, as much as Hannah cared for Samuel?

If you say, "Samuel was a child, and so are those whom we see continually devoted to Christ in Holy Baptism; they had not other things prepossessing their hearts; but I am of such and such an age, and my heart is unhappily full of other things; how can *I* devote myself to God?" If you feel such a scruple as that, I own it is a sad thought, but not a thought to make you despond. Again I remind you, "with God all things are possible." Remember the Baptism of Saul, who was afterwards called Paul. Whose heart was ever more full of thoughts contrary to Christ than his? Yet when the Light of Christ shone upon him, he turned at once towards It, saying, "Lord, what wilt Thou have me to do?" And he never afterwards turned his back upon It; never again did he look towards the world, the flesh, and the devil. His vow helped him; and if you will, by the grace of God, your baptismal vow shall help you. When you are tempted, you will say in your heart, "I have opened my mouth to the Lord, and I cannot go back." So will hard duties become easy, pleasant sins will become hateful, and the Light towards which you have turned will shine on you more and more until the perfect Day.

SERMON XX.

COLOSSIANS ii. 13.

"Buried with Him in Baptism, wherein also ye are risen with Him."

WHEN the child by his sponsors has stood to his Baptismal Covenant, the Church, as you know, goes on to commend him to God in four very solemn prayers; as if a father, sending his child a journey, should first give him instructions what to do, then make him solemnly promise to do it, and lastly cause him to kneel down, and bless him very religiously before he set out. If that would be a comfort to the child undertaking the journey, so ought it to be a great comfort in our journey through life, whenever we call to mind these affectionate intercessions, which our loving Mother the Church offered up for us, before she put us in Christ's Arms to be baptized, and so to take the first step (and the greatest but one i. e. death) in our spiritual journey. There were four intercessions which she then offered up for us; and three of them, following Holy Scripture, represent our Christian condition by a sort of parables. The first is, "O merciful God, grant that the old Adam in this child may be so buried, that the New Man may be raised up in him." This likens Baptism, as you see, to death and resurrection. The second is, "Grant that all carnal affections may die in him, and that all things belonging to the Spirit may live and grow in him." This likens the soul of a Christian to a garden, in which are some foul weeds, carnal affections, which we pray may die; others, good plants, things of the Spirit, which we pray may live and grow. The third prayer is, "Grant that he may have power and strength to have victory, and to triumph, against the devil, the world, and the flesh." This collect has also its parable, and it is very plain what it is. It likens our Christian life to a warfare against the three enemies of our souls; as after Baptism, when we are signed with the Cross, it is said to be in token of our fighting under Christ's banner against sin, the world, and the devil, and of our continuing to our life's end His faithful soldiers. Thus then each of the three prayers which are offered up for the child, immediately after the covenant and before the Christening, refers us to something which we well understand, in order that our duty, when we come to know it, may sink the more thoroughly into our minds, and be more easily recollected on all occasions. The fourth prayer will be considered by itself another time.

The first of them, as I said, compares Baptism to death and burial. It asks that the old Adam in this child may be buried. You know what is meant by the old Adam; or, as St. Paul calls it, the old man. It is the old bad nature, which we brought with us into the world. The child who is going to be baptized, be his parents who they may, has, we are sure, his part in the old Adam. He is of his own nature corrupt like the rest, and inclined to evil, and if he be left to himself, will surely go farther and farther from God. This is as certain as that he is born of flesh and blood, and cometh of the seed of Adam and Eve.

Well, the Church's prayer is, that this old bad nature may be buried in the child who is being brought to the Font; that it may be dead and buried, done away with and put out of sight. A great miracle, greater than raising the dead, and only to be wrought by the Almighty power of the Spirit of God, yet most surely wrought in each child that is truly baptized, as our Lord himself taught: "Except ye be born again of water and of the Spirit, ye cannot enter into the kingdom of God." This is the great baptismal change, which God wrought for every one of us in the beginning of life; and the whole business of our after-life ought to be, the behaving ourselves worthy of it. What should we fancy right behaviour, in any person who had really and literally died, and been raised from the dead, e. g. in Lazarus of Bethany? Surely it would disappoint us, we should think it strange and unnatural, if such an one still went on as if there were no other world, or as if he had no soul to be saved or lost eternally in it. In like manner, well may the Angels wonder, and be filled with holy indignation, when they see an impure and unworthy Christian; rather I should say, when they see a Christian who is not really striving to purify himself, even as Christ is pure. For this is the purpose of Almighty God in killing and burying the Old Man, that the New Man may be raised up in his stead. The New Man is the image and likeness of God, renewed and brought into being again in the baptized soul and body by the power of the Holy Ghost making the child a member of Christ. As the Old Man is the likeness and nature of fallen Adam, so the New Man has the likeness and nature of Jesus Christ; and this is what we pray to have raised up in our children, when we bring them to Holy Baptism. Think for a moment, what a great thing it is we ask for them. Think of them *as children*. We may ask that they may grow up like that Holy and Blessed Child, Who was the very Word and Wisdom of the Father, Incarnate, and dwelling among men: Who, as He grew, waxed strong in Spirit, filled with wisdom, and the grace of God was upon Him: Who, when He was parted awhile from His parents, was found in no other place than His Father's House, in no other employment than about His Father's business; Who abode quietly with His parents, and was subject unto them, increasing continually in favour with God and man. This is He, Whose Image and Likeness you pray that you may see in these little ones; and surely we may see a great deal of it, if we will but watch, in their loving and confiding ways, in their little acts of self-denial, in their contrivances how to be kind and dutiful and obedient. Yes, indeed, he that will reverentially look, may in many things discern the New Man in the behaviour of baptized children; and much, very much more, would be to be seen, were parents and elders such as Christians should be, especially in their cares and prayers for the lambs of the flock; and perhaps it may help some of us to remember our duty to them, if we will sometimes recollect, that when they were christened, prayer was made especially that they might be changed into the Image and glory of Christ, and how fearful it would be, if through any fault of our's they should be found rather to have put on the horrible image of Christ's Enemy.

But we pray besides, that all carnal affections may die in the babe which is about to be baptized, and that all things belonging to the Spirit may live and grow in him. Carnal affections are the lusts of the flesh; all undue appetite for meat and drink and pleasures; all those many thoughts, fancies, wishes, habits, which get hold of men who give themselves up to this world; and are like so many foul and weak and noisome weeds, overgrowing the garden of the soul. Concerning all these, we pray that they may wither and die; but for the things belonging to the Spirit, i. e. for "all holy desires, good counsels, and just works," for these we pray, that they may live and grow in that child; even as fair flowers and precious fruits thrive in the good soil of a kindly and well-managed garden. And it should be particularly noticed, that we pray not only for their *living*, but for their *growing*. We pray, and therefore we should labour, that in every baptized person there should be the spirit of improvement, not of continuance only. We are not contented if the plants we set merely just keep alive; if they leave off growing, we consider that more or less as a sign of decay. So it is not enough for a man to say to himself, I have not gone back that I know of; I believe I am no worse than I was; but he ought to have some reasonable ground of hope that on the whole he may be advancing. *That* is the necessary token of spiritual life. Thus, if you have left off telling absolute lies, still you are not to be satisfied with yourself; you must practise *every day* to be more tender and exact in your regard for truth; and so of all other virtues; as we read of the Holy Child, that He did not continue in one stay, but increased in wisdom. For as no garden is ever so perfect, but a great deal may be done in it, so no Christian's soul is so exact in any good thing, but it may be greatly improved—there are yet more things belonging to the Spirit which may be introduced into it, to live and and to grow there; and those which are there already, may be cultivated into higher beauty or more abundant vigour. Remember this, Christian Brethren and Sisters, when you are tempted to be weary and fall back. Remember, it was prayed over you, the first time you were brought here, "may all spiritual things not only *live*, but *grow* in him."

And remember, lastly, that the Church prayed for you as for young *Soldiers;* that you may have power and strength to have victory and to triumph against the devil, the world, and the flesh. She did not pray that you might be at rest and entire peace from all temptations; this, the Church knows, cannot be had in this world; she did not pray that you might have no warfare, but that you might get the better in your warfare. Two things she prayed for, victory and triumph; victory here over the enemies of your soul, triumph hereafter on the great Day, when God will finally put under the feet of His saints all the powers of evil, to rise again no more. This, your Spiritual Mother asked on your behalf of the Great King as a very precious baptismal gift; and you cannot doubt that He would grant her request. You may not doubt, you must earnestly believe that God has given you power and strength to have victory and to triumph against the world, the flesh, and the Devil. If you do not fight, or if fighting, you do not prevail, you may be quite sure it is not for want of power and strength given you in Holy Baptism. It is not for want of such a gift, but for abuse and forfeiture of it. Put this home to your own hearts, dear brethren. The victory is in your own hands if you will. Neither the devil nor any other power, can make you sin against your will. He may dart evil thoughts into your mind, but if you turn away from them at once, and decidedly, they will hardly be so troublesome again; at any rate, they will do your soul no harm. And then imagine the triumph at last; how the Great King will come in person, and all His holy Angels with Him: how from the innumerable multitude before Him, He will in some marvellous way single out each one separately who has pleased Him, with a "well done, good and faithful servant, enter into the joy of the Lord:" and so each one of us, if not found unworthy, shall meet the Lord in the air, and being blessed by Him and taken up, shall follow Him through the everlasting doors into His Kingdom.

I say, let us often think of this day of triumph, and fear greatly, as indeed we have great occasion, lest our own careless and wilful ways deprive us of our portion in it. Do you not see, when any particular Festival or Holiday is soon coming on, how much better than usual young people are apt to behave, for fear of losing their share in the Holiday? So and much more should we do our best, to secure the place graciously provided for us in that last and most glorious Procession, the procession of our Lord and His saints from Judgment to glory? It is but a short while; the day will very soon be here; and if we have many adversaries, yet a great door, by God's mercy, is open, and we have large and sufficient helps. May He grant that on that day we may each one of us look back to the day of his Baptism with joy and not with grief!

SERMON XXI.

Col. i. 23.

"If ye continue in the Faith, grounded and settled, and be not moved away from the hope of the Gospel which ye have heard."

IN taking up anew the course of Catechising which has been interrupted this year by the holy seasons of Lent and Easter, I may remind you that we were going through the Baptismal Service, and had entered on the consideration of the short prayers, which follow after the replies of the godfathers and godmothers, and come immediately before the Consecration of the water. They are four in number, and the last time we considered three of them.

The first begs for the Child the grace of regeneration: that "the old Adam in this child may be so buried, that the new man may be raised up in him." The second begs for him the grace of conversion, or continual, gradual, silent turning towards God : "that all carnal affections may die in him and that all things belonging to the Spirit may live and grow in him." The third supposes him (as he is sure to be) in a state of warfare and asks for him the grace of victorious resistance: "Grant that he may have power and strength to have victory and to triumph against the devil, the world and the flesh." And the fourth and last of those short collects, prays for the crown of all, final perseverance. " Grant that whosoever is here dedicated to Thee by our office and ministry, may also be endued with heavenly virtues, and everlastingly rewarded: Through Thy mercy, O Blessed Lord God, Who dost live and govern all things, world without end."

Consider first, for whom we offer this prayer: not for the child only which is waiting to be christened (to whom the other short collects plainly refer), but for all, " Whosoever is here dedicated to God by our office and ministry." What is *"here"*? It may mean at this Font, in this particular Church, and congregation : or it may mean generally, in this evil and trying world. The Priest, when he offers that petition, may mean something similar to that which Solomon offered concerning the Temple, to Him Whose eyes were open all night and all day towards that Holy place, that God would hear the prayers offered to Him there, or by Israelites afar off, turning that way in prayer. Or he may mean more generally, for all who have been duly baptized anywhere and by any Christian. Being so dedicated to God, they are an especial mark for the devil to shoot his arrows at : they have special need therefore to ask for perseverance, and to have it asked for them. It is a prayer of great, extensive, unbounded charity, taking in all the baptized, as the like prayer in the Communion office does all the members of Christ, in that it says; " we Thy humble servants entirely desire Thy fatherly goodness mercifully to accept this our

Sacrifice of praise and thanksgiving; most humbly beseeching Thee to grant, that by the merits and death of Thy Son Jesus Christ, and through faith in His Blood, we and all Thy whole church may obtain remission of our sins, and all other benefits of His Passion." That collect, as you may perceive, is a charitable intercession, extending the benefit of the holy Sacrifice and Sacrament which has just been offered up, far beyond the Communicants present, even to all God's whole Church, everywhere, according to their needs. Such is the love and such the prayer of the Holy Catholic Church. From every Font and from every Altar, it flows and spreads itself all around, until it have filled Heaven and earth: like a holy fire which, wherever it is kindled, will naturally lay hold of things on every side, where it can find proper materials. So that as the Apostle says, "no man liveth unto himself," in like manner we may also say, no Christian is baptized for himself alone, no Communicant receives for himself alone. All the members rejoice and are the better for the grace imparted to each one, and for the prayer of the church accompanying the gift of grace.

Consider secondly, what this prayer teaches of the condition of those newly baptized. It represents them as dedicated to God by the office and ministry of His Church, put in a way of being endued with heavenly virtues, and everlastingly rewarded, yet capable (alas!) of falling away also for ever. It is then, in short, a prayer for the gift of Perseverance. Perseverance is the great and aweful subject, on which we are led to think to day. But first I would say a few words on the account here given of the state, in which the Church prays that we may persevere.

1) It is a state of *dedication*. The child is dedicated to God by our Office and Ministry. What "dedication" means, you know. It is solemnly setting apart any person or thing to God's service. A Church is dedicated, when it is consecrated: when the Bishop, as you know, comes and blesses it with the ordained Psalms and prayers and ceremonies. From that hour the building and its furniture are taken out of ordinary and common use, taken in a manner out of this world, and made part of the heavenly world. For as the glorified bodies of the saints in heaven have no other employment, so far as we know, than to shew honour and praise to the Most Holy Trinity (as it is written, "They fall down before Him that sitteth on the throne and worship Him that liveth for ever and ever, and cast their crowns before the Throne,") so these outward and visible Churches or holy buildings, once dedicated, are never more to be put to any profane or temporal use. No more then are Christian children, once dedicated in Holy Baptism, to profane themselves by serving any other master. They are all anointed; all Kings and Priests. If I may say a bold word, they are all Christs. Woe to him who shall try to use them in ways unworthy of their heavenly dedication and nature! Woe to themselves, if they forget it, and behave as though they had not been born again, not specially consecrated to our Lord, not called, as saith the Apostle, to be saints! All this the Church would have us remember, when we acknowledge ourselves *dedicated* to God in Baptism.

2) Whereas the Church prays that the baptized

may also be endued with heavenly virtues, this reminds us of another thing, not to be doubted, nor forgotten, in our condition, viz. that for those who live beyond infancy the one gift of Baptismal Grace will not suffice to carry them to Heaven, except they have the further grace to improve the first gift by holy care and obedience, by continual turning towards God Who gave it: even as the first gift of natural life in this world will not abide either in a child or a grown up person, unless care be taken to preserve it by supplies of food and other seasonable helps. We pray then, that the spark which was lit in the soul in regeneration, may in after-life be kindled into a flame by the Unceasing Wonder-working Breath of God, i. e. by His Holy Spirit, enduing the child or man from time to time, as he becomes capable of it, with more and more of heavenly virtues. This is a Christian's intended condition, the best he can arrive at in this world, a condition imperfect and to himself always unsatisfactory, but, by God's great Mercy, always silently and secretly improving.

3) A third remark here to be made on it is, that the things in which we should be always improving are *heavenly* virtues, not the good qualities which are most in sight, and which the world loves most to praise, but *heavenly* virtues; thoughts and ways and turns of mind which can only come from heaven, and which are continually tending up thither, like fires from an altar. These heavenly and Divine virtues are more especially Faith, Hope and Charity: looking off the world and the things which we see, to the great and awful things out of sight: hoping to see God the Father, the Son and the Holy Ghost: and

loving Him above all for His unspeakable mercies in Christ Jesus. This is what we mean when, standing around the Font, we beg that all the little infants that are brought there may be endued with heavenly virtues; that the tender clinging hearts, which we know to be naturally so full of love, may be early opened to receive that perfect love, which never can in any wise fail or pass away. The sons and daughters of this world, when they look at their young children, look forward to what they will do and what they will become in the matters of this world: how they will one day take the place of their parents, and thrive, and enjoy themselves, and be respected and comfortable. But the true believer, when he looks at his young child, waiting to be christened, says to himself, "here is one who will live for ever and ever: Christ has died for him, and will now give him His Spirit, in order that eternal life may be spent with Him in Heaven, and not with the Wicked one in the place of torment. O God, grant him all heavenly virtues: give him a heart to abide in Christ: let it not be said of him, He had better never have been born."

And this is the meaning of the concluding words of the Prayer, that those who are here baptized, may be everlastingly rewarded. It is in short, as I said before, a prayer for perseverance. Perseverance is a very special grace, to be added over and above the grace of regeneration, that God's great mercy may not have been received in vain. For it is too certain, as our article teaches, that, after we have received the Holy Ghost, we may fall from grace given, may fall into deadly sin, and if we die in that state, the sin is unpardonable. Therefore our Lord so earnestly exhorts His disciples again and again, as the one thing needful, "Abide in Me, and I in you:" and as soon as we can speak, we learn in our Catechism not only to thank God that He hath brought us to a state of salvation, but also to pray for His Grace that we may continue in the same unto our life's end. This is the great thing: persevere, continue, abide. Continue in the faith, grounded and settled, and be not moved away from the hope of the Gospel. *Keep* Christ's commandments, and *abide* in His Love. We learn the Prayer in our young days, that we may continue in the same unto our lives' end: and we must never, never leave it off: in heart we must be praying that prayer night and day; for night and day there is one watching to take our crown from us. He cannot bear to see a virgin soul, a soul and body as yet unspotted with wilful grievous sin: he hates the pure white robe, and will do his best to defile it, and he surely will get us to defile it, if we permit him. He watches, to tempt and defile us: we cannot do less than watch, to keep ourselves pure. He says, "time enough, by and by, to repent and serve God; you may as well enjoy yourself a little for the present." Let us say, "the time is short; if I persevere that little while, I shall be everlastingly rewarded." O think on that word *everlastingly!*

Finally, take notice of God's most loving Condescension in counting that unutterable glory a reward for our poor services: and understand by it, how sure our place in Heaven will be, if we lose it not by our own fault: as sure as the labourers' wages in our Lord's parable, the penny a day, promised by Him Who cannot lie. He calls it our wages, though we cannot properly earn it, because He is sure to treat us as though we had earned it. Persevere, and it cannot fail you.

You perhaps know something of the joy of heart [a which God sometimes gives upon one strong earnest purpose to do, or leave undone, something, out of love for Him. You know the joy of having strongly broken off one sin, for the love of Him "Who loved you and gave Himself for you." Every good choice has such a joy. Pray God, day by day, that you may persevere in making anew, for that day also, that good choice, and you will persevere to the end. God gives the grace of perseverance to all who ask Him. And then not one thing will you have done, in any one day, for God, which will lose its reward. Not one kind word or one act, done for the love of Jesus, but you will find it there; not one fear or anxiety borne meekly for His sake, but it is stored for you there; not one tear shed for past sin, not one wish for the love of God, that you had not done it, but it will have its reward in the Infinite love of your God].

[a] The Sermon must have been finished orally. I have ventured to add some thoughts of the kind which seem to have been in the writer's mind, without attempting to imitate his simplicity. E. B. P.

SERMON XXII.

St. John xix. 34, 35.

"*One of the soldiers with a spear pierced His Side, and forthwith came thereout Blood and Water: and he that saw it bare record, and his record is true: and he knoweth that he saith true, that ye might believe.*"

As the solemn moment of the Baptism itself draws on, the supplications of the Church become more earnest and aweful, and we are taught to go back in faith to the times when our Lord and Saviour, newly dead and newly risen, did, in the most distinct and remarkable way, set His seal to that blessed ordinance. The portion of the service which so takes us back is the prayer at consecration of the water, which takes place, as you know, immediately after the four short collects. For as the child about to be baptized had been solemnly offered to God, by prayer, and by the threefold promise and vow made in his name by his sponsors: so it is meet that the water also, which is to be the outward mean and pledge of the child's regeneration, should be in its way solemnly dedicated to God. Not that such form of words is necessary for the Baptism itself, as the form of Consecration in Holy Communion is necessary for that Sacrament. For we know that in private Baptism, the case being urgent, this and all other prayers might be omitted, and only the Form itself of Baptism used, and yet we are not to doubt that the child is lawfully and sufficiently baptized. But in Church, and also in private when there is no such extreme haste, it is meet and right that this solemn prayer should be said, and the very element of water itself blessed, which is to be made the Channel of so great a good. We may consider it as the act of our Great High Priest and Saviour, applying by the Church's prayer to the particular water which is in the Font, the sanctifying virtue which in His own Baptism He had conferred upon all the waters of the earth. By His heavenly touch in the river Jordan under the Ministry of St. John Baptist, He had made *all* water apt for the mystical washing away of sin, and now the meaning of our prayer is, that the same blessing and virtue may not be wanting to this water in particular, nor to the child about to be baptized in it. That is the general meaning of this prayer at Consecration of the water. And now we are to take special notice, what are those mercies of her Lord and Saviour, by which the Church, as her manner is, pleads with His Father and our Father at the commencement of this prayer. They are two: the first is, the issuing of Blood and Water from His Side, as He hung dead upon the Cross; the other is, His commandment to His disciples, a short time before His Ascension, to baptize all men in the Name of the Most Holy Trinity. At present I have only to speak of the first of the two. You heard the particulars in the Catechising, as also some general account of their meaning. What I have now to say on it is this.

First, it is plain that there must be something very deep, deeper than we might have imagined, in this pouring out of the Blood and water from our Lord's Side after His death : seeing that St. John, who was even then waiting by the Cross, is so very earnest in bearing witness about it. "One of the soldiers with a spear pierced His Side, and forthwith came thereout blood and water; and he that saw it bare record and his record is true." Why all this care to tell us that he saw it, to affirm the truth of it over and over again, to speak of our faith as especially assured by it? *We* should not beforehand have thought it of such great consequence to our faith. There *must* be something in it, more than we can tell at first sight. And to draw our attention the more to it, the same St. John in his first epistle says, "Who is he that overcometh the world, but he that believeth that Jesus is the Son of God? This is He that came by water and Blood, *even* Jesus Christ; not by water only, but by water and Blood; and it is the Spirit that beareth witness, because the Spirit is truth. For there are three that bear witness on earth, the Spirit and the water and the Blood. If we receive the witness of men, the witness of God is greater." Put it all together, and it appears plainly, that the faith that overcometh the world, the faith that Jesus is the Son of God, as it receives of course the whole witness of God which He hath testified of His Son, so it cannot be without receiving the point that "Jesus Christ came by water and blood." There is something in *that*, quite necessary to entire belief in Jesus Christ. What that something is, was emphatically betokened by the Blood and Water which flowed by miracle from our Lord's Side when He was hanging dead on the Cross, and to which St. John so earnestly draws our attention. In a word, the Blood and Water teaches the doctrine of sacramental grace; and first and especially, the grace of Holy Baptism. Therefore the Church mentions the shedding of that Water and Blood, in the beginning of this Consecration-prayer, and says that it took place for the Forgiveness of our sins: which Forgiveness, as we all know, is first imparted in Holy Baptism: as the article of the Creed teaches: "I acknowledge one Baptism for the Remission of sins." The Church most unquestionably means us to understand, that the Water and Blood from our Lord's Side was a token and pledge of the grace of His Life-giving Sacraments. The Holy Spirit by St. John means us to understand the same, when it says, concerning this witness borne by the Spirit, the Water and the Blood, "This is the record (or witness), that God hath given to us eternal life, and this life is in His Son." He does not say, "God will give it unto us," but "God *hath* given it unto us." He gave it unto us when He made us members of His Son: and we know when that was.

To state the matter a little differently. In order that each one of us, fallen children of Adam, might be saved, it was needful not only that Christ should die for all sinners, but that the merits of His death should be applied to each individual sinner: not only that He should offer Himself a Sacrifice and a sin-offering, but that the blood of that Sacrifice should be sprinkled on each of us, one by one: not only that He should take our nature and suffer in it, but that we should be mysteriously made partakers of Him. John had baptized with water, but Christ should baptize with the Holy Ghost. John came by water only, but Jesus Christ came by Water and Blood. John's baptism was but a token of the remission of sins to be granted by and by, but Christ's was the "One Baptism for the Remission of sins," which therefore could not be without His Blood, for without shedding of blood, the Blood of the appointed Saviour, is no remission.

Thus the Blood and Water is the complete token of both parts of the grace of Holy Baptism. The Blood of Christ, to make atonement for sin, and purge the soul of the guilt of it, in the sight of God: and the Spirit of Christ, which is as living water, to apply that Blood to us, to purge our conscience from the stain of sin, to wash the sinful creature, and make him whiter than snow. For that all may go well with the sinner, that he may finally escape everlasting death, he must have both pardon for the past and grace for the future. The Blood from our Lord's Side is the token of that pardon; the water, the token of that grace. Both pardon and grace are by the law of God's kingdom conveyed to us one by one in His blessed Sacraments. First and once for all, in Holy Baptism: that is the water from the Rock following Christ's people through the whole wilderness of this world. Pardon and grace come first in Holy Baptism, and for the time they come completely: they save us, until they are forfeited by sinful relapsing: but as we grow older and temptations come on, new supplies of grace and pardon, new ways of partaking of Christ, the God-Man, are needed: and most especially the Sacrament of Holy Communion: and therefore when we read or hear of the Water and Blood of the Crucifixion, we are to think of Holy Communion as well as of the other Sacrament. We may consider that when St. John saw the wound made in the precious Side of his dearly beloved Lord, and the blood and water gushing out of that wound, it was as if a Voice had come from the Cross, and had told us all, "By this Blood and by this Water, by the merits of Christ crucified and by His Holy Spirit, the fallen children of Adam may be grafted into Him, the disease of sin cured, the image of God restored, and souls and bodies nourished unto eternal life."

Since, moreover, these blessings depended entirely on our Lord's Death, and were the price of His Precious Blood, we are particularly told that He was quite dead, before the soldier pierced His Side, and the Blood and Water came out.

And as He is called the Second Adam, in Whom all should be made alive, even as all died in the first Adam, so there is, in the history of the first Adam, a very remarkable type of the Blood and Water flowing from Christ's Side. The ancient Church always believed, that the Creation of our first mother was a shadow and figure of the building up of the Church: a figure and shadow of the way in which God would by and by form her, who would be the Spouse and Body of Christ; bone of His Bone and flesh of His Flesh. For recollect what the history tells us in Genesis. Adam had the rule over Paradise: he might eat of all the fruits but one, and all creatures were to obey him: yet he was not quite happy, he needed a help meet for him. So our Lord, in His great mercy, accounts Himself incomplete and imperfect without us: He is straitened until our Salvation through Him begins to be accomplished. He sends both for ass and colt, both for Jew and Gentile, saying, the Lord hath need of them. Therefore so far, as I said, He is like Adam needing a help.

In the next place, when we read, the Lord caused a deep sleep to fall upon Adam, and he slept; who does not see that this represents our Holy One sleeping the sleep of death upon the Cross? "Then one of the Soldiers with a spear pierced His Side;" it being so permitted by God's unsearchable Providence, even as God had Himself made an opening in Adam's side and taken out one of his ribs, in order to make of it the first woman. And it is very remarkable what care was taken by God's Providence to make sure of His being dead, before the Fountain of Sacramental grace in His Side was thus opened. The Jews, in that strange state of mind which made them particular about forms and ceremonies, while they had no scruple in commiting murder, were anxious to have our Lord and the thieves dead, that they might not hang on the cross, during the day of the Paschal Sabbath: and Pilate accommodating himself to the Jews, ordered the soldiers to see to it: but when they came to Jesus, they found Him dead already, no need to use violence as they had done to the thieves, to bring them to an end: only one of them (as it would seem, out of a kind of savage wantonness) with a spear pierced His Side, and the Blood and Water flowed out. For as St. Paul argues, when a testament or last will is to do a person any good, you must prove the death of the person making the will: as long as he lives, the will is of no force at all, but only after he is dead. So the Sacraments of the New Covenant had all their virtue from His Death and Passion: and therefore the Wound in His Side, which was the token of His Sacraments, was not opened, until after He was dead; and things were so ordered, as that there might be no mistake about this. Thus much about the sleep of Adam and our Saviour's sleep of death upon the Cross, of which Adam's sleep was a figure.

The next thing we read is, how that the Lord "builded up" the rib which He had taken from Adam's side, into the full form and stature of a woman, whom He afterwards brought to the man, who owned her to be "bone of his bone, and flesh of his flesh." I say the Lord "builded her up" to be a woman; for that is the proper meaning of the word used in this place, as you may see in the margin of some of our English Bibles. Now consider this word "builded her up," how exactly it expresses the building up of the Church, out of millions of Christians, one by one, added to it by Holy Baptism. You will thus see, how the Church was really taken out of our Lord's Side, as Eve was taken out of the side of Adam. Eve was "builded up," i. e. formed by degrees, one limb after another, from the rib taken out of Adam's side, as the Church was formed, and is even now formed, by degrees, by the Blood and Water, the Baptismal grace which flowed from our Saviour's Side.

But further; when God brought to the man the

woman thus newly created, and Adam said, "this is now bone of my bone and flesh of my flesh," it was added, " therefore shall a man leave his father and his mother, and shall be joined unto his wife and they twain shall be one flesh." That is, Holy Matrimony, the nearest union that can be on earth, is a type and shadow of the mystical Union, that is betwixt Christ and His Church. And as a man being joined unto his wife, has leave to quit his father and his mother; the old home passes away, and he has a new home, a new state of things altogether; so it must be with us, when by Holy Baptism we are made members of our Lord's Body. The whole world, and all things in it, must be quite different to us from what they would be if we had never been baptized. As the Heavenly Spouse Himself teaches; " whosoever will come after Me, let him deny himself, take up his Cross and follow Me." "I have made Myself altogether his : I grudged him no drop of My Blood ; it flowed altogether out of My pierced Side; therefore neither must he grudge anything of his to Me : he must make himself altogether Mine."

This is the doctrine of Sacramental Grace, the great doctrine which Holy Church proclaims, in teaching every one of us to say, when we come to Holy Communion, " I acknowledge one Baptism for the Remission of sins." . This is the great, the unspeakable mercy which we acknowledge most thankfully to our Heavenly Father, when, just before the Baptism of a child, we put Him in mind that His Most Dearly Beloved Son Jesus Christ, for the forgiveness of our sins, did shed out of His most Precious Side both Water, and Blood. And for a continual remembrance of it, you will observe, that in all the pictures of our Crucified and Risen Lord, He has this Wound in His Side, along with the four wounds in His Hands and Feet. As they are the token of His Perfect Sacrifice, offered once for all on the Cross, so is this the token of His communicating Himself to us one by one in His blessed Sacraments.[a]

[a] It appears from some short heads written for this Sermon, and preserved with it, that it too was finished orally. The following, which form the concluding heads, were not expanded in writing;

"Thomas could not own Him without the wound in His side, and we always look for it.

"Therefore we must cling to the faith of **His Sacraments**.

"Fearful view of the sins of Christians.

"Blessed view of their privileges."

SERMON XXIII.

St. Matt. xxviii. 19.

"*Go ye therefore and teach all nations, baptizing them in the Name of the Father, and of the Son, and of the Holy Ghost.*"

THERE are two very solemn moments in our Lord's Ministry on earth, to which we are carried back by the address at the beginning of the Prayer at Consecration of the water. The one, just after His Death; the other, just before His Ascension. The one, of which you heard something last Sunday, was the piercing of His Sacred Heart with a spear, for the pouring out of Water and Blood. The other, of which you heard in the catechising just now, was His meeting with His Apostles in Galilee, and giving them that great commission, in virtue of which the Holy Church has by their ministry gone forth into all the world: in virtue of which, from time to time, in presence of the Holy Angels and in all our presence, little children are admitted into fellowship with the Most Holy Trinity.

Now those two things are connected one with another, as the shadow with the Substance, the reality with the type. Christ's Side pierced, the Blood and

Water flowing out in the sight of those who stood by the Cross, is the shadow and token of the great things which He was about to do for His people one by one, invisibly and inwardly, to be witnessed not by sight, but by faith. As the Blood from our Lord's Side flowed not alone, but mingled with Water, so we may understand that even His Perfect Sacrifice saves us not, except it be applied by His Sanctifying Spirit in Baptism and Holy Communion. We must be made and continue members of Him. *That* is being saved by Him. Again, although in Baptism water only is visible, faith looking back to what happened on the Cross, discovers in the Font precious Blood, saving Blood, the Blood of our Lord Jesus Christ mingled with the water, to wash our souls clean both of the guilt and stain of our sins; so that the Almighty shall take off His Hand from punishing, the All-seeing shall cast our sins behind His Back, and no longer behold on us the sad taint and pollution of them. Thus, the flowing out of the Blood and Water has respect to the Baptism which was afterwards to be instituted; and the Baptism, when it was instituted, was understood to bring with it the virtue of the Blood which is not seen, as well as the cleansing power represented by the water which is seen.

When I speak of the Institution of Baptism, I mean, as you will all understand, what our Lord did at that meeting with His Disciples in Galilee, of which you heard just now. For although our Saviour had mentioned Baptism on more occasions than one before, especially in His discourse with Nicodemus, and although His Baptism had been distinctly foretold by St. John, yet He had never in form ordained and appointed it before His Death, as He had done the other Sacrament of His Body and Blood. His Disciples had indeed baptized, but not with His Baptism, but rather with such a Baptism as that of St. John, as a mere token of the purity and cleanness of heart which God requires, and which He would hereafter give by His Blood and His Spirit. They had baptized with water, but our Lord was now about to begin baptizing with the Holy Ghost, His proper Baptism; and so, in a very solemn manner, He lays down a law concerning it, makes His people a covenant and an ordinance. He meets them, after long notice given, and three times repeated, on a mountain in Galilee. He appears in some very wonderful way, which caused some of them to doubt at first whether He was their very Lord Jesus or no. He comes close to them and takes away their doubts, and then He delivers the Law of His Baptism in those plain and well-known words, " All Power is given unto Me in heaven and in earth, Go ye, therefore, and teach all nations, baptizing them in the Name of the Father, and of the Son, and of the Holy Ghost." Then He instituted Baptism, not before. His words to Nicodemus were but prophetic of what He would do by and by. "Except a man be born of water and of the Spirit, he cannot enter into the kingdom of God." But then this could not be until the great Day of Pentecost; for then was the Kingdom of Heaven first set up. That saying was prophetic of Baptism, as the Holy Communion was foretold in St. John, ".[a] Except ye eat the Flesh of the Son of man, and drink His Blood, ye have no life in you." What

[a] St. John vi. 53.

it was to eat the flesh and drink the Blood of the Son of Man, the Disciples could not well imagine, till they saw Him take Bread and Wine into His Sacred Hands, and heard Him say, "This is My Body," and, "This is My Blood." So neither could they at all make out, how people are to be born again, born of water and of the Spirit, until our Lord distinctly enjoined that all should be baptized in His Name. And although water was not mentioned, yet they would be quite aware that it must be done with water: for the Jews never baptized with anything else. Thus was the law of Holy Baptism first laid down in the Church.

I would next remark that it seems to come in as the first, if not the chiefest law of the Pastoral care. When our Lord had spoken of the matter before, I mean of their meeting Him in Galilee, He had always seemed to allude to it in connection with our care of His flock. He speaks to them as the Head Shepherd might sometimes speak to the under-shepherds. Thus in the night of His Last Supper, while they were yet gathered round the Table; He told them, "All ye shall be ashamed because of *Me* this night, for it is written, smite the Shepherd and the sheep shall be scattered." I, the Chief Shepherd, in My Coming Agony and Death shall be forsaken of you the sheep: but fear not, I am not going to cast you off, much as you perhaps deserve it. "After I am risen again, I will go before you into Galilee." As shepherds go before their flocks, so our Lord promises to go before St. Peter and the rest, when they shall have to travel into Galilee. It was to be altogether a pastoral meeting. A Shepherd calling to Him those of

His flock whom He saw fit to put in trust with the rest: calling them into a place apart, where all might be together "in peace." And the same expression, "going before into Galilee," is twice repeated after His Resurrection in directions to the same under-shepherds. To the women the Holy Angels say, "go tell His Disciples and Peter that He goeth before you into Galilee, there shall ye see Him as He said unto you." And He Himself, afterwards meeting the same women, repeats the message: ": Be not afraid, go tell My brethren that they go into Galilee; there shall they see Me." The whole was as when a flock that has been scattered is gathered again in a particular place.

And then observe, what place. It was not any where in Galilee, they might go to look for Him, but He appointed unto them one particular mountain; *the* mountain: perhaps the same mountain where our Lord with all authority spake His Beatitudes, and the rest of His gracious Sermon to His Apostles especially, as to those who should be the salt of the earth. The Mount of the beatitudes was a place for pastoral instruction: their meeting in that place, therefore, may be taken as a sign that the Great Shepherd was about to say or do something important as concerning the care of the flock.

And indeed what could be more important than what our Lord goes on to tell them, that now He has taken on Himself the full office of Universal Shepherd; saying, "All Power is given unto Me in heaven and in earth?" And next He gives them their commission as under-shepherds, "Go ye therefore and teach all nations," not the Jews only, but all the nations, all the tribes and families of the earth. As all power was given Him, as He was to be not only King of the Jews, but King of kings and Lord of lords, nay, even King over all the Angels in Heaven: so they were to go with His message to all nations.

And what was their errand? Merely to say their message and be gone, like a person delivering a letter which requires no answer? Nay, it was much more than that. Our Lord's word is, "Make disciples of them;" not merely, teach, but cause them to become My disciples. Now the disciples of Jesus, we know, were His inseparable attendants and servants, trusted to wait on Him in all things; nay more, they were His chosen friends, trusted to know His Heavenly secrets. For His Word is, "I have called you friends, for all things that I have heard of My Father, I have made known unto you." In a word, the favour now to be offered through the Apostles to all the world, to all the Gentiles, to every one of the fallen race of Adam, was that they should come to be to our Lord as St. Peter and St. John, His chosen friends; not simply that they should hear and believe certain truths concerning Him and themselves, but that they should become His friends and followers, part of His family, nay, members and limbs of His Body. For so He had spoken to the disciples before, "I am the Vine, ye are the Branches;" and now He will have all the world to be His disciples.

So far then was plain: all people were to be made Christians: but how? Was it to be merely by teaching; as people are taught to understand and believe things, which they could never get to understand and believe of themselves? Would that be enough to make them Christians, simply that they should believe with the heart and confess with the mouth the great things concerning Jesus Christ? We, or some of us, might have thought so. But our Lord's law is far otherwise. As He redeemed our whole race, not by teaching, but by making Himself one of us, and dying for us, so it is His Will to save us one by one, not by mere teaching, but by making us one with Him. He took our Flesh, that we might be partakers of a Divine Nature. And to seal and convey this blessing, and to work this wonder in us, He ordained His blessed Sacraments. "Make Christians of them," He saith, not by "instructing," not by "reforming," not by "educating and training them up," but by "baptizing them." Baptism then is the beginning of Christianity, the pledge and means of our being in Christ at the first. "As many of you as have been baptized into Christ, have put on Christ." Until one is baptized, he is not properly a disciple. This, my brethren, we all know and believe. I only wish we considered as deeply as we ought, what a deep and aweful change this our Baptism made in us; such a change as we shall feel through all the endless ages that are to come: we shall feel it more and more through all Eternity. We who are baptized shall be for ever and ever more like Angels, or more like devils, than as if we had not been baptized. This is our blessing, this also is our burthen. God give us a heart to know and feel it rightly. And that we may do so, consider the next words, the words in which our Saviour appointed the very Form of Baptism; for He did not only appoint the water, but the Word also. "Make disciples of them by baptizing them in the

Name of the Father and of the Son and of the Holy Ghost." He does not say with water, because that would be understood, as it has been understood and practised by all Christians. But the form of words He expressly adds; and it is such a form, as ought to fill every one of us with deep fear and dread and anxiety, lest he lose a soul, his own soul; lose it for ever, after that Jesus Christ has spoken such a word to it. Attend, brethren. When the Priest says, "I baptize thee in the Name of the Father and of the Son and of the Holy Ghost," or rather, when our Lord says it by the Priest, he does not merely mean, "I do this by the authority of the Father, the Son and the Holy Ghost," and by their commission which they have given me: as a constable or magistrate among ourselves might say, I do this or that in the Queen's name and on her behalf; or as one standing for another speaks, our own godfathers and godmothers for example; "they did promise and vow three things in our name." Far more than that was meant when our Lord commissioned His Apostles to baptize in the Name of the Most Holy Trinity. The Form, "in the Name," here means "into the Name." It means that we are partakers of the Name, and may in some sense be called by it: that we are joined to the Almighty God, the glorious Being, whose Name it is; as I said before out of St. Peter, "We are partakers of a Divine Nature;" as it is written in the Psalm, "I said, ye are Gods." What could be said or done for us more?

There will perhaps be more hereafter to be said of this Form of Baptism. The chief thing now to be noticed is, how in our Lord's way of appointing it, it is connected with keeping His commandments—not one commandment, but all. For after fixing the sacred Form, "In the Name of the Father and of the Son and of the Holy Ghost," He adds, "teaching them to observe all things, whatsoever I have commanded you." If we are wholly joined to God, we must be wholly His: we must not leave out any part of our Sacrifice, but purpose and endeavour to do *all* that He bids us. And it may be that our Lord in this saying, "All that I have commanded you," meant especially what He had been saying to His Apostles during those forty days, in which, as St. Luke says, He was speaking to them of the things which concern the Kingdom of God. They were to build up the Church by Baptism, and to order it by the rules and laws in which He had been instructing them. So doing, He promised them His Own especial Presence, the greatest of all encouragements. "Lo, I am with you always, even unto the end of the world." "I am with you always;" with you My Apostles, with those whom you shall ordain to be in your place, with the Church which you shall establish. "I am with you always," with all Christians, faithfully desiring and endeavouring to abide in your Communion.

If Christ is with His Apostles and with all faithful Christians always, we are to make sure that He is not absent when He is called upon to sanctify the water, in which one of those for whom He died is presently to be baptized. The child cannot have done anything to drive Him away; and no one's unworthiness, but our own, can possibly hinder the effect of a Sacrament upon us. We are not then to doubt of the grace of our Baptism, but to give God thanks for it day and night. But one thing we must never forget: that at the same time when our Lord commanded us to be baptised, He commanded that we should be taught also to observe all that He had told His Apostles of: all the rules of holy and Christian living. If we be wilfully wanting in any of these, Christ indeed will be with us in a way in which He is not with the heathen, but it will be to our judgment and ruin, not to our salvation.

As then we bear His Name, as we carry about with us (in some sense) the Holy Trinity, Father, Son, and Holy Ghost, as He is with us in all our days; so in all our days and in all our doings, let us remember Him.

What sort of days, in the world's account, the days which are to come will be, no man can tell. This only we know, that if He be with us, they will be good days to us: and He will be with us, if we drive Him not away by our sins. Thus, the remembrance of our Baptism may be an anchor to our souls, sure and steadfast. Thou art among us, O Lord, and Thy Holy Name is called upon us. Thou wilt not forsake us, if we do not forsake Thee.

SERMON XXIV.

Zechariah xiii. 1.

"In that day there shall be a fountain opened to the house of David and to the inhabitants of Jerusalem for sin and for uncleanness."

The Prayer at the Consecration of the water, before administering the Sacrament of Holy Baptism, is, like most Collects and prayers, made up partly of acknowledgement of God's past favours, partly of petitions for mercies to come. The past favours we acknowledge are,

1) The opening of His Side, and the pouring out of Water and Blood on the Cross;

2) The regular Institution of Baptism, when He bade His Disciples go, teach and baptize all nations.

The mercies to come, for which we then beseech Him, are three:

1) That He would sanctify the water then in the Font to the mystical washing away of sin:

2) That the child now to be baptized therein may receive the fulness of His grace:

3) That it may ever remain in the number of His faithful and elect children.

The address or thanksgiving part we considered

last Sunday. Now we go on to the petitions. The first, as I said, is for the Sanctification of the water. "Sanctify this water to the mystical washing away of sin;" Sanctify, i. e. hallow and bless it: set it apart, or separate it, from the common uses of water, to this most sacred and heavenly use, "the mystical washing away of sin:" so that it shall be a profane thing to apply it to any other purpose; as it would be profane to take the vessels of the Altar and use them for mere ordinary refreshment.

And not only so: the prayer goes beyond that, it asks for more than such Sanctification as every thing has, which is devoted to God's service and honour. For it uses words which in one of the former Collects had been used concerning our Lord's own Baptism by St. John. It prays that the water may be, not simply sanctified, but "sanctified to the mystical washing away of sin." Now in the other Collect just mentioned, acknowledgment was made, that by the Baptism of His Well-Beloved Son Jesus Christ in the river Jordan Almighty God sanctified water to that same purpose, "the mystical washing away of sin." The prayer therefore here is, that He would grant to this water especially that blessing which by our Lord's Baptism He granted to all the waters of the earth, viz: that being duly applied, they might be effectual to the washing away of sin. We are taken back in thought to the Baptism of Jesus Christ: we seem to stand by the banks of Jordan, and to see the Holy Baptist, in fear and religious wonder, pouring the water on our Saviour, and over Him the heavens opening and the Holy Ghost descending in a bodily shape, like a dove: and in spirit we hear the gracious Voice,

"Thou art My Beloved Son, in Thee I am well pleased." All this, if we have any faith, is brought before our minds' eye, although with our bodily eye we only discern the stone Font and the Minister standing by it with his surplice, and the child waiting near with its attendants. And we understand that, as Christ our Lord by then descending into the waters of Jordan, set apart not only that river, but all the waters of this lower world to be used Sacramentally, when needed, for our regeneration, so in this prayer, He renews the same blessing especially to that particular water over which the prayer is said. It is a part of the general course of God's unspeakable mercy to us sinners, to heal us by the Touch of our Incarnate God. When He was here on earth, His Hand was from time to time laid on persons to heal them, and on things to make them healing. "Come and lay Thine Hand upon her and she shall live," was the kind of prayer with which He was constantly approached by those who had belonging to them any sick and distressed. And to shew that it is His Will to confer blessing not always simply by His Own Touch, but through the persons or things which He had touched, He healed the blind man in St. John, not by simply putting His hand upon his eyes, but by spitting on the ground and making clay of the spittle, and so anointing the eyes of the blind man with the clay. And to certain handkerchiefs and aprons long after, He gave power to be of use in healing diseases, and in driving away evil spirits, as being brought to the sick from the body of St. Paul. He Who did all these things, in an extraordinary way, at the first beginning of His Gospel, now in an ordinary way is so present in our Baptisms to sanctify the waters in our Font by the prayer of His Church, that we may be quite sure of the sanctifying power of those waters. When we see the Priest leaning over them, and offering up that devout supplication according to the purpose of our Mother the Church, we are to make no manner of question but that the Power of the Lord is present to heal the souls that shall duly be baptized therein. The gift obtained by our Lord at His Own Baptism is applied to that particular water, as the Holy Spirit Which came down on all at Pentecost, is applied to each one of us severally and particularly, by our own Baptism and Confirmation.

And this whole process, you see, is called "mystical:" i. e. secret and invisible. We see not, nor feel, nor at all reason it out; but it is not the less sure and certain. We may not doubt God's part: He will surely give His creature of water the Power which He has long ago promised to give it in behalf of His sinful creature, man. Doubt not His Presence nor His Mercy. Bow yourselves humbly down, and make sure of it. But see that with all your heart you go on and join the Priest in the petitions which yet remain, and which are two,—two very deep and grave prayers, in their meaning and virtue reaching the whole way from the moment of the child's Baptism to the last Day, and onward through his Eternal state.

The first of these petitions relates to the child's improvement in this world. "Grant that this child now to be baptized therein may receive the fulness of Thy grace." What is the fulness of God's grace? More and more of it; full measure, according to all that the redeemed soul can need, either in this world or in the world to come: as it is written, " of His fulness have all we received, and grace for grace;" i. e. each one who is made a member of Christ by Baptism has his portion in Christ's wonderful Incarnation; for in Him dwelleth all the fulness of the Godhead bodily; and we in our turn and in our measure are mysteriously made partakers of the Blessing, partakers of the Divine nature. God giveth it not scantily nor by measure. It is poured out richly according to every man's power of receiving it. And so we ask for each child that is christened, that it may receive the fulness of God's grace: that no unworthiness of our's who make the prayer, no craft or assault of the Devil, may either diminish the blessing now, or tend hereafter to the forfeiting and making it void; that as the child will now by his Lord's lovingkindness receive the full blessing of Regenerating grace, so, as soon as ever he is capable, he may be helped with more grace to turn to God more and more, giving up every thought to the obedience of his Saviour, and that all his life long from time to time he may so turn himself, till his conversion be quite perfect: and more especially may we understand that the Church, in asking for us, the fulness of God's grace, meant especially to ask that our *Confirmation* might be very blessed: that we, coming worthily and kneeling before the Bishop, and feeling his fatherly hand over us, might be strengthened by the Holy Ghost to keep all our Baptismal vow. And is there not another time besides Confirmation, to which that prayer did especially look on? Yes, surely, my brethren, it looked on very especially to the holy times of Communion in the Blessed Sacrament, to which, more than to anything else, belongeth the fulness of God's grace in this present world. O think of these things; think, as your time of Confirmation draws on, that it was in the mind of those who prayed for you at the very moment of your Baptism; The Holy Spirit, Who will have all men to be saved, Who then came to regenerate you by His free grace, was even then preparing for you this additional grace of Confirmation, and the still greater gift of the Lord's Body and Blood. Will you make His good purpose void? Will you not put on the wedding garment and come? Will you coldly and unthankfully say to your Saviour, "Thou hast indeed been good to me in giving me Baptism, without any thought or trouble of mine, but this other grace which Thou offerest me I care not to accept, because it will cost me pains and trouble: I shall have to deny mine own will, and keep myself in order, and that, as yet, I have no mind to do." Will you deal thus with your God and Saviour, even while the Blood and Water, the Life-giving grace of His Sacraments, is flowing abundantly from His pierced Side for you? Alas! what grief to the Holy Angels, who waited so lovingly round you at your new birth; what grief especially to your own Heavenly guardian, who then took charge of you, that you reject the fulness of God's grace, and think scorn of His overflowing mercy! Nay more, it is grief to the Heavenly Comforter Himself: for we read, "grieve not the Holy Spirit of God, whereby ye are sealed until the Day of Redemption." The Holy Spirit has put His Own Seal, the Name of the Trinity, upon you, to save your souls alive in the great day: and, of His condescending Love, He calls it a grief to Him, if we slight this exceeding favour. Grieve Him not by careless dealing with Baptismal grace. And we do deal carelessly with Baptismal grace, if we trifle with those other graces which naturally come after Baptism. You are young perhaps and unthinking, or you are trusted with the care of some who are so, and it seems to you but a natural kind of weakness, a pardonable thing, to trifle about preparing for Confirmation and First Communion. O think again; think more seriously : think what it must be to grieve our God. Remember Christ's rule is, "He that hath not, from him shall be taken even that which he seemeth to have: " i. e. If you seek not to grow in grace, the Lord will take away what He has already vouchsafed to you.

For lastly, there is yet one special and crowning gift, over and above those gifts which are properly called Sacramental: a gift, without which all the rest will only increase our condemnation; and that is the gift of Perseverance. We had prayed before that all *who are here baptized* might be endued with heavenly virtues and everlastingly rewarded, that is, for the fulness of God's grace, and for the gift of perseverance: and now the same prayer in substance is offered *for the infant just about to be baptized*, that he may receive the fulness of His grace ; and that he may ever remain in the number of God's faithful and elect children. You see, the Prayer Book makes no doubt that our infants are all by baptism made God's faithful and elect children: what it earnestly asks for the little one to be christened is, that it may ever remain in that number: as our Lord said to His disciples,

"Now ye are clean through the word which I have spoken unto you: abide in Me."

This then is the point which the Church would have all Christians well to consider, when they are coming to the end of their devotions just before an infant is christened, that by its christening it is made one of God's faithful and elect children, and that, in order to continue such, it will need very special grace and prayer. And if the child, at whose Baptism you are assisting, will be made faithful and elect, so, be sure, through God's mercy, were you made at your own baptism. Consider this well, and never forget it. I speak to you all, one and all, to men, women, boys, girls, and little children: to every one who is but just old enough to understand what I say, consider well and never forget it, that in your Baptism you became a child of God, faithful and elect; faithful, not then by any faith of your own, for of course you were too young for that, but by the faith of your Holy mother, the Church, who by your Parents' or nurses' hands, or by the sponsors whom she herself appointed, offered you to be baptized in the faith of Jesus Christ. By the faith of the Church you became faithful, in the happy moment of your Baptism. And in the same moment God Almighty declared you one of His elect; one of those whom He has chosen out of the world to be members of Christ, children of God, and inheritors of the kingdom of Heaven. This may seem to some of us no such great and peculiar favour, because it is what we are used to in the case of all children born among us. But it is a favour, shewn in comparison to very few of the children of Adam. It was shewn to none of those who died before God the Son was made man. Not even Abraham Isaac and Jacob were in their life-time made members of Christ. And even now it is believed that not nearly one half the inhabitants of the world are Christians. See then what a favour it was on God's Part to you and me and each one of us, that we should be born in a Christian country: see how truly we may be called His chosen and elect, even as the Jews were of old His Own elect people, set apart from among all the other nations of the earth.

And think, my brethren, how it is with you, if at any time you are chosen out, without any virtue or merit of your own, to receive any special favour. Do you not feel that it binds you to be very thankful, that the person behaving so kindly will have a great deal to say against you, if you prove ungrateful afterwards, and undutiful to him? Suppose a class of children at school, and that some great and wealthy king were to come in and choose out so many of the children, and say he would adopt them to be his own, and so take them home to his palace, and bring them up as young princes and princesses, should you not say it was doubly shameful, doubly inexcusable in those children, if they turned out ill and ungrateful? So it is, and much more, between you and God Almighty. Here are you, elected and set apart from all the heathen and Jewish children, to be brought to Christ in your infancy and put into His Arms, to be adopted children of God and made partakers of the Divine nature. So many, by far the greater part as yet, of the children of Adam, lie in darkness and the shadow of death: but you, from no desert of your own, have light in your dwellings.

What ought you to do, what can you do, but shew yourselves in every way thankful to Him Who hath so favoured you? He hath chosen you; what can you do less than choose Him? You have found special favour with God: remember her, who of all mankind, nay of all the creatures of the Most High, was most blessed and highly favoured. Remember the Blessed Virgin Mary, whom He chose to be His own Mother, as He hath chosen you to be His brethren; and let your return be like hers. She, the pattern of God's elect, instead of at all lifting herself up, said in all lowliness of heart, "Behold the handmaid of the Lord; be it unto me according to thy word." Do you, in like manner, give yourself up to Him, and reject all that would turn you from that good mind. Do so, day after day, as often as ever you are solicited to anything that you know to be wrong. Pray, and strive in earnest to do so: and you will be helped; you will not fall from grace given: and He Who chose you in the beginning to be a Christian, will choose you again in the end to be a Saint in Heaven. It is all His Gift, but you may make sure of it, if you will.

SERMON XXV.

Rev. iii. 12.

" I will write upon him My new Name."

WE are now come to that part of the Baptismal service, which all of us, perhaps, know best; that part which even when we were little children most drew our attention to it. For even very young children are apt earnestly to look towards the Font, and to mind what is going on, when it comes to this part of the service. When, after the prayer at the Consecration of the Water, there is silence, and the Priest takes the child in his arms according to the next direction of the Rubric, it is to the eye a very simple and ordinary thing, that the clergyman should receive the infant into his arms in order to christen it, but to the eye of faith that simple action is full of high mysterious meaning. For when we see it, we are not to think of this or that particular minister who happens to be then doing duty. As St. John Baptist many times told us, we are to think of the One only real Baptizer, Jesus Christ, of Whose Presence the mortal and visible Priest is but a type and figure and shadow. We are to think, as nearly as we may, just as we would have thought, had we been present when

He took the little children in His arms, when He laid His hands upon them, sanctified and blessed them. Had any one of us been by at that time, we might perhaps have recollected in our minds what is written in the Old Testament, "He shall feed His flock like a Shepherd, He shall gather the lambs into His Arms, and shall carry them in His Bosom." The good, the kind, the considerate Shepherd looks most especially after the lambs. Of all things He will not suffer them to be forsaken and neglected: not only because they are the hope of His flock, and, if they fail, there is no chance of His Shepherd's work prospering in time to come, but also out of real pity for their helpless tender delicate condition. For which cause also the Prophet adds, "He will gently lead them which are with young." Or we may call to mind the saying of the great Prophet Moses, when he puts the children of Israel upon considering the love and care, which they had experienced for so many years in the wilderness. "The Eternal God is thy refuge, and underneath are the Everlasting arms;" i. e. He bears thee up strongly, securely, and lovingly, as a nursing father carries his sucking child: there is no fear of His growing tired or letting thee go: you may feel His arms under you, and be quite sure that you are safe. Or, as the same prophet utters the blessing of Benjamin, the youngest of Jacob's family, the child of his old age, his darling and best-beloved; "The beloved of the Lord shall dwell in safety by Him, and the Lord shall cover him all the day long, and he shall dwell between His shoulders;" i. e. on His Bosom, supported on both His arms, as one may often see fathers carrying young children. And as we feel, when we see it, what safe and tender care the children are in, so, and much more, may we imagine the perfect peace and security of these little ones, when Christ, the Great Shepherd, the Eternal Nursing Father, has just taken them up in His merciful arms. Of all which, the Priest receiving the infant from the nurse, and holding it in his arms by the Font, is a lively Image and Type.

We are also to consider from whom the Priest receives the child. Of course from the parents or sponsors: for the nurse who presents it is but their attendant and minister; and they themselves are in truth but attendants and ministers of the Church. This should be considered more than it is. The godfathers and godmothers are not there as friends of the parents only, but as persons appointed by the Holy Church to offer and present the young child to its Saviour, and put it into His arms. As Hannah brought young Samuel to Eli, who stood in the place of God to receive the child, so the nurse, the Godmother, or the mother, brings a little infant now to the Priest, who stands in the place of Jesus Christ, to take it up in his arms and bless it. And as, when you see the Priest, you are not to think of him, but of our Lord: so when you look upon a woman standing by the Font with a child to be christened in her arms, you are not to think of her, but of the Church of God, the Mother and Nurse of us all, who brings us one by one in her arms to our Saviour when we are infants, presents us to Him, and makes the engagements in our name.

Thus we have explained what is meant by the Godmother or nurse presenting the child, and the

Priest taking it up in his arms. The next thing is for the Priest to enquire the child's name, saying to those who presented it, "Name this child." Now why should the Child have a new name given him at Baptism? Because a new name is a token of a new nature, or at least of a very great change of condition. It signifies that the person receiving it is in some material respects not exactly the same as he was before. He may be better off or worse: but he cannot be exactly the same. Therefore those who seek the very best things for their children, naturally desire that God should give them a name, for a token and pledge that He will not deny the blessing. He having all power and wisdom, when He gives the name He will also give the thing, and when He changes the name, He will change the thing. So it was from very old times indeed; the times, of which we read in the Bible, the times of Abraham and Jacob, of Joshua, St. John Baptist and others. As often as we read of God's putting a distinct name upon any of those whom He delighted to honour, we may well think of Christian Baptism, and of the gift of God, properly so called; i. e. the Holy Regenerating Spirit. Thus, God changed Abram's name; changed it to Abraham, and we know the meaning of that change. Abram means simply a great father: but when God, in His Mercy, chose him openly for His own, and entered into solemn covenant with him by the sign and token of circumcision, He saw fit to change Abram's *name* also. He changed it to Abraham; a father of many nations; because not only so many peoples, in and around the Holy Land, were to be of the seed of Abraham after the flesh, but, what was a great deal more, all of us, all Christian people, all who to the end of the world shall be made members of Christ, are at the same time made truly and really children of Abraham, the father of Christ after the flesh. And so it came to be a custom, that to every Israelitish man-child, when he was admitted into Abraham's covenant by the solemn rite of circumcision, God gave a new name for a seal and token of that covenant. And this new name, to the people of Israel, signified always two things; first, that they belonged specially to God; secondly, that they had an especial blessing from God. Our Christian names, my brethren, signify the same two things to us. As often as ever we are called by them, it is a token and pledge to us (whether we consider it or no) that we do indeed belong to God, to His holy nation and peculiar people; we are bought with a price, and cannot be as if we had no Divine Master. Again, our Christian name is, to every one baptized in infancy, a token how greatly Christ has blessed us: that we are among His highly favoured, His own family, whom all generations shall call blessed. In these two respects, as set apart to be Christ's own, and as looked upon by Him with extraordinary love and pity, we resemble our fathers, the Jews of old: but in that which I am next to mention, we have greatly the advantage of them. Our Christian Name, besides all that has been mentioned, is a token of our new and heavenly nature, given to us in Holy Baptism; because we are then made members of Christ. This is more than had been promised to the greatest Prophet before our Saviour: but it is given at our Fonts to every little child. And the greatness of the gift you may partly understand by considering what was signified and given to those, whose names were from time to time changed and made new by God Almighty: how Jacob, for example, had his name changed to Israel, because he should be a mighty prince and king before God. This was a token that we Christians should be to our God a sort of kings, to reign over our own hearts and imaginations, and to command and order all outward things so, as that they shall work together for our good, we truly loving God: for such is His Promise. Again, Joshua had his name changed and made new; it meant "a Saviour," and it was altered so as to signify, "The Lord shall save:" and this was a token and pledge to him, that he should bring the people into the Holy Land; as our Christian Name is a pledge to us, that the great Almighty God hath indeed come down, suffered, and triumphed, to redeem us, and guide us to our everlasting Home, and help us to win it. Again, consider the names which were bestowed on different persons by our Lord Jesus Christ Himself, and see what a blessing they brought with them in each case. We may reckon as one of them the name of St. John Baptist, which was sent down from Heaven by special message through an Angel: and was given him, when the time came, not without remarkable miracles. That name John signifies gracious, and was a sign and token of God's true graciousness to every one coming to Christ. Again, when Simon son of Jona came to our Lord and He gave him the name of Cephas or Peter; i. e. of a Rock, firm and immoveable; this betokens the sure and certain hope, the unswerving faith, of one keeping baptismal grace. And so all along: Christian names, or names which were meant to prepare men to be Christians, as they have always in reality been given by Almighty God, so have they no less really brought each one its special blessings from Him.

Such names we know are commonly chosen by friends and parents, for love's sake : for love of some departed one, whom the new name will always bring to remembrance. And it is very well indeed, so to call to mind earthly friends departed. But it is far better, if we call to mind the whole body of heaven-friends, the saints and martyrs of old time, those who now reign with Christ, but with whom we are truly now in Communion, by virtue of the Communion of Saints. It is far better that whatever a man's own particular name may be, he shall never forget the Name which he bears in common with all his brethren, the holy Name of Christ, by which all Christians are called.

I would wish to put this very earnestly both to parents, kinsmen and friends, in regard of their children's names, and to each one among us in regard of his own name. Have we ever turned our minds, thoroughly and distinctly, to what Scripture tells us of the true meaning and virtue of the christian names which we all bear ? For instance we read in the book of Revelation in the verse out of which our text is taken, and it is our Lord Jesus Christ Himself Who pronounces the words, " Him that overcometh I will make him a pillar in the temple of My God, and he shall no more go out, and I will write upon him the Name of My God, and the name of the city of My God, new Jerusalem which cometh down from Heaven from My God: and I will write upon him My new

Name." As much as to say: He that keeps his baptismal vow, Christ will give him a sure place in His Church, a strong place, a glorious place, where he shall be not only safe himself, but shall adorn and support in his measure the holy society to which he belongs, as pillars adorn and support a consecrated building. On that man, the finger of Christ will write, as it were, three names; the Name of the Father, the Name of the Church which is the New Jerusalem, and His own New Name. And these three names shall be so far one, as that they shall be written on each one of us by the gift of one Name which is called our Christian Name. Yes, Christian Brethren, however little we may think of it, the very name by which we are ordinarily named, the name by which our friends and neighbours address us, is the name of God sacramentally written upon us. As a man might write his name in a book, or have it engraved on an implement or article of furniture, or marked on a garment, that all might know it to be his, so the Almighty Everlasting God hath written His Own Name upon you and me, and upon all who have received a Name in Holy Baptism; from those who came to St. Peter on the Day of Pentecost, even unto the little babe, whose christening we have just now witnessed, we all truly bear written upon us the Name of Almighty God as our owner. Angels, good and bad, see the great Name written upon us: the bad with hate and fear and envy longing to to steal us away for ever from Him Who so vouchsafes to own us; the good, with an earnest and longing desire to do His Will in watching and guarding us.

But further: as men for greater security commonly write the name of the place they belong to, as well as their own name in a book or anything else; so we see our Lord represents Himself as writing on each one of us, not only the Name of His God and Father, but also the Name of His City, New Jerusalem, the Church of God. Our Christian Name is a token that we are God's Own, not only as all creatures are His, but as belonging to His holy Church.

Thirdly, our Lord says,—they are wonderful and mysterious words,—"I will write upon Him My new Name:" we are not only marked as belonging to His Father, and to His Church, but also as being parts and members of Him, in such sort that His Name is ours: the Name of Christ is the Name of each Christian: and the Name of Christ is our Lord's new Name, because it was not His Name from eternity, but began to be His Name when He came into the world to redeem us: to be made Man, taking our nature upon Him. And thus each one's Christian Name is in a manner three names in one, the Name of the Father to Whom we belong, the Name of the Church wherein we abide, and most especially the Name of Christ,' Whose members we are, and through Whom we have our other blessings.

Now, Christian parents and friends, fathers and mothers, brothers and sisters, god-fathers and god-mothers, kinsmen and kinswomen (I speak to you all, for which of you is there, who is not in one or other of these ways concerned with one or more of these little ones?) might it not be well for you to think more deeply than hitherto what a Christian Name is: what deep and high things we speak of when we talk of a Christian Name? You see a young child in the cradle, or an elder child moving about the house, and it is a delight to hear that child called by such and such a name, which brings back it may be the thought of some dear parent, kinsman or friend far away, or departed this world. What if you were to think also of that other and greater and more blessed Name, which the same child surely bears written upon him, the Name of Christ, marking him as belonging to God, as abiding in His Holy Church, as a member of His Son? And if we think of this in respect to the young children in any way committed to our charge, surely we must think of it in respect of ourselves also. For we too, brethren, both old and young, have each of us a Christian name of our own. It was one of the first things we learnt in our early childhood: we may see by other children now, how we ourselves, many years ago, began to call ourselves by that name, and in our lisping way to make what we could of it. O that we would make much also of the Name of Christ, our Lord's new Name, which He wrote upon us also at our Christening, which we bear along with us through the world, and which unites us to the great Family in Heaven and earth, thè Holy Catholic Church throughout all the world! O that Christians would learn to think a great deal of the name Christian, the true token of the real high birth of us all, and would take a holy and loving pride in walking worthy of their Baptismal Name! The Almighty Lord give us that good mind! that when the names of the whole world shall be called over at the last Day, we may answer to our names without that fearful confusion which must needs overwhelm all those, to whom their very Christian name will be a reproach, because they will be found to have led unchristian lives.

SERMON XXVI.

Prov. xviii. 10.

" The Name of the Lord is a strong tower: the righteous runneth into it and is safe."

THERE are two Names which come into the actual administration of the Sacrament of Baptism, the Name of God, and the name of the child: and the wonder and the mystery is, that these two names are in a manner made one. The child is so united to God Almighty, that from thenceforth the Name of God is in a manner the child's name. But as to the child's own name, that which is commonly called his Christian name, we said something of it in our last Catechising. Now let us go on to the other, the most Holy Name, that Name which by an ordinance for ever is annexed to the Sacrament of Baptism, so that without it there can be no Baptism: the Name of the most Holy Trinity, the Father, the Son, and the Holy Ghost. For such is the foundation law of the kingdom of Heaven, enacted by the Great King at the moment when He was just about to take to Him His great power and reign. He met His Disciples by special appointment in Galilee, on the same mountain probably, where He had spoken in the hearing of the same Apostles His eight Beatitudes and the rest of His Divine Sermon; which mountain may in some respects appear to hold the same kind of place among Christians, as the mountain of Sinai among God's ancient people. Consider Him with His Apostles, on the mountain in Galilee, and mark what His words are. It is the King meeting His chosen officers and giving them their instructions for nearly the last time, as to how they should order the Kingdom in His absence. And this is the Proclamation He makes: "all power is given unto Me in Heaven and in earth: go ye therefore, and teach all nations, baptizing them in the name of the Father, and of the Son, and of the Holy Ghost." These are the words or Form of Baptism, settled once for all by Him Who baptises all. For however many and various are the persons baptized, and the circumstances under which they are baptized, the real Baptizer is always one: as the Forerunner said, "This is He which baptizeth with the Holy Ghost:" and the words used by the priest are always the same, "In the name of the Father, and of the Son, and of the Holy Ghost."

On this Sacred and mysterious Name I have first of all to observe, that here is the most express acknowledgement of the Faith of the Holy Trinity, ordained by our Lord Himself at the very entrance into His Kingdom. No one can be a disciple of His, i. e. no one can be a Christian, without this solemn acknowledgement: that the God to whom He belongs is both One and Three: One, for it says, "I baptize thee in the *Name* of the Father, and of the Son, and of the Holy Ghost; not, "in the Names," but "In the *Name*": there seem to be three Names, but in reality it is One Name: because the three Persons severally named are One God; and this God, our God, for ever and ever. He is Three also; therefore the Three Personal Names are added, the Father, the Son, and the Holy Ghost. The Father, the One Fountain of all good, from Whom in eternal unspeakable ways the other two Divine Persons have their Being: The Son or Word of God begotten from everlasting of the Father: The Holy Ghost proceeding from the Father, and sent out by the Son; or, as we acknowledge in our Communion Service, "Proceeding from the Father and the Son." In the One Divine Name of these Three Persons our Lord hath commanded us one and all to be baptized. He will have us love, trust and serve them all alike, they being so inseparable, that whatever obedience love and honour is paid to One is paid to all: although with respect to that One of them Who vouchsafed to be made Man for us, we must have special feelings turned towards Him as He is Man, doing and suffering so much for us, feelings which we cannot have as concerning those, Who never were Incarnate. However, it is quite plain, that our Lord has here put the Faith and Name of the Father, the Son, and the Holy Ghost at the very door of His House and Kingdom, so that no one can enter in, without taking that Name and that Faith upon him.

Now by this we may understand, secondly, that our Lord expects each one of us to keep up and practise the same faith continually: even as the priest enquired of us when we were brought to the Font, "Wilt thou be baptized in this Faith?" and we answered by our godfathers and godmothers, "That is my desire."

We desired to be baptized into the faith of the Father, the Son and the Holy Ghost, and He graciously granted our desire: you see then how we are bound, in all duty and thankfulness to go on living in that faith. What is "living *in the faith* of such and such a doctrine?" It is, turning our minds to it, recollecting it continually, making very much of it in our thoughts and in all our behaviour. You would not say a man lived in the faith of Christ, if he never thought of Christ, never made any difference in his doings for Christ's sake, and in order to please Him. So neither ought you to consider yourself as living in the faith of the Holy Trinity, unless you very often think of the Trinity, and lift up your heart in prayer and praise, in love and worship, to the Divine Three in One. Are you accustomed so to do, my brethren? Do you carefully use the opportunities which the Church, in her wisdom and charity, gives you of acknowledging the "Holy Blessed and Glorious Trinity, Three Persons and One God:" giving glory to the Father, the Son, and the Holy Ghost? You know how often she invites you to do so, at the end of every Psalm and Canticle. Do you always endeavour to answer her invitation with all reverence and earnestness of heart? There is fear of our not doing so.; and if we do not, it cannot but prove a serious harm to us, for the very reason that the opportunity occurs so often. In truth, if you have not hitherto taken *special* care on this point, there must have been more or less inattention and irreverence, though you were far perhaps from meaning it: and it may have been silently hurting others as well as yourself. Let me beseech you then, brethren, henceforth always to pay special regard to the most Holy Trinity, the Three Persons in One God, making some act of reverence, if not in body, yet at least in mind, as often as you read, hear or speak of them. Those Divine Three are ever present in all their love, wisdom and power. Whenever and however they are mentioned; the mention of them is their own providential way of putting you in mind of their Presence. Can you do less than notice and acknowledge it?

Certainly you cannot do less, if you at all believe what I am next going to point out to you, as the undoubted teaching of Holy Scripture concerning our portion in that Holy Name: viz., that we are baptized not only *in*, but *into* it. We have the Name of the Most High God, Father, Son, and Holy Ghost, so put upon us, as that we shall be rightly called by it; it becomes in a manner *our name*. We are called by the Divine Name, as being made partakers of the Divine Nature. So St. Peter tells us; referring particularly to the regenerating grace of the Holy Ghost, making us members of Christ, Who is God, in the moment of our Baptism. But let us consider how the three Sacred Names, the Names of the Father, the Son, and the Holy Ghost, are each severally *our* Names—how we are in a manner called by each of them.

First, we are called from God the Father, of Whom the whole family in heaven and earth is named. Being admitted into His family, we are called from Him, as being called His children: for all children have their being and their name from their Father. In Baptism we are regularly adopted to be His children, and His Name is thenceforth called upon us: and the angels looking upon us, think of Him, and of the love which He hath towards us: just as we, meeting with any child whom a great rich person had adopted, should naturally think of that person, and of the love which he had shewn to that child. Can we then help saying to ourselves, "He is our Father; where is His honour? I am His child, His adopted child: how can I ever reverence and love Him enough?" Such as these ought to be our thoughts of God the Father, seeing we are called by His Name.

And then as to the Second Person, God the Son, we are baptized into His Name, as you all know without my telling you, in that we are by that Holy Sacrament made members of Him, Bone of His Bone, and Flesh of His Flesh, and as truly united to Him, as a wife is joined to her husband in the holy and mysterious ordinance of matrimony. And therefore, as the wife from thenceforth takes the husband's name, giving up her own; so the baptized person is thenceforth called a Christian after the Name of Jesus Christ: and of his own earthly names and connexions he ought to think little in comparison, as they are indeed nothing to compare with the honour and blessing of becoming a member of Christ. Has it been so with us, brethren? is it so even now? We know that we are members of Christ; those who know least of their Catechism can hardly be ignorant of *that:* how often in the day are we used to remember it? When we are tempted to sinful or doubtful liberties, either in thought, in word, or in deed, do we regularly check ourselves with remembering, "Nay these members of mine, this heart, this tongue, these hands, this whole body and soul, are the heart, tongue, and hands, the body and soul of Christ Jesus: shall I take the members of Christ and make them the members of an harlot? Shall I tell lies with the tongue of Christ, steal with the hand of Christ? God forbid." And on the other hand do we encourage ourselves in every good word and work with the sure and certain hope, "It is not I, but the grace of Christ which is in me? I may hope for a blessing, since it is not I, poor frail unworthy being, but Christ that dwelleth in me, He doeth the works." Do we say to ourselves, "Come let us be up and doing: let no good opportunity pass away; we have our Lord's eyes to see with, our Lord's hand to work with, the tongue of Christ to utter our words, the mind of Christ to order our thoughts: we are inexcusable if we bear no good fruit: whoever else may be slothful, we may not." If we are really members of Christ, this is how we ought to quicken ourselves, and not let our time and all our blessed opportunities pass away as in an idle dream. And this, because we are baptized unto God the Son, into the Name of Christ.

But, thirdly, we are also baptized into the Name of the Holy Ghost. We are the children of the Father, being members of the Son: and how are we members of the Son? by the work of the Holy Ghost. Therefore we are called regenerate, sanctified, spiritual persons; i. e. the Name of the Holy Spirit is put upon us, no less than the Name of the Father and of the Son. That blessed Comforter, uniting us to Christ, has also united us to Himself and to the Father. It is a three-fold Cord: who may break it? Who shall separate us from the love of the Holy blessed and glorious Trinity? from the God who made us His own, before we could think or know anything?

Here then is the saying of Solomon wonderfully accomplished, "The Name of the Lord is a strong tower; the righteous runneth into it, and is safe." We are here in an evil and trying world, encompassed with many and great dangers. Storms are in the air, they may come down upon us any moment: whither shall we fly for shelter? To our earthly homes and friends? Alas, they are under the same sky as ourselves, they are subject to the same tempests: they, no less than we, may this very hour be swept away suddenly and without warning. Shall we set to work and build ourselves up a shelter, a tower, as some did of old time, whose top might reach unto heaven, a great Babylon of our own contrivance, in which we may have our own way undisturbed? We know beforehand it will be all in vain: the experience of near 6000 years has told us, and the most simple among us knows it as well and as certainly as he knows his own existence, that all such devices are in vain. And so, when we have looked far and wide, when we have thought and dreamed all things over, we shall find but this one refuge, this one hope and shelter; the Lord God Almighty, Who hath taken us to Himself, putting His own Name upon us in our Baptism. To Him let us hasten, as children run to their parents. Why should we seek any other refuge? His own saving Almighty Name, the Name of the most Holy Trinity, is ours, if we will use it, for a sure defence, and strong weapon against all that our enemies can do to hurt us. To flee away to any other, neglecting this, is in reality setting up the Evil One against God: it is the sin of witchcraft, so called in the Scriptures: it is trusting in names and divinations and charms: but may our trust always be in that worthy Name whereby we are called, in the Name of the most Holy Trinity, which we carry about with us ever since our Baptism! Whatever else we use, and thankfully use, to help and comfort us for awhile on the way, let us never trust in anything but in this One Holy Name, this glorious and fearful Name, the Lord our God, the Father, the Son, and the Holy Ghost. Into this Tower we will run, and there by His mercy we shall be safe: only let us remember to what manner of persons this is promised. The righteous runneth into this strong hold and is safe, i. e. they who by sincere obedience or true repentance have kept or recovered that righteousness of Christ which He bestowed on them in their Baptism. But if you turn back to your own wickedness, to the evil works which were your own by nature, the holy Name which should have been your Salvation will turn in the end to your more dismal ruin. Preserve us, O Lord, from that worst of sin and misery.

SERMON XXVII.

Romans vi. 4.

"*We are buried with Him by Baptism into death that like as Christ was raised from the dead by the glory of the Father, so we also should walk in newness of life*[a].*"*

The Priest, having the child in his arms and naming it as directed by the godfathers and godmothers, who are appointed by the Church to bring it to him, proceeds at last to the actual Christening, the manner whereof you well know. The words which he repeats we have already considered: that Most Holy Name which is the stay and strength, the hope and refuge of every one of us: the Name of the Trinity, which thenceforth the child is to bear with him through this world, and to take with him into Eternity to be either an Eternal blessing or an infinite aggravation of Eternal punishment. This Name is put upon the child; he is as it were sealed with it; but not by merely saying the words: it is God's Will, that the words should always be accompanied with the act which is called baptizing, in itself so

[a] A second text was added in the margin, quoted at the end of the Sermon Cant. v. 3, "I have washed my feet how shall I defile them?"

simple, in the mystery and meaning so great. The two together, the words and the act, make up (as the Catechism says) the outward visible Sign or Form in Baptism. It would not be Baptism, were a child washed or dipped in water in silence with only good thoughts: no, nor if he were washed or dipped with the best and most beautiful Prayer: it would not be Baptism, unless the very words which our Saviour appointed were used, "In the Name of the Father and of the Son and of the Holy Ghost." So on the other hand neither would it be Baptism, were this Most Holy Name ever so solemnly repeated over the child, with the Amen of the whole Church. This would not, I say, be Baptism, unless the child or person at the same time were actually washed or dipped in the water. There have been indeed and are persons in the world, who call themselves Christians, yet make light of this ordinance. What can we say of them, but that they are like Naaman the Syrian who would not believe that his leprosy would be cleansed by washing seven times in the river Jordan? Had he persisted in that scornful way of thinking, his leprosy would never have been cleansed. And so we may well fear, regarding those who go on making light of the actual washing of Baptism, that they are sadly trifling with Christ's way of Salvation. They may seem to themselves wise and knowing; they may think to be more spiritual, further advanced in Gospel grace than others: but even as that mighty man of Syria, Naaman, was better instructed by his own servants, when they remonstrated with him on his rude way of rejecting what God had told him by the prophet; so the most learned and clever of us all, if we at all feel disposed to make light of God's Holy Sacraments, may well learn a lesson from the simplest. Yes, brethren, the poorest, the meanest, the most ignorant in this or any other Christian congregation, who has learnt to behave himself respectfully at Holy Baptism, does by his behaviour give the best rebuke to those who are so ill-instructed as to disbelieve in its virtue. Without speech he seems to say to us, "If the Prophet, the Great Prophet Jesus Christ had required of you some great thing, would you not have done it? how much more when He saith unto you, 'Wash and be clean!'" I cannot help having somewhat of this sort of feeling, when I observe how in our congregations, the simple, quiet, believing worshippers turn reverently towards the Font, when the holy Service of Baptism begins: how they listen with all reverence, how earnestly they watch all that is said and done, either by the Priest or sponsors. It is a part of the Church Service, in which the dutiful children of the Church, the little ones of Jesus Christ, join, as it appears, with most especial affection and dutifulness: and when one sees them, sometimes it may come into one's heart to think, what if one of those should be here, who by any sort of wrong training has been taught to have little faith in Holy Baptism, to think of it as of a mere ordinance, surely, whether he were unbelieving or unlearned, the sight of a whole congregation so devoutly assisting at a child's Baptism may very well move him to have other thoughts. As St. Paul says of one in a like case, he may be convinced of all, "he may be judged of all," he may humble himself in heart, and believe and confess that God is in Holy

Baptism of a truth, in a way which he had not before thought of. Thus by the reverent behaviour of those who may seem only babes in Christ, He may correct and convert some of those who, in their seeming wisdom and prudence, have as yet the glory of God's Sacraments hidden from them.

But let people's thoughts and behaviour be what they may, the Holy Sacrament is, as I have said, the same, and the Divine Presence equally attends it. And now let us consider some of the things which were mentioned in the Catechising, as to the manner in which that Sacrament is administered.

The words of the Rubric are, " Naming the child after the sponsors, if they shall certify him that the child may well endure it, he shall dip it in the water discreetly and warily," saying the aweful and blessed words. Evidently then the Church prefers that way of baptizing, in which the child is plunged entirely into the water. For which cause also it is directed, that at Baptisms the Font should be *filled* with pure water: that there may be enough to dip the child. Why does the Church prefer this way to the other, supposing it were quite certain that the child may well endure it? First, perhaps, because the word *Baptize* properly means this sort of action, and not merely pouring on a little water, much less sprinkling it. Secondly, because the action of dipping sets forth to the very eye the proper force and meaning of Christian Baptism, how that it is both a Death and Resurrection; the pouring of the water scarcely gives that meaning at all. This is what St. Paul so often alludes to, "buried with Him by Baptism, wherein also we are risen again with Him, through the faith of the operation of God, Who raised Him from the dead." And in the text, "We are buried with Him by Baptism unto death, that like as Christ was raised from the dead by the glory of the Father, so we also should walk in newness of life." Yes, we are buried with Him even bodily; buried in the baptizing water for a moment, and in the next moment raised out of it: whereby are shown forth to the very eyes and ears of the bystanders a lively Image of the Death and Resurrection of Christ Crucified, an Image also of the spiritual death and Resurrection of every one of us, the death unto sin, and the new birth unto righteousness. And in this way no doubt, the more part of Christians, in hot countries, have been baptized: the very form and gesture, as well as the words and the water, serving to shew them the nature of the action they were performing, and to remind them, ever after, of their true condition towards God. But with us in these northern parts, it would plainly be very dangerous, in many cases, to insist on this way of baptism, and in all countries there would be instances in which it would prove inconvenient and next to impossible. And, therefore, He Who will have mercy and not sacrifice, has given us plainly to understand that pouring the water on the child or person, with the proper words, is sufficient. There is a tradition in the Church, that He Himself was baptized in this way, as you may see in the usual pictures of our Lord's Baptism. Therefore the Holy Church in her charity has added, as you know, to the Rubric which recommends dipping, another Rubric which permits us merely to "pour water on the child if it be certified that the child be weak."

And now, the child being taken out of the water, the Priest, before he restores him to the arms of those who are trusted to take care of him, has to make upon him the sign of the Holy Cross. But before we go on to speak of this, let us take time to think earnestly on this great thing, that now this child is really made partaker of a holy Resurrection, answering to our Lord's rising from the grave: nay more: not only answering to Christ's Resurrection, but, in inward and spiritual power, really and truly partaking thereof: so that it is said in Holy Scripture over and over again: "Ye are risen with Christ; ye are risen again with Him; ye are partakers of His Death and Resurrection; now it is not ye that live, but Christ liveth in you. Because, being made members of Christ, you are at once made to share in all that Christ did and suffered for you. You are dead with Him, you are buried with Him, you are risen with Him, you are ascended with Him."

As then our Lord's Blessed Body was changed and glorified at His Resurrection, so did our souls, yea, and our bodies too, begin to be changed and glorified at our Baptism, to be henceforth spiritual as was His glorious Body; but in Him the change was all in a moment, in us it is to go on gradually through all our time of trial, and to be completed only at the last day. The Almighty Spirit of God, Who came to us at the Font, dwelleth in and shall be in us to accomplish this change; and our work is to obey His godly motions, to be workers under Him, in renewing our own souls, and in keeping our bodies chaste and pure, that they also may be renewed hereafter. This is our new life, answering to the Life of our

Risen Lord, that as He, being raised from the dead, dieth no more, so we, being raised in Baptism from the death which Adam brought on us, should sin no more. As He during those forty days was only preparing for His Ascension, so we for the short, the very short, time that we have to abide here on earth, should be only preparing for that other and eternal world. What indeed have we else to do, since God has so graciously ordered our concerns, that all our other innocent cares, our love for our friends and kinsmen and the like, may be turned that same way, may be made steps towards heaven? Think then, brethren, day and night of your Baptism. You cannot think of it too much; only take care to think of it in this way, that being so risen with Christ you have but one thing to do, to seek those things which are above, where Christ sitteth on the Right Hand of God.

One thing more, and it shall be something which all may understand. When you think of Baptism, you think of washing; for Baptism, you know, is a washing with water. Now what is the use of washing? Of course, to make one clean. Baptism is ordained by Almighty God to make our souls pure and clean, not by any virtue which it has in itself, but through the most precious Blood of our Only Saviour Christ Jesus, which it pleases Him to apply to our souls in that way. Remember this: you have been, once at least, effectually cleansed: once at least there was a time when our Lord might have said to us as He said to His Apostles: "now ye are clean through the word which I have spoken unto you." In whatever degree we have become unfit to have the same word spoken to us now, we know whose fault it must be, and the same consequence of it. Those who are careful to be neat and clean in their houses, their persons, and their clothing, and to keep all belonging to them the same, know how provoking it is, when things which they have been taking trouble with, are wilfully and wantonly stained and sullied again. It is a very great trial of temper. Now by this you may judge how angry our Lord must be, when, having washed us clean in His own most precious Blood, so painfully shed for us on the tormenting Cross, He finds us by our own fault all foul and filthy again. Let us beware that it be not so with us. Remember the King coming in to see the guests, and what became of him whose dress was not what it ought to have been. When temptation comes near, say with the spouse in the song of Solomon, "I have washed my feet, how shall I defile them?" Alas! how many at the last Day will wish that they had borne these things in mind, when it will be too late!

SERMON XXVIII.

St. Matt. x. 38.

"*He that taketh not his Cross and followeth after Me, is not worthy of Me.*"

WHEN the child has been christened, the Priest does not, as you know, immediately restore it to the nurse's arms, but keeps it in his own arms until he have made the sign of the Cross upon its forehead, saying at the same time those noble words, known, as I trust to a great many, if not to the greater part of you. "We receive this Child into the congregation of Christ's flock, and do sign *him* with the sign of the Cross, in token that hereafter *he* shall not be ashamed to confess the faith of Christ crucified, and manfully to fight under His banner, against sin, the world, and the devil; and to continue Christ's faithful soldier and servant unto *his* life's end."

In order to have proper thoughts of this part of the service, we must consider, what is the use of signing and sealing things among men, how Holy Scripture teaches us to apply that use to the things of God, and what use we ourselves ought to make of our Lord's own sign and seal, the sign of the Cross, which we thus received at the time of our Baptism. I say, at the time of our Baptism, not *in* our Baptism: because I would wish carefully to guard against the error which some, I know, fall into, of accounting the sign of the Cross part of the Sacrament itself of Baptism. The Sacrament is complete with only the water and the word; as it is given, when an infant, being seriously ill, is baptized at home. In such case you know there is no sign of the Cross. *That* is added afterwards when the infant is brought to Church; yet we are not to doubt that the infant is lawfully and sufficiently baptized.

What is the use then of the Holy Sign, if it is no part of Baptism? The Priest's words, when he makes it, are sufficient to explain its use, if only we bear in mind what is men's purpose in signing or sealing anything. Generally speaking, a sign or seal, put upon anything, is put for one or both of two uses. To keep the thing safe, and to make known whom it belongs to. Thus the chief Priests made our Lord's Sepulchre sure, *sealing* the stone, as well as setting a watch: and thus Jezebel when she wrote that wicked letter about Naboth, not only wrote it in Ahab's name, but sealed it also with Ahab's seal, that there might be no doubt of the letter coming from Ahab.

And now we know what the uses of a seal are, we shall the better understand how the sign of the Cross is, as Christ's Seal, put upon each of us, immediately after we have been made members of Christ in Baptism.

For first of all, the Priest with the infant in his arms says aloud in his own name, and in that of all the congregation and in the name of all Christian people, "We receive this child into the Congregation of Christ's flock." It may be asked, what need so to receive the child? since, his Baptism being complete, he is already a member of Christ, bone of His Bone and flesh of His Flesh, and therefore much more is he already one of Christ's congregation and flock, and no doubt the inward blessing is already complete: the child cannot be more entirely baptized, more truly and really joined to Christ than he is. But the Church has always thought it well, that what has been inwardly and spiritually done should be outwardly and visibly accepted and declared; that Christians should acknowledge each fresh Christian, coming or brought into their assembly, with such solemn words of welcome. "We receive this child or this person into the congregation of Christ's flock," into the Holy Catholic Church and the Communion of Saints, into the blessed brotherhood and family, named of our Lord in Heaven and earth:—and surely, as the words are said, they may well go deep into each one of our hearts, husbands and wives: and as those who truly and religiously love one another had thoughts which cannot be put into words, when they listened to the Church pronouncing that they were man and wife together, so, and even much more, ought the thoughts to be very deep and blessed, which come into a Christian man's mind, when he hears infant after infant solemnly received into the flock, and considers that he has himself been so received. He may consider with himself that these words were, in deed and in truth, the voice of all Saints and Angels greeting him, as he enters within the Holy Household; they are the pledge and earnest of the yet more unspeakable greeting which the same Heavenly hosts have in store for him, against the time when, if it please God, he shall pass through the everlasting doors, and with open face behold the things in which now he only believes.

But now mark how the Service goes. The Priest says not, "We receive this child into Christ's congregation," but, "into the congregation of Christ's flock," putting us in mind that all we are sheep, that the Church is our Fold, Jesus Christ our Shepherd, and the infant of course who has just been christened, can be no other than a lamb, a lamb of Christ's fold, newly born, and of course an object of the good Shepherd's very special care. Now we know what shepherds do, in order that their sheep and lambs may be kept safe. They put their master's name, some letter of it, or some mark belonging to their master, upon each sheep or lamb separately, and so turn them out, when they have been washed and shorn. Even so is the Name and Mark of Christ put upon His lambs by His under-shepherds, when they mark them, newly baptized, with the sign of the Cross. That sign is the Name and Mark of our Lord Christ, put upon them, to tell whose they are, and to protect them from dangerous enemies: as sheep, when properly marked, wander at large in mountainous countries and are safe, because men see whom they belong to, and are afraid of the peril and trouble of stealing them. Let us consider a little how the signing of our foreheads in Baptism may be a protection to us in ways which we little dream of.

One might naturally say, how can this be, seeing that the sign itself is not really made in our forehead? It is not stamped or painted there, as it is on the sheep; but only the Priest's fingers, for one very short moment, trace the figure in the air close to the child's brow, leaving no trace when they are taken off. To all outward appearance the babe is the same as before. But, my brethren, there are others by, spectators and witnesses of the child's Baptism, of whom we may well believe that they see the print of the Cross remaining, although we do not see it. These are the good Angels, especially that one to whom, according to the Church's old opinion, the care and guardianship is committed of the child's own soul particularly. The good Angels, I say, looking on a newly christened child, see that blessed and saving Sign in its clear baptismal brightness, not as yet dimmed nor sullied by actual sin; and, generally as they go about the world, we may well believe that they see who among mortals have Christ's mark upon them, and that, for the love of Christ, they are always ready, always forward to do all they can for the help of those whom they perceive to belong to Christ? Just as any friend or faithful servant of a man owning sheep upon the mountains would look after those sheep or lambs on which he saw his master's or his friend's mark. Thus the Baptismal Cross, though to our eyes it leave no mark remaining, may yet be traceable by the eyes of the good Spirits, and we may have by it the more of their care and help. And, on the other hand, the evil spirits also discerning it may be abashed and afraid; the Sign of the Cross may discomfit and drive them away, as it discomfited and drove away Amalek when fighting against Israel. Amalek, we read, gave way and was overcome by Moses lifting up his hands in the shape of a Cross:

and so, if we steadily keep and cherish the Cross in our foreheads by prayer and holy obedience, we shall overcome our spiritual enemies, or they will fear to attack us so fiercely.

This use of the holy Sign to frighten away bad angels, and secure the help of good, appears to be referred to more than once in Holy Scripture. Not unlike it is what happened at the time of the First Passover. An Angel, a destroying Angel, an Angel of God's vengeance, was to pass through the guilty land at midnight, and enter into each house and slay the first-born only. Into those houses, on which he should see the token of Redeeming mercy, the sprinkling of the blood of the lamb, into those he was not to enter, but to pass them over. Now the sprinkling of the lamb's blood over the door was not unlike making the Sign of the Cross on the forehead; the one, as well as the other, might well serve for a token to our invisible friends and enemies, causing the one to draw back, the other to watch over us.

Again, we read in the Book of Joshua how that when Jericho was taken, one woman, Rahab the harlot, had her house and all that belonged to her spared: because she had dealt kindly with the men whom Joshua had sent to search the land. The men gave her a sign; they bad her hang out a scarlet thread at her window, which when the armies of the Lord should see, they would know it was His sign, and would spare the house when they saw it. What was that scarlet thread but a type of and token of Christ's saving Blood? In other words it was a sign of the Cross.

Again, and yet more remarkably, God revealing

Himself to the Prophet Ezekiel shewed him this vision: he seemed to himself to be in the Temple, and to see all manner of wicked idolatries carried on there, in the very sight of the glory of the Lord: and therefore he saw also, how that the Lord appointed six ministers of vengeance who were to pass through the city slaying all sorts, but before they set out on their errand, another, a merciful Priest, was commanded to go round and seal those who were penitent and better than the rest, to seal them in the forehead with a certain letter, which is believed to have been of the very shape of the Cross. *That* being done, the Angels of vengeance went forth and slew all the rest; but whomsoever they saw thus sealed, him they passed over. Not otherwise will those glorious beings deal with us sinners at the Last Day: they will sever the wicked from amongst the just, to be cast into the furnace of fire: but those, on whom they shall see our Lord's mark, they will pass over, leaving them to be admitted by our Lord Himself into Heaven.

And to make us sure that this kind of sealing has something like it in the Gospel and Church of Christ, you heard, out of the Book of Revelations, concerning the four Angels which were appointed to hurt the earth, and the sea and the trees, how that they were commanded to forego any such thing, until they should have sealed the servants of our God in their foreheads. With all this Scripture authority, no wonder that our first fathers in the faith, the Christians in the next generation after the Apostles, made very great use indeed of the sign of the Cross: insomuch that we find one of them saying, "In all our travels and movements, in all our coming in and going out, in putting on our shoes, at the bath, at the table, in lighting our candles, in lying down, in sitting down, whatever employment occupieth us, we mark our forehead with the sign of the Cross." The saving sign, which both we and they need continually, they kept repeating in act: we, who do not so, must be the more careful to repeat it very often in mind.

Thus you see in a general way, why Christ's sign or seal should be put upon the new-baptized. It is placed, to mark them for Christ's own, and to protect them from evil spirits. Now why that sign should be the Cross, rather than anything else, you all know very well. By using the Cross and no other figure, we declare our faith not simply in Christ, but in Christ Crucified, in God Incarnate, dying on the Cross to be the Sacrifice for our sins. We say the same in gesture, which St. Paul said in words, when he told the Corinthians, "I determined to know nothing among you, save Jesus Christ and Him Crucified." By that act we profess obedience to the many sayings of our Blessed Master, in which He bade us take up and bear the Cross: the first of which sayings, in point of time, is that which I read to you for our text to-day, "Whosoever taketh not up his cross and followeth after Me is not worthy of Me." Those words were addressed to the twelve Disciples by our Lord, when He first sent them out to preach in His Name; they are part of our Master's original instructions, in first forming His Divine Kingdom and Household. If you would be worthy of Me, take up your Cross. Well is it then, that on each one of us, on our entrance into that Holy Family, the very mark of the Cross was put, our Lord's own mark, uniting in one His Truth and our duty, Faith in Christ and denying ourselves for His Sake. Well is it for you and me, that, even as infants, the Cross was thus laid upon us, to mark us for Christ's own and to keep off the powers of darkness. Well is it for us so far; but it will be very ill for us if, being come to years, we decline the loving and blessed burden so graciously laid upon us. Observe our Lord's Word. He says, "Whoso *taketh* not his cross and followeth not Me is not worthy of Me." We must *take* it, i. e. willingly accept and receive it, when we are old enough to know what it is. We must *bear* it, i. e. carry it along with us on our journey through this evil world; we must not pretend or wish to part company with it. Now what do I mean, when I talk of parting company with the Cross? I mean, putting by our duty when we find that it becomes unpleasant; as for instance there are some here who, being come to the appointed age, are now preparing solemnly to take upon themselves the Cross which was laid upon them in their Baptism. They are preparing themselves to be confirmed: let them well understand what our Lord expects of them. He will not give them His confirming Spirit, unless they come to Him taking up their cross, i. e. with a mind set to do their duty, however unpleasant. Now it is plain *they* have not yet such a mind, it will be no blessing to *them* to be confirmed, if they have not yet the courage to do unpleasant duties; and I am sorry to say concerning some of them, that it is too plain, there is one duty at least, and *that* a very serious and sacred one, which they have not yet courage to do: I mean the duty of behaving well in Church. I take this opportunity, brethren, of giving as public notice as I can, that we shall not consider any person as fit to be presented to the Bishop for Confirmation, who shews by his behaviour that he is not trying to behave well and reverently at Church. However well he may answer all questions, he ought not to be confirmed and he will not be confirmed here, if he be noticed as commonly rude and irreverent in God's House. Neither he nor his friends must complain, if he be disappointed in the end when he asks for the Bishop's Blessing. Better by far for him to be disappointed, than to draw near with an untrue heart, and affront his Saviour. But how very foolish, how very sad that any Christian youth or maiden should lack even the little courage and conscientiousness to behave with outward decency and reverence for the few hours in the week, which we spend here in Church. Surely in vain, so far, has the sign of the Cross been put upon such an one, since the fear of being laughed at, or dislike of the little trouble of keeping himself in order, is of more avail with him than the fear of God and the feeling of Christ's Presence. I hope there are not many such. But some I too greatly fear there undoubtedly are. At any rate I have given them plain warning, not however plainer than the word of God has given, concerning all those who, by evil doing, shall be found at last to have worn out of their foreheads the mark of Christ, made there in their Baptism. He will profess unto them, "I know you not: depart from me, ye that work iniquity." O God, grant that those words may not be spoken to any of us.

SERMON XXIX.

St. Mark viii. 38.

" Whosoever therefore shall be ashamed of Me and of My words in this adulterous and sinful generation, of him also shall the Son of Man be ashamed when He cometh in the glory of His Father with the Holy Angels."

THE point of time in the Service for Holy Baptism on which we are to think to day, is while the priest holds the new-baptized yet in his arms, and is in the act of signing it with the Sign and Seal of Christ. That Sign and Seal, I need not tell you, is the Cross. We considered about it last week; and of how great use it may be in keeping off Evil spirits and in inviting the help of the good. Now the next point to be considered is, why this mark should be made upon the *forehead* of the child, rather than any where else. We see it always was so; according to that in the Revelations, "Hurt not the earth, neither the sea, nor the trees, till we have sealed the servants of our God in the forehead." And the beast, the great evil Power on earth, is said in the same Book of Revelations to cause them that worship his image to receive a mark in their right hand or their foreheads. There must then be a special meaning in having the mark in that part of the body; nor is such meaning hard to find. The Service points to it, "We do sign him with the Sign of the Cross, in token that hereafter he shall not be ashamed?" How is it a token that he shall not be ashamed? For this reason especially, because it is made in the forehead. For, if a person were ashamed of Christ, surely the forehead, of all places, is where he would least wish to have Christ's mark upon him; because the forehead is the most plain to be seen of any part of the body, and any mark set there is, in a manner, more public than any where else. To put the mark of Christ then upon the forehead, before the child can at all know, is as much as to pledge him that, when he does know, he will never be ashamed of Christ's mark, he will always bear it openly upon him; that he will never be ashamed of it, come upon him what will. We do sign his Forehead, especially, "with the Sign of the Cross, in token that he shall not be ashamed to confess the faith of Christ crucified."

It should seem then, as though baptized children were in some special manner in danger of being ashamed to confess Christ. Let us consider how this is.

We will suppose a good and simple child, going about for a while in his own simple way. He knowingly encourages no ill thoughts, he is kind and gentle, he speaks the truth, he will not be greedy, he does as he is bid, he tries to mind his prayers, he is the same, in sight and out of sight. How happy is that child! But it is sad to think how sorely he may soon be tried. Before long he may find himself among other children, or even among grown-up people, who have been brought up in very different ways from these, and who, to keep themselves in countenance, will be too likely to laugh at his childlike goodness. They will laugh at him, perhaps, for his strict honesty; he would not for the world take what is not his, without leave. But they have been used to deal freely with other men's goods, and help themselves boldly to what they please, when they think they can safely do it. If they see you backward to do the same, they will laugh at you; they will say, you want sense and spirit, you know nothing of life, you are altogether poor and contemptible. Can you bear it all? Will you go on just the same, as strict and exact in your honesty, as if you had never been laughed at for it? Or will it not rather have this effect upon you, that, although you were greatly shocked at first with their talk, you nevertheless cared for it so far as this; that you rather kept your honesty out of sight, you were a little uneasy when you thought it was going to be noticed; and soon you were tempted to relax a little, not to seem so strict and particular and so unlike other people; (for that is how these tempters will talk of you;) and when you have got so far, to hide your honesty for fear of being laughed at, I fear it will be found but a very little step farther, to join those whom you mind so much, in something positively dishonest, or to follow their bad example in ways of your own. Perhaps it is not so much dishonesty, by which the simple young heart is tried, as that most sad and painful temptation of impurity. Too often those who in any manner are losing themselves in this grievous sin, become so like the evil spirit, as to grudge others their goodness and innocence, and they will mock and jeer at them for being ignorant of sin, and afraid to fall into it. For such company there is but one rule; as soon as ever you perceive what they are about, avoid them, come not near them, stop your ears, look another way; you know not what incurable defilement you may bring upon yourself by any willing intercourse with them, though it be but for half an hour. Shut your eyes from seeing of evil, whether it be in books or in the ways of living people; never mind their sneers and their scorning; never mind what they will be sure to say about your want of spirit, your unmanliness, your pitiful ignorance of life. Remember the Lord's mark in your forehead, and be bold and courageous to despise all this, or, if the tempter's agents take another course with you, if they despise and mock you for being respectful to those whom God has set over you, for minding them when they are out of sight, this again is often a sore trial, through the sad frailty of our nature; but it is not a trial in which a well-disposed mind can have any doubt of its duty. Arm yourselves, then also, with the sign of the Cross, *His* sign Who was not ashamed to live thirty years at Nazareth in quiet subjection to the poor Carpenter and his wife, and, having that sign, be bold to disregard those who would taunt you with your precise notions of duty; let them, if they will, mock on, but let no sayings or doings of theirs make you less respectful, loving, and true.

How plain is all this, as we speak and hear of it, how very foolish to be ashamed of keeping either of God's holy Commandments, on account of what a few thoughtless persons may say! yet how few of us, alas!

can say that we have been, or even are now, quite above being tempted in that way. Both open ridicule, and secret scorn, are to many most painful to be encountered; many a good resolution has failed before them; many an one, who seemed like a rock, has wavered, from being ashamed of Christ. The very first sin that was committed in this world seems to have been partly occasioned by this. Eve knew perfectly, and answered exactly, what command God had given concerning the Tree of Knowledge. But the Serpent said, in the tone of scornful unbelief, "Ye shall not surely *die*," as if he should say, you "are not quite so foolish as to believe *that;*" and she was so weak that she listened to it. There are too many places, too many companies, where young people who know their duty are tempted much in the same way. Their dread of another's ridicule or secret scorn comes dangerously in, to aid their other bad inclinations. This was partly the temptation at the High Priest's door, when St. Peter, young in eagerness if not in years, was tempted to say with oaths and cursings, "I know not the Man." It would not seem to have been merely fear for his own life, but he did not like, so it may appear, to be accounted one of so strange and unaccountable a set, whom nobody could understand well enough, either to pity or respect them. Take care, my young friends, lest you too in some unguarded hour should utter words which come to the same, "I know not the Man, I care not so much for this or that point of the Creed, this or that form of words," and yet in your hearts you know or ought to know that the points of the Creed, the form of sound words, are to be cared for by Christians even unto death. Take care that in none of these respects you so forget the Cross in your foreheads, as to seem to agree with sin and unbelief, for fear of differing with other people. I think it very likely that some, perhaps many of you, may be tried in this way. A time is at hand, in which very holy things will be freely talked of in all manner of companies. Holy Baptism, and those who believe in it, will be more and more a scorn and an offence to the children of this world. Take care that none of you ever be tempted by fear of standing alone, or by fear of being laughed at, to say any thing like, "I know not the Man."

Our time is in some respects a time like that in which the gospel was first preached, when it was "to the Jews a stumbling-block and to the Greeks foolishness." So now Jesus Christ in His Sacraments is a stumbling-block to those who think they know better, and have a more spiritual religion, and He is "foolishness" to the ordinary sort of people, who will not believe their own high calling, nor be told how bad their sins are. At such a time and in such temptations, the Cross in our foreheads, seasonably thought of, may help us very greatly. We were told, when it was marked there, that it marked us not only as Christ's sheep, but also as His soldiers and servants. We are "manfully to fight under our Lord's Banner;" that is what is required in soldiers. What is our Lord's Banner? the Cross, that Sign of the Son of Man in Heaven, which, as many have believed, will be carried before Him when He shall come with His armies at the last Day. Under that Banner, i. e. the Banner of self-denial and of suffering, we are to fight against sin, the world, and the Devil. We are not to have an hour's peace with them; the warfare on which we enter at our Baptism is to continue unto our life's end. And how are we to fight? in one word, "manfully;" we are to be courageous, loyal, persevering, in one word, to quit ourselves *like men*. Bear this in mind, my young friends. You are ready enough in general and glad enough to be reckoned men and treated as men. Not seldom you are seeking and contriving to be so before the proper and natural time, in a great hurry to leave school, to be your own masters, to be dealt with as if you were grown up. Well then, if you want to be men, shew yourselves manly where Christ requires you to do so; i. e. in striving against sin, in never being ashamed of Christ. Nothing so unmanly, as to be put out of countenance, when you are standing up for your King, your Master, or your parent; and still more for Him Who is all these in one, and more than all these, your Saviour. Nothing so truly manful and courageous, as to go on simply and plainly in the way of duty, whether those around us regard and respect us, or no.

We must be manful and we must be faithful; manful to enter on the fight, faithful to continue it unto our lives' end. This indeed is great part of true manliness, not to be "like children carried away with every blast of vain doctrine," but to be ordered and established in the truth of Christ's holy Gospel. Surely, if you would be men, (as you all wish to be) this spiritual and inward manliness will be all in all to you. Keep to it firmly, yet humbly and devoutly, and all besides will be sure to come right.

Finally, remember, Brethren, that we are *slaves*, given up entirely by Jesus Christ as a living Sacrifice to our Lord; and this is one reason more, why we bear the Sign of the Cross; we are to continue His faithful soldiers *and servants*. Slaves in old time bore their master's mark in their foreheads; I believe it is so in some countries even now: it is the mark which shews to whom they belong, and by which they are found out if they forsake his service: they no doubt, poor creatures, are often unwilling enough to bear it; but let us with all joy and willingness wear our mark, the Cross of our Saviour. He made Himself a Slave for us, when He took our nature upon Him; as He says in the Book of Psalms, "Mine ears hast Thou opened," i. e. I have made Myself Thy servant, and Thou hast taken Me to be Thy servant for ever. "Lo, I come to do Thy will, O my God." Thus did He make Himself a slave for us all, and we were taken by Him to be His slaves, when He had us signed with the sign of the Cross. Let it be all our joy and glory, as it is our only hope, that we are not our own, but His, whether we will or no. We are His servants; let us see to it that we are faithful servants. Our Master is away out of sight: let us take care to be awake, when He returns. For blessed are those servants, whom the Lord when He cometh shall find watching. Therefore the Church, in signing us with the Sign of the Cross, put us in mind of our life's end, which will be but a short time. The Sign was to make us recollect, that we are pledged to continue Christ's faithful soldiers and servants unto our life's end. So be it, O Lord. May we so lead our short lives here that Thou and Thy good Angels may own us to be Thine, seeing Thy mark upon us in the Day of Resurrection.

SERMON XXX.

St. John xv. 3, 4.

"Now ye are clean through the word which I have spoken unto you. Abide in Me and I in you."

THE infant having been solemnly admitted into the congregation, and Christ's mark put upon his forehead, the Priest restores him to his nurse's or Godmother's arms: in which action when we behold him, we may think of Jesus Christ, how He is even now committing this little lamb of His, newly sealed with His own Name, to the care of its Spiritual Mother the Holy Church, which promises and is bound to nurse and to teach him. Every woman, thus receiving a newly baptized child from the Priest, is for the time a figure and type of the Holy Church of God, receiving infants from Christ, and would do well to consider what a serious thing it is, what a great wonder and mystery, in which she is so permitted to bear a part, and so she should keep her attention from being wholly taken up with the child, and should try to think as much as she can of the great work which God has just been doing for its soul.

When the Priest has so given back the child, he proceeds to invite the congregation to join him in thanksgiving and prayer; "Seeing now, dearly beloved Brethren, that this child is regenerate and grafted into the Body of Christ's Church, let us give thanks unto God for these benefits, and with one accord make our prayers unto Him, that this child may lead the remainder of his life according to this beginning."

Now the first thing to be observed upon this is, that the Church directs us to speak the words over every baptized infant alike. Whatever be the child's name and his parents', be they rich or poor, high or low in the world, nay whatever their character be, good or bad, religious or irreligious, to the child it is all one, so far as this: that the Church commands us to thank God for its Regeneration. We are to say distinctly, "this child is regenerate;" if there were any doubt, the Church, I suppose, would bid us say, "*we hope* that this child is regenerated." There is no reason against our saying that, if it were more according to the truth, according to our Lord's sayings, and the mind of His Holy Church. We might say, we hoped this child was regenerate, just as we say in the Burial Service, "our hope is" that our Brother or Sister is now resting in Christ. The word would have been just as easily spoken. But instead of saying, "we hope," we say, positively, "it is regenerate." We say it concerning every child: no distinction is made between this one and that one. Why should we say it, if we are not to believe it? Surely the Church meant us all to believe it: and if we will be true Churchmen, we must believe it. I say it over and over again, and I wish you to take notice of it, and always to remember it, that over every child without exception, immediately after it has been baptized, the Priest is desired to say, "This child is regenerate:" not, "it may be," or, "we hope it is," but plainly and distinctly, "it is." Supposing any person should come up at the same moment and say, "Perhaps it is not so, we cannot tell, we can only hope that it is so," would you not say that person contradicts the Prayer-Book? Surely this matter is so plain, that no one can help perceiving it, unless he chooses to be blind. And we ought to be very thankful that the matter is so plain. For unhappily there are too many who for various reasons wish to make it out that we need not believe all infants to be regenerate in Baptism: and they have many subtle things to say, which may perplex the hearts of the simple; and we all know too well that Satan is very busy in this matter, for it exactly serves his purpose, if he can get men to imagine that their sins are not so very bad, because perhaps they have never had grace given them; and since unhappily even well-meaning persons have somehow got to persuade themselves that the Prayer Book does not say, *all* baptized infants are regenerate, I fear, I greatly fear, that the evil one will be more than ever busy in deceiving us. Therefore I say, we ought to be very thankful that God has given us such a plain and direct answer to him. We have but to point with our finger to this one place in the Baptismal Service, "this child is regenerate;"—words to be spoken over every single infant that is christened. We have but to point to these in faith, and the adversary must go away ashamed. And this is what I should advise you generally to do, instead of entering upon long arguments. Keep close to the simple saying, this child is regenerate; let nothing drive you from it: so may the simplest who now hears, be a sound and effectual witness to God's holy truth. O! who can thank our Merciful God enough, that His good Providence has caused our Church-Prayer-Book to be so very plain and distinct upon that one point especially, which in our age people are most apt to scorn and disbelieve.

And to make it, if possible, still more distinct, observe what we are directed to say, when a child is brought to Church that has been christened at home. The Priest takes *it* also in his arms and makes the sign of the Cross in the regular form: but when he invites the people to give thanks, instead of saying, "this child is regenerate," he says, "this child is *by Baptism* regenerate," not by the prayers of its friends and sponsors, nor by some unknown gift before Baptism, but by Baptism itself. What can be plainer?

And you will observe further, that this thanksgiving, to which the Priest invites us all, refers to certain prayers which had gone before. Before the child is christened, we pray that it may be regenerate: after it has been christened, almost the next moment after, we thank God that it is regenerate. How should that be, if Holy Baptism has nothing to do with regeneration? O my brethren, others must do as they please: let us for our part, you and me, keep our faithfulness to the old and good ways. We ought rather to die, than willingly to sacrifice any portion of the Church's treasure, any one Article of the Faith?

But now observe, we have been truly regenerated in Baptism. Every one of us here present has indeed been born again: every one of us, being by nature born in sin and a child of wrath, has been truly and really grafted into Christ, truly and really made a member of Him. We are taught it in the very first answer of the Catechism. For there every one of us, one as much as another, was brought up to say, "In my Baptism I was made a member of Christ." We do not say, "perhaps I was so, but I cannot be quite certain." We make no doubt of the fact, no more than we do of our own birth. We have been regenerate, and we have been made members of Christ, every single one among us. In that respect there is no difference. "As in Adam we all died, even so in Christ have we all been made alive." What then? are we to go on at our ease, taking no care of ourselves, because He hath done so much for us? why, only just consider how it is in regard of our natural life, the life of the body, the life which we had from our parents at our first birth. You know very well that if no care had been taken, no meat and drink, no lodging nor clothing, no help nor watching, that life would soon have passed away: and yet it was a true and real life; none of us ever doubted *that;* you would think a person out of his senses who should say, "I see that such and such a child is dead: I conclude therefore that it never was really born." And you may be quite sure, it is much the same grievous mistake, when you hear it said, as it often is said, "I see that such and such a person is dead in sin: how can I believe that he ever was born again?" As if there were no such thing as dying after birth: as if it were impossible to depart from grace given: as if we had never heard of the fallen angels nor of Judas

Iscariot, nor of the Prodigal son in our Lord's parable. Never, I beseech you, listen to any one, however good and wise, and greatly to be regarded in other respects, who shall come teaching you such a doctrine. Say to them in your heart, if not with your lips, "I cannot, I must not believe you:" the Church says plainly in every case, "This child is regenerate;" the Holy Scripture says just as plainly, "as many of you as have been baptized into Christ have put on Christ." But when you have said something like this in your heart, as concerning those who would lead you into false doctrine, say a good word, I beseech you, to yourself also. Go on and think to yourself, "yes indeed I was regenerate and grafted into the Body of Christ: but where is my spiritual life now? am I at this moment a working limb of that Blessed Body, not dead nor palsied, not yielding to wilful sin?" O my brethren, it is a sad confession to make, but there can be no doubt at all of it: if we, who know that we were baptized and born again in Christ, had been always careful to maintain our life in Him; if we had always walked worthily of the great unspeakable gift; if we had never quenched the Spirit; no one would ever have thought of denying the great truth of baptismal grace. It is our sins, which have given occasion to the enemy so to blaspheme and to weak brethren so to stumble. O may the merciful Spirit, to Whom we have made so ill a return, humble us more and more with the most true and sorrowful conviction, that all this confusion and unbelief is in reality the doing of such as we are, who knew ourselves to be the members of Christ, but did not the works of Christ.

When we were christened, Holy Church after pronouncing us regenerate, invited all her children to give thanks to God for so great a benefit. Each one of us then in turn has had the thanks of the Church spoken over him; not only of the persons then present, but of the whole Body of Christ. For Faith perceives and owns the presence of the whole Body, wherever there are but two or three persons gathered round the Font in the Name of Christ. Reflect, my brethren, what an honour and blessing this is: that when, after the christening of a child, rich or poor, it makes no matter, the Priest invites us to return thanks, not only we who see one another, not only all our friends far and near, who may be aware of our christening-day, but the Angels also in Heaven whom none of us can see, and perhaps too the blessed Saints departed in Paradise or in Heaven unite in one and the same joy with the parents and friends of that little child. As it was at our Lord's Nativity, so it is at the Spiritual Nativity, the new birth of all who are made His members. There is a glory round each one of them, as there was round Him in the manger; and as Mary and Joseph and the Shepherds and the Angels joined in praising God for what they saw that day, so doth the glorious company of Heaven join with Christ's people on earth, and especially with the parents and sponsors of the new-baptized, in praising Him, for that He hath regenerated this infant by His Holy Spirit. Some of us may remember, what joy there was when our Queen's eldest son was born. But what was that, what is the inheritance of all earthly kingdoms put together, in comparison with the glorious condition of a child just made a member of Christ, and sure, if it die as it is now, of an everlasting kingdom in Heaven. Depend on it, there is joy in the other world and in this, at the Baptism of the meanest infant, far deeper, far more transporting than all that is felt here on the birth-day of an heir to the greatest and most beloved prince.

But observe this also very particularly, that along with her thanksgiving the Church then offered her prayers. "Let us give thanks," the Priest said, "unto Almighty God for these benefits; and with one accord make our prayers unto Him, that *this Child* may lead the rest of *his* life according to this beginning." For here, as all along, from beginning to end of the Baptismal office, two doctrines go together, or rather two parts of one doctrine. The one, that every baptized babe without exception is regenerate by the Holy Ghost, the other that every one who lives to the age of actual sin will stand in need of further grace,— the grace of perseverance and of improvement, most likely of conversion also, that he may not after all be a castaway. These two are necessary parts of the Church's doctrine of Baptism, and we have no right at all to leave out either of them: neither we in our teaching, nor you in your belief. And therefore it is, that both thanksgiving and prayer are necessary parts of the duty of the congregation, and are therefore both made part of the office, after the Sacrament has been administered. Because the child is regenerate, we give thanks; because it will surely fall away without further continued help, therefore we pray for more grace. We are invited to pray that the favoured and happy child, having really been made a member of Christ, may "lead the rest of his life according to that beginning." What "beginning?" Surely a reality, not a mere fancy and shadow, not a set of words without meaning. Surely what the Church means is, that we all, not doubting that the infant has received the heavenly life, should unite in praying, that it never may lose that life, but may go on from strength to strength, and finally appear before God in the heavenly Jerusalem. This is the prayer, which was made over every one of us. My brethren, let me beseech you with all earnestness, not to make that prayer void. Void indeed it cannot be, any more than the Baptism can be, on which it follows: it must be either a great blessing or a great curse. You, by His mysterious Providence, are left free to choose which it shall be. The prayer of the Angels and of the whole Church was, that you might "lead the rest of your life according to that" good "beginning." That is, that as your Baptism was the greatest of changes, so your life should be all new; quite different from what it could have been, if you had not so put on Christ. Then, that as you were washed in pure water, so your souls and bodies might continue pure from all stain of wilful, deadly sin. Then, that as your Baptism grafted you into Christ, so you might never, never be cut off from Him, according to His Own blessed Promise: "Now ye are clean through the word which I have spoken unto you: abide in Me, and I in you."

This was the prayer: and by God's great Mercy it rests with yourself, whether it shall be fulfilled or no. And it may do you good, sometimes to think thus with yourself, that the same company which then offered this prayer for us after our Baptism will be once again assembled around us: we shall meet them all face to face, both Angels and Saints, and Parents, and Sponsors, and neighbours, and friends present and absent, openly before the Judgement seat of Christ. Who can express the joy that it will be, if they find their good prayers fulfilled? or the misery, if our folly and wickedness force them even to bear witness against us, and consent to our condemnation, as they gave thanks at our Baptism. The Good Lord enable us to keep this thought in our hearts!

SERMON XXXI.

1 Thess. v. 23, 24.

"The very God of peace sanctify you wholly; and I pray God, your whole spirit and soul and body may be preserved blameless until the coming of our Lord Jesus Christ. Faithful is He that calleth you, Who also will do it."

WHEN our young children have been baptized, the Church their Holy Mother does not send them home without special prayer to God, that they may never lose the benefit received, special thanksgiving to Him for bestowing it, and special directions what they must be taught and how brought up, in order to walk worthy of it. The special prayer is first the Lord's Prayer. It had not been used in the Baptismal Service before, though in many services it forms the very beginning. This may be, because the Lord's Prayer is in an especial sense the Prayer of Christians; the Prayer of regenerated persons, the Prayer of the faithful. Therefore, until we are faithful, regenerate, Christian Persons,—in one word, until we be baptized, we have not, strictly speaking, any right to say this Prayer. We cannot so properly call God our Father, until we have been graciously made

His adopted children; and the early Christians kept this rule, never permitting an unbaptized person to use it.

But now that this has been assuredly done;—now that this present infant has, without any manner of doubt, been made the child of God by faith in Christ Jesus: (for having been baptized into Christ he has put on Christ,) the Father sees him now, not as he is in himself, but as he is in Christ:—this being so, we all, in that child's behalf, kneel down and say the Prayer which the Lord Himself taught us.

And see, my brethren, consider, you all more especially, who have ever had children of your own christened,—what a deep and affectionate meaning the words of this prayer carry with them, as they are used on this particular occasion. Our Father, Thou Who hast now been pleased to adopt this child to be especially Thine Own, uniting him by Thy Holy Spirit to Thy True and Eternal Son Christ Jesus; Thou art now to this little one a Father in Heaven: and hast prepared for him a place in Heaven, if he lose it not by his own miserable falling away. How can those, who are his earthly parents, ever thank and praise Thee enough for this Thine unspeakable mercy to him? All the love they have to their child is but a drop poured into their hearts from Thee Who are the only Fountain, or rather the unexhausted Sea of Love. All they can ever do for him is nothing, less than nothing, and vanity, compared with what Thou hast done, in making him, by this Thy Baptism, a member of Thine Only Begotten Son, and so a partaker of Thine Own Divine Nature. We can but fall prostrate and praise Thee.

But since we are all as yet in a world of trial; since the child is as yet only entered into a state of salvation, not finally and entirely saved; we must add to our humble acknowledgements a no less humble prayer. For this child we pray; and our prayer is, "Hallowed be Thy Name." May Thy glorious and dreadful Name, which has even now been called upon this child, be ever kept sacred by him and in him: may it never be blasphemed through him or his doings. May he always remember, even in his most secret thoughts, that he bears about with him in very deed the Name of the Father, the Son, and the Holy Ghost: he is trusted with it: he has taken it on him: and if he be found at last to have taken it in vain, the Lord, we know, will not and cannot hold him guiltless. Our very first prayer, then, for this new-baptized infant, must be that he may always honour God's holy Name and His Word: that instead of being a reproach to it by any kind of sin, he may honour it always by all kinds of holy obedience, and may be a happy instrument, at least by good example, of bringing others to honour it also. And with all our hearts, kneeling round the Font, we say for the new-baptized infant, "Hallowed be Thy Name."

Next, since the infant has also just been made by Baptism an inheritor of God's Kingdom, we pray also that God's Kingdom may come to that child, not only as it cometh to children, but more and more, until every thought word and work is brought into the obedience of Christ, and that which is now a little babe, having but the seed of Holiness implanted in it, shall have become a full-grown man in Christ Jesus, a perfect King and Priest unto God and the Father.

We pray, thirdly, that this tender babe may be a blessed instrument in God's Hand to work His Will in all things: that, as long as he lives, he may be a Priest as well as a King, sacrificing himself and all that belongs to him to the great God, the Giver of all. This is what we ask, when we say on behalf of the newly christened child, "Thy will be done on earth, as it is in Heaven." And those moreover, to whom the child is especially near and dear, may well have such a thought as this following: " Now, by God's great mercy in Christ Jesus, the great point is for the present secure: if my child die as he is now, he will undoubtedly be saved through Christ for ever. In this faith I cheerfully trust him to the Saviour Who died for Him; being sure, that He Who loved him so dearly will deny him nothing that is really for his good. Thus may parents, in their deep anxieties, support themselves by the thought of their child's Baptism. He is safe in Christ's arms for the present: they have but to pray and strive, calmly and earnestly, that he may never lose his place there.

Therefore they go on to ask for the little one the daily blessings of support, pardon and grace: that He Who has given him life will not leave off to give Him bread: by His Almighty Spirit continuing and supporting the Heavenly life which He has just breathed into him. Give unto us all, and especially to this child, his daily bread, the continuation of his part and portion in Christ, without which he cannot live to God. Give him this precious gift this day and all the days of his life. This is our especial meaning when we say at the Font, "give us this day our daily bread." In old time, at least in many parts of the church, the words had also another very special meaning. They related to the Holy Eucharist, which was then given immediately after Baptism, even to infants. Now, this has ceased to be the general custom of the church: still there is no harm in thinking of Holy Communion, when at the Font we come to this part of the Lord's Prayer: there is no harm in thinking then of the child's first Communion, and praying in one's heart that he may live to be worthily confirmed, and worthily to receive his Saviour's Body and Blood.

Since also he has just been made partaker of the "One Baptism for the Remission of sins:" when we go on and say, "Forgive us our trespasses," we may well look forward to the time, when he will like others be exposed to sin and temptation, and we may understand ourselves as saying, "Forgive, O Lord, this child, whom Thou hast now taken into Thine Arms and blessed, all the sin that he shall hereafter fall into, through the unhappy stain of his nature, the original sin which cometh from Adam, abiding in him even now after his Baptism. Preserve him by Thy grace from all deadly sin, and cause him speedily to recover from all sin of infirmity, and carefully to watch against it. Who can tell how much good it might do to those whom we love best, if we followed up the first gracious beginnings with such prayer as this, earnest and persevering, and above all things, recommended by repentance and seriousness of heart?

Again, when one thinks of that malicious one, how even in Paradise he went walking about, seeking whom he might devour: how, wherever the sons of God are, there he also is found among them, how natural does it seem, to say in one's heart, "Lead not this infant, just made Thine Own, lead him not, O Lord, into temptation: watch around him and keep him from the evil world. Leave him not to the devices of his own heart, and of all things deliver him from evil; from the Evil One, from the crafts and assaults of the devil." In former times, it was a part of the Baptismal service, to exorcise the child, i. e. to command the evil spirit to depart from him, since all children are by nature born in sin, and under the power of Satan. We, my brethren, may piously believe, that devoutly saying these last words of the Prayer of our Lord may help in like manner to keep him off from our children.

And having thus prayed as our Saviour taught us to pray, and said Amen with all our hearts, we in the Name of the whole Church may solemnly thank Him for what He has done for the child, adding him to the number of His elect, and putting him into a state of salvation. This we do in the words following. "We yield Thee hearty thanks, most Merciful Father, that it hath pleased Thee to regenerate this infant with Thy Holy Spirit, to receive him for Thine own child by adoption, and to incorporate him into Thy Holy Church." Here, are three unspeakable blessings, for which we thank Almighty God on behalf of the new-baptized. The first, Regeneration, the second, Adoption; the third, Incorporation into the Church. Concerning each of the Three we are directed to speak quite positively. We are not to say, "we hope it hath pleased Thee," but, "it hath pleased Thee." What can this mean, but that we are not to doubt, but earnestly to believe, the Regeneration of each baptized child? As surely as ever we see him at the Font, the priest pouring the Water and saying the Words over him, so surely are we to believe that he is born again of water and of the Holy Ghost: that God for Christ's sake has adopted and accounts him His child: and that he is grafted as a real member into the Church which is the Body of Christ. He may hereafter (God forbid it, but he *may*) turn out an undutiful child, a rotten unfruitful branch, and then his new Birth will do him no good but harm. It will but serve, unless he repent, to his greater condemnation: still he will have been new-born: for what is done cannot be undone. But for the present, being as he is a simple child, who cannot do anything to frustrate the grace of God, his Baptism, we are sure, is a mere blessing, a cluster of all blessings to him. We are *sure* he is born again to a new and heavenly life, we are *sure* he is adopted into our Lord's own family: we are *sure* he is united to Him, and made a member of Him. What a thought is this to fill all the heart of a father or mother who truly loves his Child! and what a sad calamity, what a grievous loss will it be, if we listen to those who would disturb us in our faith and thankfulness, and say the child's blessing is doubtful: all indeed are baptized alike, but only some, we cannot tell which, are blessed. Surely this, though not so intended, is both unthankful to God and unkind to man. Far be it from those who gather round this our Font, this our blessed Laver of Regeneration, to have any such doubt in their hearts. The Angels, who are with us invisibly, have no such doubt. As they gave thanks to God with no uncertain sound at the Birth of the Lord Jesus Himself, so do they, depend on it, at the new birth of any of His little ones. Fear not and doubt not: only try to praise Him as they do, and humble yourselves, as unworthy of so great a blessing.

After the Thanksgiving, the Church falls to Prayer again: Prayer for improvement, and Prayer for perseverance: for those are the two graces which the infant now stands in need of. As for improvement we humbly beseech God to grant, that this child, being dead to sin and living unto righteousness, and being buried with Christ in His Death, may crucify the old man, and utterly abolish the whole body of sin. You see, the Prayer takes up the notion of Death and Burial as representing our Christian condition. The child is so far dead to sin, as that the guilt of its original sin is clean washed away, and as yet it has no power to commit actual sin. It is also alive unto righteousness; for it has within it the Quickening Spirit, the Lord and giver of the Life which is in Christ: so that in Him it can do all things, though of itself it can do nothing. Still there is abiding deep in the heart of that child, the sore and plague-spot of what we call original sin: that is to say, the old man, the likeness of Adam, that, of which comes the body of sin. This then we pray, that the child may be always crucifying, and at last that he may utterly abolish it. For the Christian's calling is, not simply to overcome sin, but to crucify it, i. e. to get the better of it by the Cross of his Saviour: putting it down by faith in the Cross, and by real mortification and self-denial after the pattern of the Cross. We pray that the child may be doing this continually, that it may be his daily and hourly exercise, all his life long. And it is perhaps but the same prayer in other words, when we add, that as he is made partaker of the Death of Thy Son, he may also be partaker of His Resurrection. The child is baptized once for all into Christ, into His Death; he is once for all made partaker of the benefits of His Death. But during the child's whole life and being afterwards, God graciously means, and we are humbly to pray, that the child may partake of the Resurrection, i. e. of what is sometimes called the Risen Life of our Lord: that as Christ dieth no more, so the baptized may sin no more: that as Christ ascended into Heaven, so we may in heart and mind thither ascend. Thus we ask for each little one the grace of improvement: and we end with asking the grace of final perseverance: "that finally, with the residue of Thy Holy Church, he may be an inheritor of Thine everlasting Kingdom." Thus from the beginning we look on with hope unto the end. We stand in the strait and narrow gate, the lowly baptismal entrance into Christ's Kingdom, and we look along the strait and narrow way, and see the glimmering, more or less clearly, of Eternal Life at the end. We look on in faith and charitable prayer, as St. Paul looked on for his Thessalonians: praying that God would "sanctify them wholly, and preserve their whole spirit and soul and body blameless unto Christ's" awful "coming." This is our prayer, our hope is stedfast: for we know how faithful He is. He hath called us: He will do it. He for His part is most sure to hear His Church's prayer, and to keep us in the right way. Only it rests with each one of ourselves to confirm His mercy or make it void. It is an aweful burden: may He give us grace to bear it, and turn it into a Crown at last.

SERMON XXXII.

1 Sam. i. 22.

"I will bring him, that he may appear before the Lord, and there abide for ever."

It is Hannah who speaks these words, the mother of Samuel, that mother who shewed her love to her child in nothing so much, as in being willing to part with him. She thought not of her own comfort, but of his good; she wanted to do the very best for him; therefore she thankfully gave him up to his God. As soon as ever Samuel was weaned, just at the time, perhaps, when he was as precious to her as he could well be, and she would most entirely feel as if she could never do without him, just then she brought him to God's Priest and left him there, to pass his life at a distance from her. It was a great sacrifice, and the Almighty rewarded it with a very great blessing: as He will always richly reward those parents, who for love's sake give up their children to Him. No doubt it was, for the time, very trying. Samuel was as yet her only child, much prayed for, long waited for: and it must have gone to her very heart to leave him there, where for the future she would only see him for a short time once a year, when she and her husband came to offer the yearly sacrifice. But Hannah had faith, and therefore she willingly endured it: and God made her one of the happiest of mothers, a true type of her whom "all generations shall call blessed," Mary the Mother of our Lord Jesus Christ, who brought her Child also in His Infancy to present Him to God in His Temple, but did not for the time leave Him there, as Hannah did Samuel. He, the Child Jesus, willed for the time to be redeemed with an offering of turtle-doves or young pigeons: but His mother only took him back, to part with Him by and by, in a way infinitely more grievous and trying, when she had to stand by His Cross, and the sword was piercing her own soul also. One cannot imagine any other parting like that. Still, Hannah's parting with Samuel was in some respects an image of it: even as are all partings of Christian mothers with their children, for heavenly love and duty's sake. And Hannah's words, in preparing for it, as they speak a real parent's mind, so are they not ill fitted to express the mind and purpose of a Christian godfather or godmother, standing in a parent's place. Therefore I have made mention of them on this occasion, when I am to say something to you on the last portion of the whole Baptismal Service, the admonition to the godfathers and godmothers.

Hannah's words in themselves are very plain and simple; "I will bring him, that he may appear before the Lord, and there abide for ever;" a short and easy saying, yet, if I mistake not, sufficient to remind us of the whole duty of those whom we call godfathers and godmothers. For they set before us two things;

first, Hannah's act which she was about to do, the bringing the child to Eli the Priest; secondly, the purpose for which she was to do it, that he might appear before the Lord, and there abide for ever. Now these are just the two purposes, for which godfathers and godmothers are appointed: first, they are to present the child to be baptized; in which respect they stand for the whole Church, which is our true Mother in God. The Church brings her children to be christened, as Hannah brought her child Samuel: and she makes their profession for them by the mouth of the sponsors, as Hannah declared to Eli that Samuel should thenceforth belong to God only. "For this child I prayed, and the Lord hath given me my petition which I asked of Him: therefore also I have lent him to the Lord: as long as he liveth, he shall be lent to the Lord." That saying of Hannah, you see, comes to very nearly the same as the promise and vow which infants make by their sponsors: "I desire to be baptized in this faith, and I will keep God's holy will and commandments, and walk in the same all the days of my life." This is the duty of godfathers and godmothers, so far as it is set down in the first part of the baptismal office: to present the child for Holy Baptism and make the promise and vow in his name; and this is why they are called "sureties." For sureties, you know, are persons who answer for another, and become bound for them: as, when a man is put into a place of trust, and some friend pledges himself in writing, that the man will perform the duties of the place, and agrees to forfeit so much if it prove otherwise, then you would say he became surety for his friend. Something like this, though not exactly like it, is that which sponsors do, in making the answers required of them in the Baptismal Service: and therefore, you know, they are called "sureties," both in the Service itself and in the Catechism afterwards to be learned. In the service the Priest says to them, after rehearsing Christ's part of the covenant, "Wherefore, after this promise made by Christ, this infant must also faithfully, for his part, promise" so and so, " by you that are his sureties." And again in the Catechism, when we were asked, why should infants be baptized, if Repentance and Faith be required, they as yet not being capable of either; our answer, as you know, was, "because they promise them both by their sureties."

But now it is very plain, that, when any persons have engaged for another that he will fulfil certain duties, if they have it in their power at all to help him or encourage him in doing so, they are bound to do their best for that purpose: just as Hannah, presenting her son to the Lord, was bound to do her best, that he might continue always the Lord's servant; for she says, herself, that she brings him, not only that he may appear before the Lord, but also that he may abide with Him for ever. In this sense Godfathers and Godmothers are not only sureties, but trustees also; they are to do what they can towards the child's abiding for ever with the Lord, to Whom they have brought him: and this is what the Priest reminds them of in the very end of the Baptismal office. "Forasmuch as this child hath promised by you his sureties to renounce the devil and all his works, to believe in God, and to serve Him; ye must remember, that it is your parts and duties to see that this infant be taught, so soon as he shall be able to learn, what a solemn vow, promise and profession he hath here made by you." Now it is very much to be noticed, that this instruction, and the words which follow it, do in fact draw out a short plan for the Christian education of all children, a short and simple plan, but a very complete one, and sufficient, if carried out, to make them good and happy for ever, through Christ Jesus. Therefore this is a part of the Prayer Book, which concerns not godfathers and godmothers only, though it is specially addressed to them, but it concerns all who are engaged in the care of young children, and most nearly and dearly does it concern all fathers and mothers. Surely it is their part, even more than the sponsors', to see that these infants be kept as near as can be in that happy state of pardon and salvation into which they were brought by Baptism. Surely it will be a fearful hearing, one day, for that father or mother, to whom the Judge shall have to say, "where is thy flock that was given thee, thy beautiful flock?" thy beautiful flock of sons and daughters, lent unto Me, for all their life long, in Holy Baptism, and committed to thee to be taken care of for Me? Where are they? What is become of them? Why are they on the left hand, in the wrong place? Oh how shall we look up, when that question is asked of us, if our own hearts shall bear the sad and shameful witness against us, that our neglect was too much the cause of their being where they are, of their losing Christ out of their hearts? Some of us may have had such a thought as this: "Nay, I do not willingly neglect those under my charge; but it is so great a matter, that I know not how to set about it, and so I neglect it from day to day, and can only hope that God will forgive me at last." But we ought not to talk or think so; indeed, we ought not. Only just consider these few short sentences, which you hear as often as you are present at Holy Baptism. "It is your parts and duties to see that this Infant be taught, so soon as he shall be able to learn, what a solemn vow, promise, and profession, he hath here made by you." Here is the very principle and beginning, the corner-stone of Christian teaching. Fix very deep in their young hearts, that of all things their vow in Baptism is to be kept. It is that, which the Church mentions first in her short account of your duties: and if you live to lie upon your sick bed, and to be in need of Church ministrations there, this matter, of the Baptismal vow, is the very first which the priest will begin impressing upon you: "I exhort you," will he say, "first of all, to remember the promise which you made unto God in your Baptism." O fathers and mothers, can it possibly be, that you think it too much trouble to use your children in good time to that, which will be their greatest help on their deathbed? What if you are no scholars? What if you cannot understand long discourses? Thus much surely you can understand, that it is your duty and your children's duty, to keep a promise when you have made it, much more when it is made to God: and therefore that both you and your children, to keep the vow, must have it continually in mind. That is the first thing: and if you heartily set about it, you will soon find that the most ignorant, by God's gracious help, may understand and remember it to good purpose. None so ignorant, none so dull, but he may ask himself, and teach his children to ask themselves, "is this which I am going to do, agreeable to what I have vowed or no?"

Next, the godfathers and godmothers are told, "that he may know these things the better, ye shall cause him to hear sermons," i. e. as I understand it, you shall make him regularly go to Church, as soon as ever he is of age, and you shall see, as well as you can, that he attends to the holy lessons which are there taught him. This is one among the many reasons, why children should be brought to Church very early, and very early instructed to make a religious difference between the Church and other places: not only for the prayers' sake, (though that is a most sacred matter which ought never to be forgotten), but also for the instruction's, sake, that, being all their lives long trained to attention and reverence in the holy place, they may be ready and disposed to receive the sermons and lessons, when they shall be able to understand them, into their very minds and hearts. And this, about hearing sermons, which cannot be without going regularly to Church, is set down specially in these directions to the godfathers, not only, I suppose as being a needful part of the child's Christian education, but also as being a thing in which the godfather may be of special use in many cases. For if he misses the child often from Church, he ought to take some friendly way of remonstrating with the parents about it: if he may see him inattentive, or otherwise ill-behaved, a quiet word or two from him can hardly be out of season. And this is a part of a young person's duty which all can see and take notice of; so that the godfather, if he see it neglected, can hardly be thought wrong in interfering: and here is one among the infinite reasons, why all, who are in any way trusted with others, should be very diligent themselves in their Church duties. For how can you really and truly cause your children and godchildren to hear sermons, if you do not set them the example, and consequently are not yourself at Church to see that they are there, and that they behave properly?

The next caution relates to the Catechism. "Chiefly ye shall provide that he shall be taught the Creed, the Lord's Prayer, and the ten Commandments in the vulgar tongue, and all other things which a Christian ought to know and believe to his soul's health." This plainly binds it upon all godfathers and godmothers to do their best to make sure that the young persons for whom they answer, shall be properly taught the Catechism. They ought to look to it early, and to see about it from time to time. If they find it neglected, they should put the parents in mind, not minding if they are sometimes a little affronted. One day, they may depend upon it, both parents and children will own, that they ought to have thanked their baptismal sureties for any such kind and Christian interference. No one can say, how much good might be done by a word, now and then spoken in due season, seriously and lovingly, for the souls of these tender little ones, by those who are so bound to look after them; or how much it might strengthen the hands, both of their pastors and of those who have to teach them at school. What a blessing it might bring down upon the charitable godfathers or godmothers themselves, if they put themselves a little out of the way, according to their vows, to do good to the children's souls! May God give grace to all who are concerned, to think more and more of it! Of course, when parents do their duty, the cares of the godfathers in this respect are greatly lightened. But then too there ought to be this very serious thought; "What if the child, otherwise in a good way, should take any hurt or hindrance by my neglect or ill example?" And there should be constant prayers and endeavours that he may prove not only *good*, but *very* good: not only escaping damnation, but going on or, as the Church says, "daily proceeding in all virtue and godliness of living." But of this I must speak next Sunday, when I hope, if it please God, to finish what I had to say on the service of Holy Baptism. In the mean time I wish we might all pray, that He, Who baptizeth with the Holy Ghost, Who never fails to be present at our Fonts, may give unto us all, and especially unto all parents and godfathers, and to all whom He has entrusted with young children, grace to think more and more of Christian perfection, as it is written of those whose strength is in God, "they shall," not merely abide in Him but, "go on from strength to strength," better, purer, more loving, and more humble, each new day, than they were the day before.

SERMON XXXIII.

Ps. lxxxiv. 7.

"They will go from strength to strength, and unto the God of gods appeareth every one of them in Sion."

IF you look back to the commencement of the Holy Baptismal Service, you will find that it began with setting forth to us our natural condition; "All men are conceived and born in sin;" and this is declared to be the reason why the child is brought to be baptized. Our Saviour Christ saith, "None can enter into the Kingdom of God, except he be regenerate and born anew of water and of the Holy Ghost." "I beseech you, therefore, to call upon God the Father through our Lord Jesus Christ, that this child may be baptized with water and the Holy Ghost, and received into Christ's Holy Catholic Church, and be made a lively member of the same." Thereupon the prayers are offered, the covenant made, the child baptized and signed with the sign of the Cross, and thanks given to Almighty God. Is the child then left to itself, to work out its own salvation without any special help from above? Far from it. Baptism, great as it is, is but the beginning of an endless stream of mercy. The Good Shepherd is not contented to have found the lost sheep, but He layeth it also on His Shoulders rejoicing, and beareth it all the way home. And thus, as the Holy Service begins with declaring what we are by nature, and how we may, by God's mercy, be put into a better condition, so it ends with declaring what we are made by grace in Baptism, and how we may go on to improve the gift unto the end. For that is the meaning of the last words of the exhortation to the Godmothers and Godfathers, to which we are now come. "It is your parts and duties to see that this child be virtuously brought up, to lead a godly and a Christian life, remembering always that Baptism doth represent unto us our profession." Thus, before we go away from the Font, we are reminded once more of the great work which has been wrought there, and by it of all our future duty. We are put in mind, how in those few minutes a great change has been wrought, a great miracle; how very different the child's condition is now from what it was when he was brought into Church, although to the outward eye there is no difference. As saith the Scripture, "The world knoweth us not, because it knew Him not;" the world, which could not see the difference between God Incarnate and a mere man, neither can it see the difference between a child of wrath and a child of God. But Faith has eyes to see the difference; Faith acknowledges in the little child, given back from the Font to the Church's arms, an instance of God's miraculous mercy in raising a soul from death to life: Faith sees in Holy Baptism a lively image of the Death and Burial of Christ, and of His rising again from the dead. To him that believeth, Holy Baptism, especially if it be done by immersion, represents our profession; when he sees it, he sees with his mind's eye both the Creed and the Life of a Christian. Just consider this for a moment. First, when you see a child christened, you see things done, which are indeed most simple in themselves, yet, taken altogether, they contain in them very many of the chief truths which we are bound to believe. The three Immersions, or Pourings, with the Threefold Holy Name, represents to us the mystery of the Trinity in Unity: the plunging of the child in the water is like the Death and Burial of Jesus Christ: his rising up again is like Christ's Resurrection: the water represents the sanctifying Power of God's Spirit: the ministering Priest represents Jesus Christ, God and Man, pouring that Good Spirit upon us, or, as St. John Baptist said, baptizing us with the Holy Ghost. Thus does Holy Baptism represent our profession, in respect of what we are to believe of God's saving mercy; and no less does it represent our profession, in respect of what we are to do, that we may not forfeit that mercy. It is an outward and visible sign, both of our blessing and of our duty. It is a sure pledge, whenever we think of it, that we are dead unto sin and risen again unto righteousness: and no less is it a lesson which cannot be mistaken, how we are to lead the rest of our short lives here on earth. It represents unto us, how that we have promised and vowed to follow the example of our Saviour Christ, and, by God's mercy, to be made like unto Him: " that as He died and rose again for us, so should we, who are baptized, die from sin and rise again unto righteousness." We should "die to sin," i. e. we should account it as much out of the question, for us who are baptized to commit and indulge wilful sin, as for a dead body to do the works of a living one. "He that is dead," says the Apostle "is freed from sin," i. e. a dead man can no more commit murder, nor steal, nor swear, nor add to his account by any sin here committed: so ought a Christian to try and behave himself, as if he were, (as indeed he is if he will be,) freed from all necessity of wilfully sinning, free to serve God in holy obedience continually. This deliverance, this inward death and resurrection, the outward act of Baptism both represents and seals and conveys to all receiving it as infants, or receiving it worthily after they are grown up. But it represents also the life which God expects us to lead: as is explained in the latter part of this exhortation to the sponsors. Baptism, so far as it is like death, is like that which a Christian should be always practising, i. e. our daily dying unto sin; and so far as it is like Resurrection, it no less resembles our daily rising again unto righteousness. At the Font we died with Christ; let this remind us that we are daily to mortify all our evil and corrupt affections. At the same Font we rose again with Him: let this equally remind us that we are daily to proceed in all virtue and godliness of living. Holy Baptism then, by what is done in it, not only teaches us some of the chief points of the Creed, but also what we ourselves are to do: it sets before our very eyes both God's part in the mystery of our Salvation, and also (if without offence I may so call it) our own part. Whenever we see a child christened, whenever we remember our own Christening, it is something to put us in mind of our present duty. We should say, when temptations are troublesome, "I was dead and buried in Baptism, how can I let my sins be so awake and alive in me, as that I should do this wrong thing?" And when we are inclined to be slothful and lukewarm and to omit any part of our duty, we should say, " I am risen again in Baptism, I am made partaker of the new life in Christ, how can I lie still like a dead body, and suffer the hour and the day to pass, without doing any thing to show that I live, or rather that Christ liveth in me?"

In this way, says the Church to the Godfathers, "you are to take care, that the child be brought up;" and with a view to this, you must even now be put in mind of his Confirmation, which is to obtain him health of spirit, and strength to do all that he has promised. "Ye are to take care that this child be brought to the Bishop to be confirmed by him, so soon as he can say the Creed, the Lord's Prayer, and the ten Commandments, in the vulgar tongue, and be further instructed in the Church-Catechism set forth for that purpose." Why are the Sponsors to take care that the child shall be brought to be confirmed? Because Confirmation, if not exactly a Sacrament, is nevertheless so great a help to Christian people in the way of grace; for in it they receive the Holy Spirit, to encourage and strengthen them in that hard work, the keeping of the Commandments of God. And as the Sponsors' office is chiefly useful to young children, before their own mind can be made up, it seems very natural that it should be made especially useful in bringing them worthily to Confirmation: at which time they are supposed capable of full consideration and of choosing their own way of life: and so the Sponsors' office does in a manner cease. And what so natural, as that they should take leave of them by presenting them to God's minister to be confirmed? so leaving them, as it were in *His* Arms, Who Alone can guide them safe through the world. Accordingly the Church directs, that each person at his confirmation should have a sponsor to witness it: and I wish this to be taken notice of.

Finally, the Godfathers and Godmothers are told what the young Christian is to be taught, in order to be a worthy candidate for Confirmation. He must be able to say, word for word, the Creed, the Lord's Prayer, and the ten Commandments, and he must be so far further instructed in the Catechism, as to be able to answer, if not in exact words yet in their meaning, the questions contained in it. That is the least which the Church will accept as the groundwork of Christian Knowledge. But that being once learned and the person otherwise well-disposed, in ordinary cases the Confirmation should not be put off. The Prayer-Book says, "They shall be brought to the Bishop *as soon* as they can say the Creed, the Lord's Prayer, and the Ten Commandments, in the vulgar tongue, and be further instructed in the Church-Catechism set forth for that purpose." Bishops indeed ordinarily direct us, not to bring our young persons till they are about fifteen years old. But if there be any young person who is really well informed and well-disposed, the Bishops generally allow us to bring such an one for Christ's blessing, though he be a year or two under the age which they have marked out.

And so, the Baptismal Service being all over, we return to our places in the Church, and go on with the regular Service, the Holy Angels rejoicing with us, that another soul is taken out of Satan's kingdom, another son or daughter born into God's Family.

The Angels, my brethren, rejoice greatly; we may not doubt it. But what, in general, are the thoughts of us mortals, who are most nearly concerned with the blessings and mysteries of Baptism? Alas! too often we think very little of it; a child is christened; very well, we say to ourselves: that is no such extraordinary thing. Nay we are very little careful to remember our own Christening, and, when we are put in mind of it, we do not make much of the thought. And yet a King's Son, a great Prince, one born to a royal inheritance, as he would find plenty to put him in mind of it, so he would commonly think much of it himself. We are sons of the great King, ourselves made Kings and Priests unto Him. Can we so entirely forget our own dignity and the treasures freely given and carefully guarded for us, as to go on, as if nothing had happened? Alas! too often it is even so. People live and die and go away to be judged, almost without ever thinking of their Baptism. We may be sure it is so, when they take no pains to improve. If a man really and truly believed, that, he having been baptized and born again in Christ, Jesus Christ was in him by His Spirit, if he really believed this and kept it in his thoughts, would he not strive and pray to be better than he is? It must come across his mind, how very very little he is doing, in comparison with what he might and ought to do. When a man is entrusted with a great treasure, to lay out to the best advantage, and knows in his heart that he is not at all laying it out well, nor deeply considering how to do so, would it not greatly alarm him if he heard a Voice from Heaven, "The owner of this treasure will soon be here; he will demand a strict account; he will expect to find you making a profit, laying out his stores to the best advantage? What if you, hearing those warnings, were conscious to yourself that your stock had been allowed to lie dead, and you had nothing to shew for all that you had the care of? Would you not be ready to sink into the earth? to "say to the mountains, fall on us, and to the hills, cover us," and hide us from the wrath of Him Who so trusted us, and to Whom we have proved so unfaithful? Oh my brethren! consider with me for a few moments what we might have been, every one of us, had we, according to the Church's injunction, continually mortified all our evil and corrupt affections, and proceeded daily in all virtue and godliness of living. We might, for instance, have come greatly to delight in our prayers; the sound of the Church-bell might have come to us with a real charm; we might have been able to say with the Holy Psalmist, "How amiable are Thy Tabernacles, O Lord of Hosts:" it might have been a true joy to us, both Sundays and weekdays, when they said, "let us go into the House of the Lord." This might have been our lot, had we improved our baptismal grace. But now I fear there are few hearts which are able to feel in this way. Again, had we attended to the Church's good advice, and believing that "Christ was in us of a truth, had we continually mortified our evil and corrupt affections, mastering and keeping down our flesh, that it might not rebel against the gracious presence of Him, the very God of Purity, how far better and happier we should have been by this time than now we are; how much more inclined to fasting and self-denial and to strict and religious ways of ordering those pleasures even, which would still be lawful and right for us. What different things would the daily meals and festive entertainments of Christians be, how differently would husbands and wives live one with another, if we were careful, as we might have been, to honour one another and the Presence of God within us, partakers as we all are of a Divine Nature by our membership with Christ! How far deeper and more perfect would our penitence be, whenever unhappily we fall into wilful sin, if we well considered what a thing it must be to sin at all knowingly after Baptism, after receiving the Holy Spirit in our hearts and bodies to join us to Christ and to change us into His likeness.

In these respects, and in our whole Christian life, what we are, we see and feel; what we might have been, we may partly understand by the word of God and the good example of His Saints: and if we had no more to think of, miserable indeed would our condition be. But thanks be to His infinite and miraculous mercy, we are permitted further to think and to hope, what we may yet be, if we will diligently and humbly make use of the little time which yet remains. We may, by His Grace, be true Penitents, bewailing and lamenting our sinful and imperfect lives, and seeking to bring forth worthy fruits of Repentance: only let us try immediately, perseveringly, and in earnest. O that it would please Him to pour out upon us even now, His good and loving Spirit, upon *us*, I say, who are here present, that we might from this very hour begin, one and all of us, to shew forth our Baptism in our lives, far more truly, far more courageously, far more lovingly, than we have yet done! And one fruit of that good Spirit will assuredly be that Parents and Teachers, Godfathers and Godmothers, will go on making more and more of their precious and tender charge, the little ones of Christ. If we make much of our own souls and of theirs, they will learn themselves to make much of them also. If we make light of them, fearful indeed is the end we must expect, both to them and to us.

THE END.

Library of the Fathers

OF THE HOLY CATHOLIC CHURCH, ANTERIOR TO THE DIVISION OF THE EAST AND WEST.

Translated by Members of the English Church.

Vol.	VOLUMES PUBLISHED.	Published price. £ s. d.	Subscribers' price. £ s. d.
1.	St. Augustine's Confessions. *Third Edition*	0 9 0	0 7 0
2.	St. Cyril's Lectures. *Third Edition*	0 10 6	0 8 0
3.	St. Cyprian's Treatises. *Second Edition*	0 10 6	0 8 0
4, and 5.	St. Chrysostom on 1 Corinthians, 2 vols.	0 18 0	0 14 0
6.	St. Chrysostom on Galatians and Ephesians. *Reprinting.*		
7.	St. Chrysostom on Romans. *Reprinting.*		
8.	St. Athanasius against the Arians	0 9 0	0 7 0
9.	St. Chrysostom, Homilies on the Statues	0 12 0	0 9 0
10.	Tertullian. *Second Edition*, Vol. I.	0 15 0	0 11 0
11.	St. Chrysostom on St. Matthew. Part I.	0 12 0	0 9 0
12.	———— on Timothy, Titus, and Philemon	0 12 0	0 9 0
13.	St. Athanasius' Historical Tracts. *Reprinting.*		
14.	St. Chrysostom, Homilies on Philippians, &c. *Reprinting.*		
15.	———— Homilies on St. Matthew. Part II.	0 12 0	0 9 0
16.	St. Augustine's Sermons. Vol. I.	0 14 0	0 10 6
17.	St. Cyprian's Epistles	0 12 0	0 9 0
18.	St. Gregory the Great on Job. Vol. I.	0 15 0	0 11 0
19.	St. Athanasius against the Arians. Part II.	0 10 6	0 8 0
20.	St. Augustine's Sermons. Vol. II. *Reprinting.*		
21.	St. Gregory the Great, Morals, etc. Vol. II.	0 15 0	0 11 0
22.	St. Augustine's short Treatises	0 16 0	0 12 0
23.	St. Gregory, Morals, etc. Vol. III. Part I.	0 10 6	0 8 0
24.	St. Augustine on the Psalms. Vol. I.	0 10 6	0 8 0
25.	St. Augustine on the Psalms. Vol. II.	0 10 6	0 8 0
26.	St. Augustine on St. John. Vol. I.	0 14 0	0 10 6
27.	St. Chrysostom on 2 Corinthians	0 10 6	0 8 0
28.	St. Chrysostom on St. John. Vol. I.	0 10 6	0 8 0
29.	St. Augustine on St. John. Vol. II.	0 16 0	0 12 0
30.	St. Augustine on the Psalms. Vol. III.	0 14 0	0 10 6
31.	St. Gregory, Morals, etc. Vol. III. Part II.	0 15 0	0 11 0
32.	St. Augustine on the Psalms. Vol. IV.	0 14 0	0 10 6
33.	St. Chrysostom on the Acts. Part I.	0 10 6	0 8 0
34.	St. Chrysostom on St. Matthew. Part III.	0 12 0	0 9 0
35.	St. Chrysostom on the Acts. Part II.	0 10 6	0 8 0
36.	St. Chrysostom on St. John. Part II.	0 14 0	0 10 6
37.	St. Augustine on the Psalms. Vol. V.	0 12 0	0 9 0
38.	St. Athanasius, Festal Epistles	0 6 0	0 4 6
39.	St. Augustine on the Psalms. Vol. VI.	0 14 0	0 10 6
40.	St. Justin Martyr	0 8 0	0 6 0
41.	St. Ephrem's Rhythms (from the Syriac)	0 14 0	0 10 6
42.	St. Irenæus. *In the Press.*		

LIBRARY OF THE FATHERS (continued).

	Published price.			Subscribers' price.		
	£	s.	d.	£	s.	d.
ST. ATHANASIUS against the Arians. 2 vols. (*Third Thousand.*) (With very full illustrative notes on the history of the times, and the faith in the Trinity and the Incarnation. The most important work published since Bishop Bull.)	0	19	6	0	15	0
——————— Historical Tracts. (St. Athanasius is *the* historian of the period.) (*Second Thousand.*)	0	10	0	0	8	0
——————— The Festal Epistles. (The work recently recovered in the Syriac translation.)	0	6	0	0	4	6
ST. AUGUSTINE'S Confessions. (*Fourth Thousand*), with notes. (Containing his early life and conversion. The notes illustrate the Confessions from St. Augustine himself.)	0	9	0	0	7	0
——————— Sermons on the New Test. 2 vols. (Clear and thoughtful expositions of Holy Scripture to the poor of Hippo, with rhetorical skill in fixing their attention.) (*Second Thousand.*)	1	8	0	1	1	0
——————— Homilies on the Psalms. 6 vols. (Full of those concise sayings on Christian doctrine and morals, which contain so much truth accurately expressed in few words.)	3	15	0	2	16	0
——————— on the Gospel and First Epistle of St. John. 2 vols. (At all times one of the favourite works of St. Augustine.) (*Second Thousand.*)	1	10	0	1	2	6
——————— Practical Treatises (chiefly on the doctrines of grace.) (*Second Thousand.*)	0	16	0	0	12	0
ST. CHRYSOSTOM on St. Matthew. (*Third Thousand.*) 3 vols.	1	16	0	1	7	0
——————— on St. John. 2 vols.	1	4	6	0	18	6
——————— on the Acts. 2 vols.	1	1	0	0	16	0
——————— on St. Paul's Epistles (excepting those on the Epistle to the Hebrews, which are completed,) 7 vols. in 6. (*Third and Second Thousand.*) (These contain the whole of that great Father's exposition of the N. T. still extant, and occupy five vols. folio of the Benedictine Edition. St. Chrysostom, besides the eloquence of his perorations, is remarkable for his care in developing the connection of Holy Scripture.)	4	0	0	3	0	0
——————— to the people of Antioch. (The celebrated homilies, where St. Chrysostom employed the fears of the people at the Emperor's displeasure to call them to repentance.) (*Second Thousand.*)	0	12	0	0	9	0

LIBRARY OF THE FATHERS (continued).

	Published price. £ s. d.	Subscribers' price. £ s. d.
ST. CYPRIAN'S Works. (*Third Thousand.*) (St. Cyprian, besides his great practical wisdom, states the doctrines of grace as carefully as if he had lived after the Pelagian heresy. He was a great favourite of Dean Milner. He is a witness of the early independence of the several Churches.)	1 2 6	0 17 0
ST. EPHREM'S Rhythms on the Nativity, and on Faith. (From the Syriac. A very devout writer of the mystical school, and full on the doctrine of the Incarnation.) (*2nd Thousand.*)	0 14 0	0 10 6
ST. GREGORY THE GREAT on Book of Job. 4 vols. (Called the Magna Moralia, from the depth of the observations on human nature of one who lived in close communion with God.)	2 15 0	2 2 0
TERTULLIAN'S Apologetical and Practical Treatises. (The treatises, especially the Apologetic, have, over and above, much historical information on early Christianity. They are full of those frequent sayings of deep practical truth, for which his name is almost proverbial.) (*Third Thousand.*)	0 15 0	0 12 0
ST. JUSTIN THE MARTYR. Works now extant	0 8 0	0 6 0
ST. IRENÆUS, the Works of. Translated by the late Rev. JOHN KEBLE. *In the Press.*		

ORIGINAL TEXTS.

	£ s. d.	£ s. d.
ST. AUGUSTINI Confessiones (revised with the use of some Oxford MSS. and early editions.)		
ST. CHRYSOSTOMI in Epist. ad Romanos	0 12 0	0 9 0
———————— ad Corinthios I.	0 14 0	0 10 6
———————— ad Corinthios II.	0 10 6	0 8 0
———————— ad Galatas et Ephesios	0 9 0	0 7 0
———————— ad Phil., Coloss., Thessal.	0 14 0	0 10 6
———————— ad Tim., Tit., Philem.	0 10 6	0 8 0
———————— ad Hebræos	0 12 0	0 9 0
Or the set	£4 10 0	3 9 0

(For this edition all the good MSS. of St. Chrysostom in public libraries in Europe have been collated, and the Rev. F. Field having employed his great critical acumen upon them, the English edition of St. Chrysostom is, so far, the best extant, as Sir H. Savile's was in his day.)

THEODORETI ad Romanos, Corinth., et Galat.	0 10 6	0 8 0

(The second volume, containing the rest of Theodoret's Commentary on St. Paul, was nearly completed by the Rev. C. Marriott, when the Church was suddenly deprived of his unwearied labours. The few remaining sheets, and the collations belonging to them, having now been found among his papers, the volume will shortly be published.)

WORKS by the Rev. E. B. PUSEY, D.D.

ELEVEN ADDRESSES DURING A RETREAT OF THE COMPANIONS OF THE LOVE OF JESUS, engaged in Perpetual Intercession for the Conversion of Sinners. 8vo., cloth, 3s. 6d.

The CHURCH of ENGLAND a Portion of Christ's One Holy Catholic Church, and a Means of restoring Visible Unity. An Eirenicon, in a Letter to the Author of "The Christian Year." 8vo., cloth, 7s. 6d.

TRACT XC. On certain Passages in the XXXIX. Articles, by the Rev. J. H. NEWMAN, M.A., 1841; with Historical Preface by E. B. PUSEY, D.D.; and Catholic Subscription to the XXXIX. Articles considered in reference to Tract XC., by the Rev. JOHN KEBLE, M.A., 1851. 8vo., sewed, 1s. 6d.

TWO LETTERS TO THE VERY REV. DR. NEWMAN. i. In Explanation, and chiefly on the Immaculate Conception. ii. On the Possibility of Corporate Re-union, and of Explanation on the part of Rome. With an Appendix in Answer to the Rev. T. HARPER's Strictures. 8vo. [In the Press.

THE MINOR PROPHETS; with a Commentary Explanatory and Practical, and Introductions to the Several Books. 4to., sewed. 5s. each part.

Part I. contains HOSEA—JOEL, INTRODUCTION. | Part III. AMOS vi. 7 to MICAH i. 12.
Part II. JOEL, INTRODUCTION—AMOS vi. 6. | Part IV. [In the Press.

DANIEL THE PROPHET. Nine Lectures delivered in the Divinity School of the University of Oxford. With a new Preface. *Third Edition. Fifth Thousand.* 8vo., cloth, 10s. 6d.

The COUNCILS of the CHURCH, from the Council of Jerusalem to the close of the 2nd General Council of Constantinople, A.D. 381. 1857. 10s. 6d.

CASE AS TO THE LEGAL FORCE OF THE JUDGMENT OF THE PRIVY COUNCIL *in re* FENDALL *v.* WILSON; with the Opinion of the Attorney-General and Sir Hugh Cairns, and a Preface to those who love God and His truth. 8vo., 6d.

THE DOCTRINE of the REAL PRESENCE, as contained in the Fathers from the death of St. John the Evangelist to the 4th General Council. 1855. 12s.

THE REAL PRESENCE, the doctrine of the English Church, with a vindication of the reception by the wicked and of the Adoration of our Lord Jesus Christ truly present. 1857. 9s.

The ROYAL SUPREMACY not an arbitrary Authority, but limited by the laws of the Church of which Kings are members. Ancient Precedents. 8vo., 7s.

WORKS by the Rev. E. B. Pusey, D.D. (*continued*).

The CHURCH of ENGLAND leaves her children free to whom to open their griefs. A Letter to the Rev. W. U. RICHARDS. 8vo., with Postscript, 5s.

LETTER to the LORD BISHOP of LONDON, in Explanation of some Statements contained in a Letter by the Rev. W. DODSWORTH. (*Fifth Thousand.*) 16mo., 1s.

RENEWED EXPLANATIONS in consequence of MR. DODSWORTH's Comments on the above. 8vo., 1s.

COLLEGIATE and PROFESSORIAL TEACHING and DISCIPLINE, in answer to Professor VAUGHAN. 5s.

MARRIAGE with a DECEASED WIFE'S SISTER, together with a SPEECH on the same subject by E. BADELEY, Esq. 3s. 6d.

GOD'S PROHIBITION of the MARRIAGE WITH A DECEASED WIFE'S SISTER (Lev. xviii. 6) not to be set aside by an inference from His limitation of Polygamy among the Jews (Lev. xviii. 18). 8vo., 1s.

WORKS edited by the Rev. E. B. PUSEY, D.D.

The SPIRITUAL COMBAT, with the PATH of PARADISE; and the SUPPLEMENT; or, the Peace of the Soul. By SCUPOLI. (From the Italian.) (*Sixth Thousand, revised.*) 3s. 6d.
———— Cheap Edition, in wrapper, 6d.; fine paper, limp cl., 1s.

The YEAR of AFFECTIONS; or, Sentiments on the Love of God, drawn from the Canticles, for every Day in the Year. By AVRILLON. (*Second Thousand.*) 6s. 6d.

A GUIDE for PASSING LENT HOLILY, in which is found for each day, Advice as to Practice, a Meditation and Thoughts on the Gospel for the Day, and Passages from the Holy Scriptures and the Fathers; with a Collect, and One Point in the Passion of our Lord Jesus Christ. By AVRILLON. Translated from the French, and adapted to the use of the English Church. *Third Edition.* 12mo., cloth, price 6s.

The FOUNDATIONS of the SPIRITUAL LIFE. (A Commentary on Thomas à Kempis.) (*Second Thousand.*) By SURIN. 4s. 6d.

The LIFE of JESUS CHRIST in GLORY. Daily Meditations from Easter Day to the Wednesday after Trinity Sunday. By NOUET. 8s. (*Second Thousand.*) Or in Two Parts, at 4s. each.

PARADISE for the CHRISTIAN SOUL. By HORST. Two Vols. *Fourth Thousand.* 6s. 6d.

LENT READINGS from the FATHERS. *In the Press.*

ADVENT READINGS from the FATHERS. *New Edition.* 5s.

MEDITATIONS and select PRAYERS of ST. ANSELM. 5s.

From the "Paradise for the Christian Soul."

DEVOTIONS for HOLY COMMUNION. (*Third Thousand.*) 18mo., 1s.

LITANIES. In the words of Holy Scripture. Royal 32mo., 6d.

SERMONS by the Rev. E. B. PUSEY.

PAROCHIAL SERMONS. Vol. I. (*Fifth Edition.*) 8vo., cloth, 6s.

—————————— Vol. II. (*Fourth Edition.*) 8vo., cloth, 6s.

ELEVEN SERMONS preached before the University of Oxford, between 1856—1865. *In the Press.*

Single Occasional Sermons.

I. THE DAY OF JUDGMENT. Preached at St. Paul's Church, Brighton, 1839. (*Fourth Thousand.*) 6d.

II. CHRIST THE SOURCE AND RULE OF CHRISTIAN LOVE. Preached at St. Paul's Church, Bristol, 1840. (*Second Thousand.*) 1s. 6d.

III. THE PREACHING OF THE GOSPEL A PREPARATION FOR OUR LORD'S COMING. Preached at St. Andrew's, Clifton, for the S.P.G., 1841. (*Second Thousand.*) 1s.

IV., V. GOD IS LOVE. WHOSO RECEIVETH ONE SUCH LITTLE CHILD IN MY NAME RECEIVETH ME. Two Sermons preached at Ilfracombe, 1844. (*Second Thousand.*) 1s. 6d.

VI. CHASTISEMENTS NEGLECTED, FORERUNNERS OF GREATER. Preached at Margaret Chapel, on the General Fast Day, 1847. (*Second Thousand.*) 1s.

VII. THE BLASPHEMY AGAINST THE HOLY GHOST. Preached at All Saints', Margaret-street, 1845. 1s.

VIII. DO ALL TO THE LORD JESUS. Preached at All Saints', Margaret-street. (*Fifth Thousand.*) 6d.

IX., X. THE DANGER OF RICHES. SEEK GOD FIRST AND YE SHALL HAVE ALL. Two Sermons preached at Bristol, 1850. (*Second Thousand.*) 1s. 6d.

XI. XII. THE CHURCH THE CONVERTER OF THE HEATHEN. Two Sermons preached at Melcombe Regis, 1838. (*Third Thousand.*) 12mo., 6d.

XIII. A SERMON PREACHED AT THE CONSECRATION OF GROVE CHURCH, 1832. *Third Edition.* 6d.

The above in one Volume, price 7s. 6d.

LIFE, THE PREPARATION FOR DEATH. A Sermon preached at Great St. Mary's, Cambridge, 1867. 6d.

OUR PHARISAISM. A Sermon preached at St. Paul's, Knightsbridge, on Ash-Wednesday, 1868. 6d.

Single University Sermons.

I. THE HOLY EUCHARIST, A COMFORT FOR THE PENITENT. Preached 1843. (*Nineteenth Thousand.*) 1s.

II., III. ENTIRE ABSOLUTION OF THE PENITENT. Two Sermons. Preached 1846. (*Fifth Thousand, and Second Thousand.*) 1s. each.

IV. THE PRESENCE OF CHRIST IN THE HOLY EUCHARIST. Preached 1853. (*Second Thousand.*) 1s.

V. JUSTIFICATION. Preached 1853. (*Second Thousand.*) 1s.

VI. THE RULE OF FAITH, AS MAINTAINED BY THE FATHERS AND CHURCH OF ENGLAND. Preached 1851. (*Second Thousand.*) 8vo., 1s.

VII., VIII. ALL FAITH THE GIFT OF GOD. REAL FAITH ENTIRE. Preached 1855. (*Second Thousand.*) 2s.

IX. PATIENCE AND CONFIDENCE THE STRENGTH OF THE CHURCH. Preached on Nov. 5, 1837. (*Third Thousand.*) 1s.

The above in one Volume, price 7s. 6d.

EVERLASTING PUNISHMENT. A Sermon preached before the University of Oxford, 1864. 6d.

WILL YE ALSO GO AWAY? A Sermon preached before the University of Oxford, 1867. With PREFACE and APPENDIX. 1s.

Lenten Sermons.

REPENTANCE FROM LOVE OF GOD, LIFELONG. A Sermon preached in St. Mary's Church, Oxford, 1857. 1s.

THE THOUGHT OF THE LOVE OF JESUS FOR US THE REMEDY FOR SINS OF THE BODY. A Sermon for Young Men. Preached 1861. (*Second Thousand.*) 6d.

THE SPIRIT COMFORTING. Preached 1863. 1s.

WORKS by the late REV. JOHN KEBLE, M.A.

THE CHRISTIAN YEAR. In Fcap. 8vo., cloth, 7s. 6d.; 24mo., cloth, 6s.; 32mo., cloth, 3s. 6d.; *Cheap Edition*, cloth, 1s. 6d.

LYRA INNOCENTIUM: THOUGHTS IN VERSE ON CHRISTIAN CHILDREN, THEIR WAYS, AND THEIR PRIVILEGES. Fcap. 8vo., cloth, 7s. 6d.; *Cheap Edition*, cloth, 1s. 6d.

THE PSALTER, in English Verse. 1840. 18mo., cloth, 1s. 6d.

SERMONS, ACADEMICAL AND OCCASIONAL. 1848. Second Edition. 8vo., 12s.

PRÆLECTIONES ACADEMICÆ. 1844. 2 vols., 8vo. 10s. 6d.

SEQUEL OF THE ARGUMENT AGAINST IMMEDIATELY REPEALING THE LAWS WHICH TREAT THE NUPTIAL BOND AS INDISSOLUBLE. 1857. 8vo., 4s. 6d.

A LITANY OF OUR LORD'S WARNINGS. WITH SUGGESTIONS FOR THE USE OF IT. 1864. 16mo., 6d.

CHURCH MATTERS IN 1850. Nos. I., II. Fcap. 8vo. 6d. each.

ON THE REPRESENTATION OF THE UNIVERSITY OF OXFORD. A LETTER to SIR BROOK W. BRIDGES, Bart. 1852. 8vo., price 6d.

A VERY FEW PLAIN THOUGHTS ON THE ADMISSION OF DISSENTERS TO THE UNIVERSITY. 1854. 8vo., 6d.

WOMEN LABOURING IN THE LORD. A SERMON preached at Wantage, 1863. Fcap. 8vo., 6d.

PENTECOSTAL FEAR. A SERMON preached at Cuddesdon on the Anniversary of the Theological College. 1864. 8vo., 1s.

WORKS by the late REV. J. KEBLE, M.A. (continued).

SERMONS, OCCASIONAL AND PAROCHIAL. In Twelve Parts, 8vo., 1s. each; one vol., cloth, 12s.

VILLAGE SERMONS ON THE BAPTISMAL SERVICE. 8vo., cloth, 5s.

Lately Reprinted.

THE CHRISTIAN YEAR: THOUGHTS IN VERSE FOR THE SUNDAYS AND HOLYDAYS THROUGHOUT THE YEAR. *Facsimile of the First Edition.* 2 vols., 12mo., *cloth*, 7s. 6d.

ON EUCHARISTICAL ADORATION. Third Edition. WITH CONSIDERATIONS SUGGESTED BY A LATE PASTORAL LETTER (1858) ON THE DOCTRINE OF THE MOST HOLY EUCHARIST. 8vo., cloth, 6s.

———— *Cheap Edition*, (the Fourth,) 24mo., 2s.

AN ARGUMENT AGAINST REPEALING THE LAWS WHICH TREAT THE NUPTIAL BOND AS INDISSOLUBLE. Second Edition, 8vo., 1s.

SUNDAY LESSONS. THE PRINCIPLE OF SELECTION. Being No. XIII. of "Tracts for the Times." 8vo., 6d.

ON THE MYSTICISM ATTRIBUTED TO THE EARLY FATHERS OF THE CHURCH. Being No. LXXXIX. of "Tracts for the Times." 8vo., sewed, 3s. 6d.

LETTER TO A MEMBER OF CONVOCATION. Reprinted from the "Literary Churchman." 8vo., 2d.

In the Press.

MEMOIR OF THE REV. J. KEBLE, M.A. By Sir J. T. COLERIDGE. Post 8vo.

A SELECTION FROM THE POEMS OF THE LATE REV. J. KEBLE. Fcap. 8vo., toned paper.

THE PSALTER, in English Verse. Uniform with the above.

www.ingramcontent.com/pod-product-compliance
Lightning Source LLC
Chambersburg PA
CBHW030729230426
43667CB00007B/649